The Sacred Isle

Belief and Religion in Pre-Christian Ireland

T0324653

dochum glóire Dé agus onóra na hÉireann

The Sacred Isle

Belief and Religion in Pre-Christian Ireland

Dáithí Ó hÓgáin

THE BOYDELL PRESS • THE COLLINS PRESS

First published 1999
The Boydell Press, Woodbridge
and
The Collins Press, West Link Park, Doughcloyne, Wilton, Cork

ISBN: 978-0-851-15856-3

Irish ISBN 1898256 74 8 (hardback)
Irish ISBN 1898256 60 8 (paperback)

The Boydell Press is an imprint of Boydell & Brewer Ltd
PO Box 9, Woodbridge, Suffolk IP12 3DF, UK
and of Boydell & Brewer Inc.
PO Box 41026, Rochester, NY 14604–4126, USA
website: http://www.boydell.co.uk

A catalogue record for this book is available from the British Library

Library of Congress Cataloging-in-Publication Data

Typesetting by Red Barn Publishing, Skeagh, Skibbereen, Co. Cork
Jacket design by Upper Case Ltd.

Contents

Introduction

IT IS DIFFICULT to say much with certainty about the religious ideas and practices of pre-Christian Ireland. The sources for such a study are plentiful enough, but the problem lies in the interpretation. Thus we find that both the archaeological and the early literary data are continually being reassessed by scholars.

The major difficulty for archaeologists is that, while the actual description of the surviving materials is carried out with great scientific skill, the lack of a living cultural context means that ambiguity can often persist. This means that even when interpretations can be offered, these can only be arrived at by degrees and by slow and laborious comparisons. The major difficulty with the early literature of Ireland is that it first came into being when Christianity had already – at least officially – replaced the earlier beliefs. We have reason to be grateful to these Christian authors for the wealth of subject-material with an antique flavour transmitted by them, but we cannot expect them to have given a full and unbiased representation of it. After all, much of the ancient lore belonged to a belief-system which they felt obliged to eradicate. What they did relay was rendered innocuous by stressing its pseudo-historical aspects, and some of it was brought soundly into the realm of the new dogma. In studying prehistoric religion in Ireland, therefore, the archaeologist must decipher what has become silent and unstated through the natural process of time, whereas the literary scholar must decode what is stated and guess at what may have deliberately remained unstated.

It need hardly be added that, in both cases, the clearest evidence refers to the higher echelons of power and influence in the ancient culture, and that there is little to indicate the beliefs and practices of the ordinary man and woman who lived their lives in relative obscurity. Furthermore, even where the evidence is impressive and therefore challenges us to attempt an interpretation, the actual processes involved in terms of organisation and ritual can only be guessed at. A study of this subject must therefore perforce limit itself generally to the concepts which prevailed at the different prehistoric periods, and to a lesser extent to the human emotions which went with these concepts. This book has grown out of a course of lectures given to students at University College Dublin on the insights which the study of folk tradition can bring to the field of archaeology.

Folklore itself presents many problems of interpretation and, in this context particularly, of chronology. One needs to reach a certain level of understanding concerning the likely age and spread of specific ideas, beliefs, customs, and narratives. Once this level of understanding is achieved, in other words when the mechanics of tradition can be grasped and the resultant insights applied, folkloristics can be of great assistance in determining how the human person experiences the surrounding world. In the belief that some interpretations can follow in this way from the archaeological and literary data, this is the approach chosen in this book.

Of the many people whose conversations have been of great benefit to me in this type of research, I would like to offer my thanks in particular to Professors Séamas Ó Catháin, Bo Almqvist, Proinsias Mac Cana, George Eogan and Barry Rafferty, and to Doctors Caoimhín Ó Danachair, Séamus Caulfield, and Gabriel Cooney. It is necessary to add that I myself bear sole responsibity for any errors or misunderstandings which may be found in this work.

DÁITHÍ Ó HÓGÁIN, 1999

– 1 –

The Pre-Celtic Cultures

THE PREHISTORY OF Ireland is several times longer than the actual known history, but it is without written record, and for this reason any attempt at an insight into the religious practices and beliefs in that long period might appear to be futile. Thanks to the expert and ever-advancing work of archaeologists, however, much knowledge has been gained regarding the material culture of the inhabitants of the country in ancient times. Such knowledge involves occupations and skills, social structures, economy, and commerce; and from it some details can be gleaned concerning the thoughts and predispositions of these – to us silent – men and women of the remote past.

People of the dawn
It is possible that some small groups of people had arrived in the country before the end of the Ice Age, but this theory of palae-olithic man in Ireland has not gained much acceptance. The earliest human settlements in Ireland are considered by most archaeologists to date from around 7,000 BC, the incomers having crossed into the northeast from Scotland over a sea which was much more shallow than it is today. They would have settled in coastal areas, and along the banks of rivers and by lakesides in the then thickly forested landscape. Few traces of these

settlers remain, apart from implements crudely fashioned from flint and chert, but their descendants survived for a long time, and by the 5th millenium BC they had spread south as far as Dublin Bay and west as far as Sligo. By that time also, small numbers of people had settled along the south coast, probably having arrived from Britain.[1]

These mesolithic inhabitants lived by hunting and fishing, and the artefact evidence suggests that they gradually improved their techniques by developing larger axes, as well as boring tools and scrapers.[2] It may be that they were being pushed further south and west by new groups of people arriving in the northeast during these long centuries. With regard to the more specific questions of culture, we may deduce some basic facts concerning customs and beliefs held by them. For example, remains of food which have been discovered at their sites include, as well as fish, such staples as hazelnut and pig[3] – both of these were so highly valued in succeeding millennia that they came to have sacred associations and were consumed at ceremonial feasts. Perhaps they already had such associations in the simple social life of that early period. The mesolithic people would have lived in small groups, composed of a number of families knit together by ties of kinship, and the system of authority would most likely have been based on individual prowess. There would have been some ceremonies within and among these groups, at the very least for the provision of marriage partners and probably also for the exchange of gifts and raw materials.[4]

These early inhabitants must have – since before they reached Ireland – had methods of thought which explained their life and environment in abstract terms. The great antiquity of religious thought is shown by the many spiritual beliefs held by human cultures which were documented thousands of years ago,[5] and by the diversity and complexity of such beliefs among the primitive societies of more recent times.[6] Direct evidence of such abstract thought among palaeolithic man in Europe is provided by the copious remains of skull and bear cults found at many sights, and most dramatically by the figurines and the cave art.[7] Whether we interpret this evidence to represent fertility or hunting magic, mythical symbolism or group ceremony,[8] it shows clearly that the sense of mystery was being ritualised at that early stage. The human mind, in its attempt to unravel a mystery, tries to concretise and dramatise its components, in other words to think metaphorically. It is this metaphoric mode of thinking which gives rise to the calcified imagery which we know as super-stition, and we can be sure that the earliest inhabitants of Ireland were just as adept at developing and preserving such traditional beliefs and practices as has man in every other time and place.

Antique peoples in general had the impression that hidden forces lay in the environment, and this was expressed in a belief that the landscape was inhabited by spirits of one sort or another. Considering the fact that Ireland was thickly forested at the time, the mystery of the depths of these forests must have impressed itself on the incomers, and no doubt the precarious nature of their existence would have added to their sense of awe. From the few artefacts which have survived them, and from their own very survival in the country, we know that they were a practical peo-ple. As in matters of daily life, therefore, they would have had a practical approach to the world of the unknown and have used elements of ritual to come to terms with it, and to placate and control it.

Their culture, or more correctly cultures, would have involved matters pertaining to both the internal group practices and the external world surrounding them. Naturally, these internal and external levels of existence would have impinged upon each other. The strong human tendency to project issues of material importance into the spiritual realm must have been at work, giv-ing validity and strength to customs and ritual practice.[9] These mesolithic inhabitants of Ireland – like human societies at all known stages – would have tended to formalise their attitudes to such things as the age and prestige of individuals, seasonal and climatic changes, and environmental variety in both physical and visual terms. Due to the small numbers of people in each group, however, we can suppose that the rationale employed by them would have been a rather rudimentary one. Their social vista was limited and their lifestyle quite basic, and their spiritual patrons would accordingly have been nature or ancestral spirits rather than sophisticated deities.

Human attitudes tend to be strongly influenced by symbolism, and primitive man did not trouble himself with acute analysis in such matters.[10] So long as symbolism does not contradict the natural and material facts of the immediate environment, symbolic connections between things and events are accepted by people as being an ordinary part of life. In this way of thinking, the imagery of things, and the nature of events, can be taken as linked together when parallels are noticed in them. Thus, for example, since blood congeals at death, it can be taken as symbolical of life and vibrancy, and its red colour represents this all-important strength and vigour. The occurrence of red ochre on some tools used by mesolithic dwellers in Ireland[11] could therefore be explained as a quasi-magical device to render these tools more effective. Ochre, indeed, of the same colour is well instanced abroad in burials from much earlier dates, the purpose in these cases undoubtedly being to provide vigour for the corpse in the afterlife.[12]

Since red was given a mystical significance, it is to be expected that – to early man in Ireland – other colours had symbolism of their own in matters of healing, magic, and ceremonial. Such ideas by their nature are perishable culture, and so would leave no direct traces. Traditional practices in more recent times included a variety of derivatives from 'sympathetic magic'[13] – for instance, using a concoction from dandelion or some other yellow plant to cure jaundice, in the belief that like appeases like; or, contrariwise the belief that like tempts like, as in the case of not dressing in green for fear that one's life might wither away just as vegetation does.[14] These superstitions may well have had their correspondences in the magical practices of mesolithic Irishmen.

Similarly with attitudes towards events in the lives of individuals. It is, of course, typical of primitive thought to regard accidents or other traumatic things which happen to a person in the course of life, as being symbolically connected to some other event. The mishap would thus have been foreshadowed, or it may have been foretold, or may have been considered the result of a deliberate act of sorcery. All of these are quite rudimentary notions in human thought, based on the logic of cause and effect. This logic of cause and effect was well-known to early man, as is clear from the ways in which he fashioned and adapted tools to his tasks, and it was doubtlessly extended by him to those matters over which he had no direct control. Anthropological studies have shown that, in situations which are of importance to them but which are fraught with unpredictability or danger, people tend to have recourse to preternatural remedies. Thus magic as a practical skill to compel favourable results, and religion as a mystical means of securing the good will of providence, were resorted to by early man as they have been by his successors.[15]

The workings of the environment, – especially the sun, moon, and stars, as well as tides and storms, and the variations in the very landscape itself – would naturally have attracted much attention, for they were crucially important in the computation of time and on them survival itself depended. The actual mechanics by which they functioned was, however, puzzling, and so there was a general tendency in ancient cultures to regard otherworld beings as responsible for all of these phenomena.[16] Such beings were invisible, but dead ancestors – who had disappeared from ordinary human surroundings – and were often connected with them. The human imagination, at its most primitive level, reflects its own feeling of personality onto other phenomena with which it has to contend.[17] In this way, the environment could be felt to be comprised of a great variety of very definite agencies, and man's encounters with these agencies were naturally to be explained in human terms. Although departed from the community, the dead had once been human in all respects, and their personalities would thus in some way be retained in their new mysterious surroundings. Human experience is registered in terms of the environment, and accordingly such spiritual personalities would become entangled with the environment and could even coalesce with it, becoming agents in its mysterious works.

The environment being 'alive' in this humanised way, the natural, and indeed the only way, in which man could rationalise it was by the performance of rites and the relaying of mythical narratives.[18] We can be sure that the earliest populations in Ireland – like all of their successors in the country – had some form of such mythico-ritual traditions. For instance, the waning and waxing of the moon is so obvious a phenomenon that it must have been given a mythico-ritual function in archaic Ireland as it has been in so many known cultures. Usually, the tendency is to regard the waxing moon as a propitious time to undertake some task, and the waning moon as an unlucky time.[19] Although we can only guess at the views and practices of the mesolithic inhabitants, there are – as we shall see – certain indications that a fundamental role was from a remote period assigned to the sun, not only in seasonal custom, but also in matters of life and death for the individual and for the community.

The more sedentary the lifestyle, the more socialised becomes living, and therefore the importance of place and locale is increased. Already in mesolithic times, it is likely that the concept of sacred versus profane would have worked itself out in a tendency to regard certain places or sites as having a particularly numinous significance.[20] The everyday world of a mesolithic inhabitant of Ireland would have been geographically quite limited, and such an inhabitant would naturally have situated the centre of that world in or near to the place where he dwelt.[21] We may presume that he would therefore gain mental reassurance from having some location or object in the vicinity of his habitation site, which would function for him as a sacred place offering some protection from the vicissitudes of daily life. Excavations have produced evidence for pits, ditches, and temporary timber structures which may have fulfilled this function.[22]

From some time before 4,000 BC, new settlers with a much more advanced culture were arriving in the country. These were neolithic farmers, who domesticated cattle and sheep and therefore were not totally dependent on hunting and fishing for their sustenance. They had developed sharper polished axes, and with these they set about felling trees and clearing the land, in order to sow crops such as barley and wheat.[23] It is likely that the earlier mesolithic inhabitants continued their own more primitive style of life for some time, but they must eventually have been absorbed by the newcomers. Within a few centuries, the population was numerous enough to construct what are by far the most striking monuments of prehistoric Ireland – the great tombs which we call court-cairns, portal chambers, and passage-graves. These megalithic tombs are built of massive stones, and over a thousand of them survive, with considerable variation.

Giants of stone

The court-cairns are the earliest of the tombs, and they predominate in Ulster and east Connacht. Stones were used to form long rectangular burial chambers, and then more stones were heaped on top of these chambers to form a large mound. At the entrance to the mound was an open space flanked by standing stones. This arrangement is of course a strong indication that some form of ceremony was involved. There is evidence for both inhumation and cremation. Remains of several individuals have been found within the precincts of these cairns, as well as pottery, implements from stone and flint, and remnants of what apparently were food-offerings.[24]

The building of massive tombs from boulders and stones was common to central and western Europe from the 5th millennium BC, and data indicating the practice of formal rites has been assembled from some tombs of the period abroad.[25] It would be reasonable to regard the spread of this great culture of tomb-building, throughout a large area of Europe, as the proliferation of a body of belief, no matter how variegated. Such a body of belief, with its spiritual and social referentials, would have had the basic traits of a religious system, and it may therefore be regarded as a type of megalithic 'religious' movement.[26]

Court-cairns are conspicuously absent from most of Britain, and those which are found in western Scotland and the Isle of Man seem to be derived from the Irish pattern. Archaeologists are therefore of the opinion that our court-cairn culture is derived from western France, where structures of a broadly similar type were raised. It could possibly be that an influence from abroad caused the existing inhabitants of Ireland to begin to bury their dead in this way, but the most likely occasion for such a massive innovation in culture would be a new and substantial influx of population. The strong suggestion is that the builders of the court-cairns were recent arrivals in the Ireland of the 4th millennium BC. They continued to construct these tombs, thus

showing that they maintained their cultural identity, for well over
a thousand years.

It is clear that the court-cairns were communal burial places,
and the ceremonies must have involved a considerable number of
people. The larger the social groups involved in such activities,
of course, the richer and more varied the ritual is likely to have
been. One would accordingly expect the congregations to be
arranged in a way which reflected differences in social and personal prestige, and the ceremonies themselves to include an
impressive array of symbolical gestures and of sacred speeches.
Perhaps even mythical narratives were recited. There would have
been time for such, for the variety of animal bones found at
court-cairns suggests that some form of ritual feast accompanied
the burials.

Other forms of tombs, of a more general international type,
were soon adopted in Ireland. For instance, the portal chambers
– popularly known as 'dolmens' – which are found in all parts of
the country but are rare in Munster. From the frequency of similar structures in Britain and France, it would appear that this
form of architecture was introduced into Ireland from these areas
– probably by the same people who had built the court-cairns.
The portal chambers consist of a number of large upright stones
with one or two other large stones raised on top of them and
sloping backwards. The gaps between the uprights were sealed
with smaller stones, and a large stone was used to seal the
entrance. In the case of these portal-chambers, also, there is evidence for both cremation and inhumation.[27]

The passage-graves are the most celebrated of all the ancient
structures of Ireland, and rightly so. Although these Irish examples of passage-graves are the most impressive, they do in fact
correspond to a type widely instanced abroad. They are therefore considered to have been constructed by people who came
up the east coast of the country from Brittany and landed near
the mouth of the river Boyne around the year 3,300 BC. Those
in the Boyne valley are accepted as the earliest of this class of
tombs; but very soon the type spread to the adjacent areas of
Counties Meath, Dublin, and Wicklow, and further afield as far
as Mayo in the west, Antrim in the north, and Waterford in the

south. The fact that court-cairns continued to be built in the north and west of the country, however, shows that the passage-grave builders did not completely overthrow the older tradition in these areas.[28] The standard passage-grave consists of a long stone-lined passage leading into a stone chamber, with this whole structure covered by a large circular or oval mound. There may be a number of recesses off the chamber, often giving a lay-out in the general shape of a cross.[29]

Archaeological investigation of the passage-graves shows that the dead were burned before being interred within them. Large stone basins found in the chambers may have been used in the rite of interment, and personal belongings were burned with the bodies. The ornaments accompanying burials included pins and bead-necklaces, as well as pendants in the shape of tools and often fashioned from semi-precious stone. The pottery vessels found were crudely ornamented, and some were gritted with sea-shells. Small stones and chalk balls were also found with the deposits. This placing of small stones within the mound, while larger ones were found scattered around the entrance to the passage, must have had some ritual purpose. It has been remarked, also, that special care was taken in the construction of some passage-graves to keep the chambers inside continually dry.[30]

All of these complicated forms of burial involved a heavy amount of labour, and thus they indicate that a substantial population was in existence. Furthermore, they indicate that a strong social importance attached to the burial of at least some members of the community, and the variously patterned arrangements of stones must have involved the extension of respect beyond the immediate social realm into some kind of spiritual dimension. It appears that the number of people buried in the passage-graves was not large, and they certainly were not communal burial-places. The largest number of attested remains is over a hundred persons in the small passage-grave later known as 'the Mound of the Hostages' at Tara in Co. Meath.[31] The most likely circumstance is that these tombs were reserved for leaders or other significant individuals, and that they were constructed with the intent of denoting the power and authority of particular dominant groups within the population.[32]

Passage-grave art

Excavations show that the ordinary dwellings of the neolithic people are in no way as impressive as the great sepulchral structures, and this strange imbalance in itself demonstrates the veneration which attached to the revered dead of the élite. It is evident that the megaliths of western Europe in general were constructed by such local élites who wished to perpetuate their power through their own particular ancestor-cults.[33] The necropolis of such a group would therefore be the sacred centre of their power. This would have been the situation in Ireland also, and some further clues as to the precise nature of the culti can be gained from the actual design and ornamentation of these passage-graves. This would be particularly true of the great 'cemetery' of such graves at Newgrange, Knowth and Dowth in the agriculturally rich Boyne valley. The population of this area seems to have consisted of several thousand people, large enough to extend their influence over a wide area of the midlands. Judging by the size and scope of the megalithic structures built by them, indeed, it would appear that they constituted the most imposing power-group in the country at the time.[34]

The political power-game would have determined, as well as hierarchy within an individual population group, a certain order of precedence among a number of different groups. This would appear to be represented, for instance, at Loughcrew in Co. Meath, where some of the tombs face their counterparts in the Boyne valley, others of them face towards the tomb at Tara, and a passage-grave at Slieve Gullion in Co. Armagh is aligned towards Loughcrew itself.[35] Such a social dimension is important, but the ornamentation is likely to reveal something of the more 'spiritual' concepts. At several of the passage-graves, we find incised ornamentation on exterior stones, as well as on stones within the passages and chambers themselves. This is generally similar to that found at megalithic sites in Brittany and in the Iberian peninsula, and must have been brought with them to Ireland by the passage-grave builders. Very prevalent are the angular and rectilinear styles, which generally take the form of lozenges and triangles. The purpose of these may have been mere embellishment, to direct attention to the sacredness of the sites.

There are also many varieties of spirals and curving lines, and of circles, and the impression of movement which they give suggests a connection with the numinous sense and with ritual activity.

The circles are sometimes accompanied by rays, and can be taken to represent the sun. There can be little doubt concerning the importance of the great orb to those who created this art. Since the neolithic people who built these tombs were farmers, it is logical that the sun would have played a leading part in their outlook on life and death. Emphasis on the sun was so great among the builders of a few of the Irish tombs that they constructed the passage so that it would receive the sun at special times, and so it is clear that seasonal festivities were taken into account in the basic design of these particular passage-graves. That similar ideology lay behind the art is apparent from the fact that the ornamentation is concentrated on the kerbstones on the southern sides of tombs with this solar orientation, such as at Knowth and at Knockroe (near Owning in Co. Kilkenny).[36]

The builders of megaliths in Britain and France seem also to have taken the position of the sun into account and to have represented its image in their art, but the Irish evidence is clearer and more plentiful.[37] It may be that solar worship was stronger and more sophisticated in Ireland. At Knowth, the east-west orientation of the passages in the dual-passaged tomb is such that the sun rises and sets directly in line with it at the spring and autumn equinoxes (20–21 March and 22–23 September).[38] This would ritually indicate the time for beginning the sowing and the time when the harvest should be completed. The most striking and celebrated instance of solar orientation is that of the passage at Newgrange, which is arranged in such a way that the sun shines right through to the chamber inside during the few days centring on the winter solstice.[39] It penetrates the tomb through a slit under the 'roof-box', which is situated over the entrance to the passage.[40] The coming of light into the tomb thus presages the end of the dark winter and the rebirth of the sun.

Given that Newgrange was a burial site, it would seem logical that this had not only a pastoral function, but was connected with the actual process of burial in the mound. It could, for instance, mean that the sun was intended to take away with its rays the spirits of those who had been interred there during the previous year. Alternately, or perhaps concomitantly, the sun, at its own rebirth, could be understood to banish death from the tomb and to restore life there. In effect, the sun may have come to be regarded as the ultimate ancestor – the spirit of all the ancestors – in the cultus specific to the Boyne valley. It can hardly be doubted that religious ceremonials of this combined social-environmental character centred on the tombs[41], a conclusion which is also suggested by the imposing size and geographical prominence of the structures themselves. At Newgrange, an intriguing question arises from the quartz-stones found near the entrance to the tomb, for if they were originally featured on the outer wall they would provide impressive reflections when the sun shone on them.[42] This would give the impression to onlookers that the sun, along with the relevant spiritual agencies, were active.[43]

The general opinion is that those interred in the passage-graves were either leaders of their communities – possibly accompanied by retainers or relatives sacrificed with them – or other individuals who in some way symbolised the interests of their people. It is noticeable that the remains of children rarely occur in this context,[44] and we can thus presume that the rituals and ideas connected with formal interments had a strong dimension of social authority.[45] That this social importance was connected with some mystical ideas can hardly be denied for, since the adult bodies were usually cremated before being placed in the chambers, the necessity of disposing of the remains of the dead would not in itself require entombment. Cremation must have fulfilled a dual purpose, social and spiritual, for fire was to pre-scientific man a powerful and mysterious element which 'ate' up substances. It dissipated the visible physical personality, and left only the internal man – the charred bones as witness to the fact that the individual had once existed.

The actual interment must therefore have been a rite, which a transcendent force of some kind was thought to attend. The lifeless body had been dissolved by cremation, but the social essence of the individual lingered on and needed to be released. Such a release was necessary for the structures of authority among the

living, but also because it rationalised death as part of the combined periodicity and continuity of time, and of life itself. Primitive man has always considered time as cyclical, the sun being
the most visible proof of this. The sun would therefore become
involved in the issue of the death of eminent personalities, due to
its function of perpetuating and rekindling social life. In this
wider sense, life was enduring and solid, like the stone used in the
construction of the tombs. One would expect the designers and
artists of these structures had a well-developed sense of
metaphor, and it is not beyond the bounds of possibility that a
three-fold symbolism was intended – the soil for productivity, the
sun for vivification, and the stone for continuity.

The overall importance of the sun as instigator is further indicated by the fact that some of the designs were hidden from view
within tombs, a practice well instanced from contemporaneous
burials abroad.[46] The inference is that these designs were
intended not so much for the attention of mortals as for some
other expected force. The general pattern of artistic ornamentation at Newgrange and elsewhere seems to direct attention
inwards to the core of the tombs,[47] and this could also have some
abstract purpose. It might even be that, in addition to the sun-
symbolism of the circles and spirals, the linear and curved art-
work referred to the sun-rays as they penetrated the tomb. That
these rays were understood to revitalise is strongly suggested by
two other examples of neolithic tombs whose passages are
aligned to the midwinter sun. The rear wall of one of these, in
Balnuaran at Clava in northern Scotland, has dark red slabs
which the midwinter sun would illuminate.[48] Another, that at
Knockroe, has two tall stones at the entrance to the inner com-
partment, and one of these is of red sandstone.[49] Just as red
ochre was used by prehistoric man to symbolise individual life,
it may be that social life was understood to be rekindled by the
sun falling on these red stones.

Communal welfare
In this way of thinking, the great tomb which honoured the celebrated dead was in fact a kind of temple. In Irish passage-graves
which have no formal art, the 'cup-mark', or picked hollow, is

often found on the stones. This age-old marking, found plentifully in rock-art abroad, has been interpreted as an image of entry
into the realm of death from which there is no escape.[50] Such an
understanding had obviously been greatly modified, and made
more sophisticated, by the metaphoric thinking – and undoubtedly accompanying ceremonials – of the great tomb-builders. To
them, the passage-grave was not only a place where the dead were
laid, but a place where continuing life was rationalised. This is the
pattern at both Newgrange and Knowth, where cup-marks are
frequent on the external kerbstones but much rarer on the internal stones. This indicates that the most arcane ceremonials, in
which death was rationalised and largely neutralised, took place
within the tombs. This would be the area where the official seers
– perhaps in dissociated states of consciousness – would commu-
nicate with the forces which they felt were at work in the mystery
of existence. The large stone bowls, found inside some of the
tombs, must have had some importance in this context, and were
probably used in some form of purification rites.

There is plenty of evidence – particularly in the Boyne valley –
that ceremonials took place in the vicinities of the great tombs,
and that these ceremonials became gradually more impressive and
elaborate. The decorated kerbstones at Newgrange and elsewhere
suggest that some form of ordered rites, or even processions, took
place. Given the solar alignments of some of the tombs, and later
ritual traditions, one would expect such processions to have been
in a right-handed, or 'sun-wise', direction. The addition of other
features to Newgrange, spanning several centuries after its construction, shows that the ceremonials developed and underwent
some alteration, and it is to be expected also that their meaning
as well as their form was somewhat changed in the process. These
features include the shaping of a 'cursus', or route between parallel banks, immediately to the east of the mound.

It is impossible to reconstruct the actual forms of ritual
employed, and the most which we can do is to speculate on the
concepts which are likely to have lain behind it. The suggestion
has been made that some of the megaliths had a sexual symbolism and, though this has not found general acceptance, it may be
relevant given that metaphors relating to sexuality are among the

most natural to the human mind. In many cultures, caves and openings in the earth are age-old symbols of the womb and of maternity,[51] and it seems no coincidence that the figuration of court-cairns and passage-graves are suggestive of the female reproductive organs. The structures and art of a considerable number of megaliths abroad are indeed strongly indicative of this symbolism.[52] It seems accurate to say that regeneration was one of the principal functions of these structures and that reference was made to it, as well as to social and economic matters, in whatever speeches or gestures were employed in the rituals. Stone objects of phallic shape have been found at both Newgrange and Knowth, indicating that fertility was an important motif in the ceremonials practiced at both sites.[53] It may also be that the oval-shaped stones which were so conspicuously included in the outer wall of the Newgrange tumulus represented a kind of cosmic egg of reproduction.

This again raises the question of the calendar connections of the alignment of passage-graves, and of the possible pastoral and social significance of these alignments. If the interred individuals were socially symbolical, their actual death must have had a symbolical function, for it would mean that something of the community's confidence or 'spirit' had died with them. In such a case, the most urgent concern of the community would be that this spirit should not be irretrievably lost, and some ritual would have to be devised which was understood to affect its restoration. Little else can be said with assurance, but we can speculate as to what might have been involved at a very basic level. The alignment of the passageway in the Newgrange tumulus with the winter solstice in itself invites an explanation. Was it in fact the intention that the sun would at this time escort the ghosts of the dead out of the tumulus, where the community had so obviously confined them? Such an explanation would mean that the coming of the new sun would initiate a new period of social time, in which the dead had somehow made their departure for ever. It would also mean that space was being made for new interments there, who would in their turn be escorted away a year hence.

However, given the perennial requirement of these pastoral tomb-builders for restoration in their economic life, a theory which encompasses the idea of continuity would be plausible. Many ancient peoples had the notion of a communal life-force, which was embodied in some strata of their leadership. By being so embodied, it could easily be linked to the individual life-force, thus allowing for beliefs in an abstract type of rebirth of some individuals, or more precisely in a restoration of the qualities thought to be inherent in these individuals.[54] The connection between the dead and their living successors could be thought of in the sense of kinship, with the spirit of a people residing in special bloodlines; or in the sense of social or political life, in which case the spirit would reside in the rite of succession itself. The discovery of remains of men, women, and children in these tumuli might suggest the kinship connections but, even if this were so, it would not rule out the social dimension, which must have had a special emphasis.

The spiral designs, rare at megalithic sites abroad, were given special development in the art of the Irish passage-graves. We have suggested that this resulted from a very strong sun-cult, with special ideological developments, in neolithic Ireland. There are indications that the cult underwent a further development in the Boyne valley and contiguous areas some centuries after the original erection of the tombs. This influence appears to have come from the passage-tomb tradition of Brittany, and it gave a much more anthropomorphic focus to the whole cult.[55] Thus we find that at Newgrange, Knowth and other sites, the concentric circles are used in combination to give the impression of a human face.[56] This would appear to represent a kind of personalised solar being, whose life-giving properties were being welcomed into the abode of the dead.

Further development of the cultus is evident, for there are some other notable, and possibly related, occurrences in this art.[57] At one of the cairns at Loughcrew, in the west of Co. Meath – which are regarded as derivatives of that at Dowth – an upright stone has a design of grouped arcs suggestive of a female human figure. This is complemented by a simpler passage-grave at Sess Kilgreen in Co. Tyrone, which has the clear form of a woman engraved large on a boulder. She is accompanied by an angular male figure, which resembles similar figures at Dowth and on the hill-top cairn at Seefin in Co. Wicklow. A human-like figure can also be deciphered in the inner end of the tomb at Newgrange. These anthropomorphic figures – paralleled by representations found in megalithic tombs abroad[58] – show that the builders of the Irish passage-graves were working with concepts of a transcendent nature.[59] Female human figurines, of course, occur abroad from much more ancient strata of culture, where they seem to have symbolised fertility.[60] Given what we have said about the solar imagery of other designs, these incised figures in neolithic Ireland could therefore have symbolised the regeneration of the life which had been lost through the death of those who had been interred in the tombs.

The circle of life

This speculation would lead to a theory of the rising sun causing a sort of social rebirth from within the Newgrange passage-grave – and perhaps from within other passage-graves also, for the possibility has been considered that there may once have been 'roof-boxes' at other sites.[61] Thus, the guaranteeing of good fortune would be expressed as a social regeneration from the bones of the significant dead. Is it not conceivable that the sun, with its blessed light of rejuvenation, released the spirits of these dead into a new and socially valuable existence? This, of course, begs the question of what exactly such an existence meant – whether it involved a second and temporary ghostly 'life' for the revered dead, or whether the spirits of these dead were needed to be embodied in their successors. The latter alternative seems to be by far the more likely one, given the suggestions that the rebirth was caused by the sun as a male agent impregnating the womb-like structure of the passage-graves. The symbolism of the primaeval couple, the male sun and the female earth, formed a common basis of belief among ancient peoples.[62] It appears very strongly in Irish tradition of a later age (see Chapter 2), a tradition which could well be a survivor of much earlier beliefs among the inhabitants of Ireland.[63]

Lingering beliefs of this nature may in fact be echoed in stories from Irish literature, even though these stories concern personages from the Celtic culture. In these stories, the father-deity

known as the Daghdha was claimed to have entered the Newgrange tumulus in order to lie with the lady Bóinn, and from this
union the wonderful youth Aonghus ('real vigour') was born
within the tumulus.[64] This father-deity was often given solar designations, and one source actually describes Aonghus as 'the son
of the ruddy-visaged Daghdha'.[65] Aonghus himself, we read, had
a 'crystal sun-bower' in Newgrange.[66] In another account, the
god Lugh brings the girl Deichtine to the Newgrange tumulus in
order to impregnate her there and thus bring about the conception of the super-hero Cú Chulainn.[67] For its part, the Knowth
alignment with the sun at the spring and autumn equinoxes may
evidence a similar rationale, except that there the beginning of
crop-growth and the end of the harvesting would provide the
birth-death complex. This would entail the abstraction of 'life'
into a clearly agricultural or economic format. It could be argued,
of course, that since Newgrange and Knowth are within a short
distance of each other and comprise part of a general 'megalithic
cemetery' in the Boyne valley, the tombs might have had somewhat diversified functions for a single large community.[68]

Diodorus Siculus, writing in the 1st century BC, gave a strange
account of an island 'no smaller than Sicily' which was far to the
north of his Mediterranean world.[69] He was drawing on earlier
lost accounts – he mentions as a source the writer Hecataeus who
flourished four centuries earlier[70] – and what he had to say was
typical of fanciful Greek descriptions of the *Hyperboreis* (those
'beyond the north wind'). Certain aspects of these descriptions,
however, seem to have been derived from the northwest of
Europe as much as from the extreme north.[71] It is thus possible
that Ireland was meant in this case by the island with a 'mild cli-
mate' which lay 'beyond the domain of the Celts' and where the
inhabitants speak 'their own distinct language'. 'People say that
Leto was born there', and for this reason 'Apollo' is venerated on
the island. There is 'a splendid enclosure and a huge temple of
rotund form' there, under hereditary rulers who are 'offspring of
Borea'.

The account, of course, is replete with the Greek culture of the
time. Furthermore, it claims that Apollo visits the island every
nineteen years, and dances continuously there 'every night from

the vernal equinox until the rise of the Pleiades'. This latter is an obvious reference to the midnight sun in the Arctic Circle, the most intriguing solar feature in geographical studies. The selection of personages from the Greek pantheon might, however, be of some significance. Leto was the mother, by the sky-god Zeus, of the brilliant youth Apollo.[72] According to Homeric lore, Boreas – who personified the north wind – once took the form of a black stallion, and thus impregnated twelve mares with fine foals.[73] The account, therefore, while confusing the geography with the extreme north of Europe,[74] features not only the sacred circular temple but also the sun-symbolism and the notion of mystical rebirth in an ancestral line. Perhaps the early Greeks had heard something of a cultus in pre-Celtic Ireland which held that the sun brings new life to an élite by penetrating a sacred tumulus near their dwelling.

A significant problem for the acceptance of such mythical concepts in connection with the neolithic monuments is, however, raised by the great variety in their designs and their alignments. On the issue of sun-worship in general, the fact that the earlier court-cairns are generally aligned in an east-west direction, with the entrance towards the east and the burial chamber to the west,[75] deserves consideration. This may have to do with an understanding that the eastern direction, where the sun rises, represents life, whereas the western direction, where the sun sets, represents death. It is noteworthy that alignments of the entrances to megalithic tombs in France, Spain, and Britain are often towards the southeast or southwest.[76] This indicates an emphasis on the sun in the rationale of life, but the lack of hard evidence to parallel the solstice phenomenon at Newgrange would lead one to conclude that, among the bulk of the country's neolithic inhabitants, sun-worship was not expressed in a homogenous or sophisticated way.

Customs and time

Many popular beliefs and practices must have been associated with the megalithic monuments and artefacts in the neolithic era, but archaeologists are rightly cautious in expressing opinions on these matters. All that is perishable has perished, and so discussion must focus on the possibilities of the situation and on the rituals which are likely to have centred on these megaliths. The settings of stones outside the tombs, for instance, must have served a ceremonial purpose, as also would the conical stone objects found near the entrances to tombs at Newgrange and Knowth. These stone objects have phallic shape, and the balls of chalk deposited within the tombs further suggest fertility as an important function in the rites.

It is likely that a political or religious leader used the splendid flint macehead, discovered at Knowth, as a symbol of social power. The angular spiral style of the design on this macehead is significant, for that is the same style as the engravings on the entrance stone and on other stones at Newgrange.[77] The import of this is that the passage-graves may have had quite wide implications in terms of religious ceremonies – such as mourning, pilgrimage, seasonal assemblies, and various rites. Such rites would naturally have included the well-being of crops and flocks.[78] It can be taken for granted that this productive function of magic was well-known to neolithic man in Ireland, and the other leading functions of magico-religious practices – protection and destruction[79] – must also have featured. Foundation sacrifices, such as the human remains excavated under the floor of a passage-grave at Fourknocks in Co. Meath,[80] attest to the protective function; while the inevitable conflicts and power-struggles[81] would have occasioned the use of destructive magic of one kind or another.

The tendency to situate structures on eminences and hill-tops in itself reflects a desire to stress the social, and probably also the spiritual, importance attributed to them. This is relevant to the locations of many of the passage-graves. Heights, which dominate the landscape, are made to function as symbols of social power and prestige in many cultures. Connected with this is the common religious idea that sacredness attaches to high points in the landscape, suggesting as they do a proximity to the skies and therefore to the powers beyond human comprehension.[82] But can such general resemblances between prehistoric cultures and the later recorded cultures be taken to indicate that much more could be held in common between them?

There is a time-honoured tendency in scholarship to attempt to decipher the culture of long vanished societies from antiquated customs and ideas which survived into more modern times. This form of deduction contains many risks, but it can nevertheless be stated that in certain ways Irish folk tradition has a quite antique flavour, definitely more antique than does the 1,500 year-old literature of the country. Referring to the evidence for the practice of agriculture in neolithic Ireland, one ethnologist has claimed that in that epoch 'the foundations of Ireland's peasant culture must be sought'.[83] The claim may be regarded as in a sense too general and in another sense too specific, but it is not without a basis.

Folk ideas, in effect, represent a continuation and survival of ancient ways of thinking. They are extremely tenacious, and their hold on the popular mind depends largely on the aura of antiquity which attaches to them. An element of traditional belief or practice may be altered in order to adapt to new circumstances, but the core idea is rarely lost, except when a general uprooting of culture occurs due to abrupt, widespread, and fundamental social change.[84] It is difficult to speculate on changes in population and culture in prehistoric Ireland, but archaeological evidence indicates that, no matter how unquantifiable, there was a certain continuum in ordinary life.[85] The data found in traditional folklore may therefore be considered as of some assistance to an effort at deciphering tendencies in the 'religious' thought of the dim and distant past.

The most obvious aspect of megalithic culture is its use of stone. This can, of course, be accounted for by the fact that stone was the best available building material to archaic man. From this practical reality has come the tendency in human culture to regard stone as a symbol of endurance and of impregnability, and it would surely have had such an image in the abstract thought of megalithic man. In other words, the builders of the megaliths would have had a reverence for stone as the element which above all else guaranteed protection for their burials. From this would have sprung a whole array of ideas connecting stone with whatever sustaining and immutable forces were perceived in the environment, and using it as a symbol of continuity in the community itself.[86]

The erection of standing-stones served the function of marking or 'socialising' the environment, thereby stressing the
spheres of influence of different groups in the population. Since
matters of social importance tend in human culture to be underlined by the attributing to them of a spiritual importance, it can
be taken for granted that such standing-stones had a religious
significance of their own. Their presence would have increased
the emphasis on the sites as sacred places, and some of the
sacred power would naturally be thought proper to the stone
itself.[87] In Irish folklore, and to a lesser extent in the literature,
there is an emphasis on the idea of supernatural power residing
in stone. The custom of swearing on stones, for instance, was
quite common, as was the notion that on certain occasions
stones could move about and even speak oracles. As an expression of their solidity, it was considered unlucky to remove rocks,
and some people even thought that a rock would of its own
accord return to its original setting. Stones were also used in a
magical or quasi-magical way to rid people of illness and, contrariwise, to cause misfortune to people. The power of stones to
provide a mutually protective barrier between the dead and the
living may lie behind the traditional gesture of respect for the
dead by placing stones or quartz pebbles on the grave, or indeed
behind the more curious practice of adding a stone to an ancient
burial cairn when passing by.[88]

Because of the physical solidity of stone projected onto the
spiritual realm, indeed, people were wont to pass underneath a
stone or between stones in order to shed their ailments. The possibility that the settings of stones in megalithic burials fulfilled
some similar spiritual function is an attractive one – probably
there was a belief in the purification of those engaged in the ceremonials by passing through these settings. Especially relevant
is the common folk belief, in Ireland as abroad, that clefts
between stones or a single holed stone can prevent bad luck
entering through them. The idea here is that stone is impene-
trable, and that it can be used in such a way as to allow only the
desired force to reach the person, moreover in condensed form.
The passing of the sun through the aperture at Newgrange
might be considered in a similar light. On the numinous level,

stone constitutes an impressive image in the landscape, and the echoes which it can produce have often been interpreted as voices from the spirit world.[89]

With regard to the sun, a whole range of folk beliefs could be cited in support of this curious phenomenon concerning the winter solstice at Newgrange. A belief held by many peoples is that the sun is the source of the life-force,[90] and we have speculated that the sun at Newgrange was thought to carry away the spirits of the dead and to affect some form of rebirth. At the end of the dying year, one phase of communal life was disappearing and was being replaced by a new phase of that same life. Irish folk tradition affords parallels for these ideas, and in a manner quite independent of formal or learned culture. It was, for example, believed that the oldest member of the household should sleep in the position furthest to the west in the home, as a sign that that person accepted his or her role as next in line to depart with the sunset. Another prevalent belief was that a young wife was more likely to conceive if she lay for a while under the full glare of the sun.[91] The relevance of the sun to both death and birth, although not in any way recognised in official Irish literary or religious tradition, seems thus to have survived as a 'submerged' tradition through the ages.

The suggested phallic symbolism of some of the carved stone artefacts in the passage-graves may be of relevance here, but the available data is hardly sufficient for a definite statement. The question of female symbolism is an even more difficult one. We have suggested that the megaliths were partly envisaged as an enduring womb of rebirth for communal good fortune. The unclear forms of the few tiny stone 'idols' discovered in the passage-graves rule out any interpretation of them, but female figurines have been found plentifully enough abroad from as early as palaeolithic times. These figurines are usually of pregnant women, and no doubt represent a desire on the part of ancient peoples for productivity.[92] Scholars are of the opinion that the specific cult of goddesses as patrons of society did not spread across Europe until the late neolithic period or even until the Bronze Age.[93] It is, however, likely that peoples who engaged in agriculture – as the megalithic peoples did – would have had some rudimentary form of female symbolism as part of their lore, and indeed some of our previous discussion would require at least an element of such symbolism. The evidence for the Irish Bronze Age offers nothing of assistance in this regard, as the few carvings of human figures which have been unearthed are rather non-descript.[94] It is only in the Celtic era that we find an obvious and fully personalised image of the goddess of fertility.

Archaic storytelling

One folklore theory goes beyond the claim for the persistence of antique beliefs and customs by insisting on the long survival of one of the most complicated of all genres in folk culture, the international folktale.[95] This form of oral narrative, which tends to have several motifs united in sophisticated plots, is known to have been popular in different parts of Europe and Asia for a very long time. Examples include short and fanciful animal-tales, wonder-tales full of fantastic happenings and adventures, and romance-tales based on more natural social situations.[96] In order to demonstrate the antiquity of some of these plots, it should be mentioned that a few examples occur on Egyptian papyri from the 2nd millennium BC, and some others in ancient Babylonian and Assyrian texts.[97] Instances of well-known international folktales are also found in early Greek literature, and it has been argued convincingly that some of these had survived from the Mycenaean culture of the same millennium.[98]

Struck by these facts, Carl von Sydow has referred to the possibility that some of the international folktales may be megalithic in origin. In particular, he drew attention to a story known to scholars as 'the Magic Flight', which appears to have originated among a Mediterranean people and is evidenced in more recent centuries from the Atlantic in the west to a wide area in southern and eastern Asia. From its occurrence in early Greek literature (in the myth of Jason and Medea[99]) we know that this story is very old. Struck by the correspondence between its geographical spread and the prehistoric spread of megalithic culture, von Sydow opined that this was no mere coincidence but that the story originated 'not later than 2,500 BC'. In brief, the plot goes as follows – a maiden assists a youth in performing difficult tasks set by her ogre father;

the youth then succeeds in selecting her from her identical sisters; finally, when the couple flee together, she throws a stone, a comb, and a flint behind them and these objects magically form protective barriers such as a forest, a mountain, and a conflagration.[100]

The occurrence of the tale – in historical times – in the same general areas in which ancient megalithic monuments are found, is a weak premise on which to base such a theory. The proven antiquity of the tale itself, however, could be more pertinent, and it employs imagery which is impressive in the context. The stone as a magical object accords well with archaic culture, and it would be easy for the neolithic people to consider its solidity in terms of the immovable mountains. Similarly combs, fashioned from pieces of timber, could cause speculation on how small sticks grew into forests. Flints, like sticks, were used to make fire – surely one of the most mysterious natural processes observable to early man; and to imagine a flint give rise to a conflagration would have been a dramatisation of this process. There is every reason to consider that such perennial elements of the environment would have been stressed in the rituals of neolithic man.

Von Sydow also suggested that another well-known international tale-type, known as 'the Swan-Maidens', resulted from a 'formation brought about by the megalithic people within an area of such immense extent'. This concerns a beautiful girl who is transformed into swan-shape but is disenchanted by a youth, who later loses her but regains her through the help of wild animals and the use of magical objects.[101] It is, of course, impossible to prove that these specific stories were known in Ireland, or indeed in any other area, at so early a period; but if – as seems likely – neolithic man used mythical narratives in his ceremonial and religious life, plots of this kind would have suited his purpose well. The formulation of such plots – with emphasis on contrasting characters, on the natural environment, and on magical processes – is of a type likely to be of great antiquity, and these 'wonder-tales' are certainly the oldest known genre of story.

The coming of metal
A type of structure, called the wedge-tomb, is found generally in the western half of Ireland. It consists of a narrow stone gallery,

higher at the entrance than at the rear.[102] The wedge-tombs are
thought also to have been introduced from Brittany, and may in
fact have originated there from the larger passage-graves. Like
these, the wedge-tombs were for multiple burial, but inhumation
was practised as well as cremation. Archaeological opinion considers them most likely to have been constructed by an influx of
people which occurred sometime before the year 2,000 BC, a
people who appear to have settled initially in the southwest.
These people are noted for their use of a new type of pottery in
beaker shape. They soon involved themselves in mining and metalwork, thus giving rise to the Bronze Age in Ireland.[103]

Other groups who came directly to the east of the country
from Britain used metal also, they being recognisable from their
own beaker-vessels and urns. As is clear from the archaeological
record, these latter groups in fact represented a variety of material cultures, but all tended to bury their dead singly and without cremation.[104] The usual type of tomb made by them was a
cist, comprised of stones sloping inwards and with one or two
overlapping slabs, within a rounded mound.[105] They also tended
to use the earlier passage-grave sites and to – at least partially –
imitate their techniques in constructing new mounds or cemeteries of mounds.

In both western and eastern areas of this 'beaker' culture, the
practice of fashioning great circles, either of banks, ditches, or
upright stones, soon became common.[106] Such circles seem to
have been related both to assemblies and to burials. In the case
of burials, cremation was the principal practice, but inhumation
is also attested – indicating again the variety in material cultures
and probably also of population groups concerned. From the
penetration of the building of stone circles into the area of the
great passage-graves in Meath, it is clear that incoming peoples
tended to either displace or assimilate existing population
groups. It is significant that the newcomers tended to take over
older sacred sites and to put them to use in their own ceremonies
– the most striking example of this is the circle of great standing
stones which they erected around the Newgrange tomb.[107] The
circular enclosures which they constructed physically marked off
the sites from the rest of the landscape. They were obviously

designed in some cases to solemnise an already sacred area, or in other cases to create a new one. The form of a circle occurs widely in magic and religion as a protective device, or a technique for emotionally controlling the cosmos.[108] It is therefore not hard to imagine that those who constructed these circles in Ireland would assemble within them on certain occasions in order to gain ritual protection for their communal, and perhaps even individual, welfare.

When circumambulation is employed in ritual practices, it is considered correct to move in the same direction as the sun. It was customary in more recent Irish tradition for a funeral cortege to walk thus, righthandedly, around a cemetery before interring a corpse there.[109] It may well be that a similar practice was followed when the remains of the dead were inhumed within these ancient enclosures. There are indeed hints from this period that the spirits of the dead were sometimes thought to depart with the setting sun. The wedge-tombs are usually orientated with their entrances towards the west or southwest,[110] and the significant number of stone circles in Munster with their openings facing either east or west[111] could entail a similar allusion. This alignment would seem to parallel the well-attested custom abroad in the same period of burying corpses with their heads towards the east and their feet towards the west.[112]

It should be stated that much archaeological evidence from the period does not suggest strong sun-worship, but there must have been pronounced variety in the religious practices of different social groups. The general preference for circular forms is, however, striking. At Ballynahatty in Co. Down a great circular earthen bank, known locally as 'the Giant's Ring', was constructed around an earlier passage-grave. There are remains of several other burials in the immediate vicinity, and beside the Ring itself, excavations have shown that a double circle of oak-posts enclosed another area. Within this double circle, on its eastern side, was a smaller double circle again of oak-posts, comprising what was evidently a mortuary where bodies were cremated or left to be excarnated before burial.[113] These structures again show the importance of the ritual circle, and sacrificial pits from this period have been discovered at Newgrange, these pits being also enclosed by a large double circle of wooden stakes.[114]

Of further interest is the strong indication that the placing of votive offerings in pits was introduced to Ireland by these 'beaker' people. Such pits have been found in several places, but most strikingly in front of one of the Knowth tombs, where they were arranged in a circular pattern, with each pit originally containing an upright wooden post and offerings such as pottery, flint, worked stone, and animal bone.[115] The offerings must have been intended for some sort of spiritual agencies residing in the soil, but this may have been easily reconciled with sun-worship, for the sun itself is seen to sink into the earth each night.

Some of the stone circles contained a burial cist or pit in their centre, which may or may not have been an original aspect of their construction. The practice of single burial in stone 'cists' within small mounds and in stone-lined pits in the ground was, indeed, long in use, such graves probably being of ordinary or less powerful individuals than those for whom the larger tombs were held to be appropriate.[116] Interestingly, at some sites – such as Lough Gur in Co. Limerick – the dead were interred within abandoned dwelling structures.[117] This would indicate that one custom was to leave the departed ones to repose in antiquated surroundings, which for their very antiquity had come to be considered sacred or otherworldly.[118] A similar way of thinking would have lain behind the custom, evidenced from the period, of burials at the base of pre-existing standing stones.[119] All of this seems to represent a rationale of death involving some kind of post-existence within the landscape.

A curious aspect of burial practice was to deposit unburnt skulls, without any other part of the body. This is evidenced from neolithic Ireland and continued into later periods. Some of these skulls were interred with obvious veneration, whereas others may have been those of sacrificed individuals.[120] The cult of skulls is well-known also from abroad, stretching back to a much earlier period.[121] It indicates the importance placed on the head as the most intrinsic or characteristic part of the body, the part in which the spirit resides. We may instance the common Irish folk belief that the soul departs at death through the top of the skull.[122] From the emphasis on the head we can further presume that variations in appearance and in facial expressions of living people would have aroused curiosity. For instance, features such as unusual formation or colouring of the eyes may have been considered to result from the work of spiritual agencies. In more recent folk belief, such traits are regarded as having a sinister import,[123] but this could be a reversal of a more ancient attitude, as earlier Irish literature often refers to them as indications of divine power.[124]

Primitive cultures have tended also to regard strange traits of temperament as an indication of the presence of spiritual power in the afflicted person. This was especially so in the case of people who exhibited unusual and dramatic behaviour, such as psychosis or epilepsy. It is very likely, indeed, that many of the individuals who officiated in religion and magic in these early communities may have had, or purported to have had, some distinguishing marks of this kind.[125] The aura of uniqueness and mystery which would attach to these individuals would be easily exploitable for the purpose of gaining prestige in spiritual matters. We have, of course, no direct evidence concerning such practitioners in the archaic communities of Ireland. In some cases, the magico-religious role may have been fulfilled by the social leaders themselves, but it is reasonable to assume that especially impressive individuals would have functioned as select intermediaries with the mysterious forces of destiny.

Such practitioners would have had a strong social role, for no clear distinction was made in ancient societies between the realms of the sacred and the secular. Prestige in material things would have been of paramount importance as a reflection of both these realms, and this is amply borne out by the archaeological record. As mining and metalwork became more general in Ireland, the occurrence of axeheads as burial deposits increased, and halberds and daggers came to be used in that context also, with the purpose of indicating the wealth and power of the deceased.[126] This may furthermore bear witness to a growth in the idea that the dead required protection, which would be a natural projection into the afterlife of power-struggles in the real world.

Ideas concerning the numinous nature of the spiritual world are less slow to change than the projections of social reality. So we find, as an interesting feature of this phase, the custom of burying the dead in a crouched position,[127] which custom had many parallels abroad from a remote period.[128] This often had a practical function in making room for the corpse, but in itself it must reflect some posture with cultural or spiritual meaning. Some scholars have suggested that it was intended as a magical device to ensure that the dead would not return, but a more likely purpose was to simulate the image of the embryo in the womb and in this way to hasten a 'birth' into the spirit world.[129] This would accord with the traditional axiom that a person leaves this world as he enters it,[130] and may have been a development on such an idea.

Especially noteworthy was the custom of some groups to cremate their dead and cover the ashes with an inverted urn.[131] Cremation itself may have originated in the notion that a dead body pollutes the community but, even if so, this would entail a sense that there was some personality exceeding the physical realm involved in a human being – or at least in some important humans. It is much more likely that – when ritually practiced as an alternative to inhumation – cremation was an assertion that the dead person was composed of both physical and spiritual essences. It therefore was a means of releasing the spirit of the dead from its former state into its new otherworldly existence. Such a mysterious element as fire would be thought an especially apt way for the powerful spiritual forces to take the dead individual into their own realm. The inverted urn would be intended to contain the already burnt body so as to allow the spirit to depart, and the placing of a smaller food vessel either within the urn or outside of it must have been of relevance to the proceedings. A possible explanation would be the provision of sustenance to the spirit both before and after it escaped from the urn.

The archaeological record shows that only a small number of individuals were buried with elaborate ritual.[132] These must have been leaders or other celebrities. It is also of interest to note that children are rarely represented in these burials, and from this it may be assumed that in the Bronze Age – as in neolithic Ireland

– one had to achieve adulthood before being regarded as a full
member of the ruling class.[133] This attitude is well documented
for traditional cultures, which regard the individual as becoming
a full member of the society only when he or she comes of age.
An individual's life is therefore divided into stages marked out
by the crucial events of birth, puberty, and death.[134] These three
points in life are ritualised, and a large amount of superstitious
belief attaches to them. As in later folk culture,[135] magical practices would have been current with the purpose of promoting the
fertility of couples and of guaranteeing healthy births, while
some element of ceremony would have attached to the attaining
of puberty, and – most crucially of all – the personal and social
disruption caused by death would have caused it to be a major
event with appropriate cultural reactions.

The problem of death

Some remarks are required concerning the way in which the
actual experience of death is likely to have been envisaged in prehistoric Ireland. The earliest sources which give precise details of
cultural interpretation of the state of the dead are the ancient
Middle Eastern literatures.[136] A basic premise in these sources is
that the spirit is a central part of the individual, possesses the
characteristics of that individual, and survives him after death.
Thus a kind of relationship persists between the dead person and
the community, and this may be expressed in various ways – such
as furnishing the dead person with food, clothes, and other
things which were thought necessary for his continued existence.

The actual nature of that existence was not altogether clear,
but in general the Middle Eastern sources represent it as a rather
weakened and gloomy form of the physical world. It was cold
and especially dry, and therefore not suitable to physical productivity, but on the other hand the dead were much more
knowledgeable than their living fellows. Allied to all of this was
the notion or the fear that the dead could be inimical to the living, and therefore a necessity was felt to placate and accommodate
them. Similar ideas are instanced by traditional cultures in many
other parts of the world, and such resemblances between unrelated cultures in the matter of death and burial is quite notable.

We may therefore assume that when faced with the great nega-
tion, the human mind tends to react and rationalise along certain specific lines.[137] Ideas of this kind must be very old in human
history, and they are also very enduring. In European folklore,
for instance, are found a complex of notions concerning death
and burial which are by no means accomodated by Christian
practice and – since they are paralleled in archaic cultures – it is
obvious that they must have at the very least predated the spread
of Christianity.

We note that in recent Irish tradition,[138] upon the expiry of a
family member, the curtains were drawn in the house, the mirror
was covered, the clock was stopped, and the cat or dog put out.
This was done, of course, with the understanding that it was a
mark of respect for the dead, but the peculiar nature of the
actions can only be explained as having originated in a belief that
the soul could leave the body and become incorporated in something else. After the burial, it was customary for relatives to leave
food-offerings, and even tobacco-pipes, on the grave, and also to
refrain from wearing the clothes of the dead person for a definite
period. In this we can detect the feeling that the spirit remained
in the vicinity of the body for a while after death.[139]

The customs of lamenting the dead, and of playing games at
wakes – though roundly condemned by Christian clergymen –
were until recently in Ireland thought of as means of honouring
the dead, but one suspects that originally they had the function
of reassuring him that he was still valued by family and friends.
Perhaps there was something more than reassurance in question,
and that – in view of the general fear of even benign ghosts – the
real purpose was one of actual placation. Indeed, at variance
with all Christian dogma, the idea persisted that the dead live on
continuously in a kind of ghostly community side by side with
our own, and that they may assemble in groups in churchyards
or even return to their individual houses at the feast of the
dead.[140]

It would not, therefore, be over-fanciful to hold that ideas of
this general kind were held in prehistoric times. The neolithic and
Bronze Age Irish, who spoke languages of which no trace
remains and who have left us no evidence except those material

things which would not decay, would have held beliefs and conceptions of a type with their contemporaries in Britain and other
parts of Europe. These beliefs and conceptions would have
included the continuation of 'spiritual' life at least for some
period after the normal course of living, the necessity to acco-
modate this 'spirituality' in the social context, and a resolution
of the issue which would negate the tension between the dead
and the living. Such a resolution is likely to have involved the
infusion of new life into the community as a direct benefit or
compensation from the realm of the dead, and the idea that
social and economic life was inextricably linked to that process.
The life-force in society must furthermore have been, to a great
extent, envisaged in terms of the male-female relationship to
which all human existence is due. Beyond this interpretation it
seems impossible to go, for the terminology, nomenclature, and
formalities which would have accompanied these ancient religious systems are lost to us forever.

Skill and sacrifice

The wide range and skilled decoration of their metal implements
– such as axeheads, spearheads, swords, shields, awls, sickles,
and cauldrons – shows the sophistication of the Bronze Age
inhabitants of Ireland. Most striking of all, however, was their
art-work in gold. From the middle of the 2nd millennium BC,
this art-work was producing torcs, gorgets, rings, bracelets,
dress-fasteners, and other objects of intricate design with a variety of raisings and engravings.[141] From the weight of some of the
adornments, it is clear that they were worn only for special occasions, whether social or ritual – several of the golden clasps and
bracelets, for instance, must have been designed exclusively for
ceremonial use.[142]

In general the motifs – whether on vessels, implements, or items
of personal adornment – served an aesthetic purpose and would
have signified mere ostentation, and it would be unrealistic to
relate them intimately to a system or systems of belief. Evidence
for belief, indeed, becomes more and more scanty as the Bronze
Age progresses, and there are little or no grave-deposits from Ireland in the 1st millennium BC. Both inhumation and cremation

were practiced in this period, sometimes apparently simultaneously, but the differing significance of the two types of burial are
not clear.

A possible indicator of belief within the art-work of the Irish
Bronze Age is furnished by the so-called 'sun-discs', about twenty
of which survive from different localities, sometimes in pairs.
They are early – belonging to the first half of the 2nd millennium
BC – and consist of rounded discs fashioned from sheets of gold,
with concentric circles and a stylised cross in the centre. Since
several of them have two holes near the centre, it is thought that
they may have been attached to cloth or leather wear. The circular and cruciform design, enhanced by further radial effects, suggests a reference to the sun and its rays, and indeed the fact that
they are of gold seems also to indicate an imitation of the heavenly body.[143] The basic pattern of cross-within-disc originated in
central Europe, but its elaboration and adoption to gold may be
an Irish feature.[144]

It seems logical to consider these, probably ceremonial, objects
as in some way connected with the other images paralleling the
sun in prehistoric artefacts. Several apparently solar designs on
rocks from the Bronze Age are of a type with earlier neolithic
designs,[145] thus showing that there was some form of continuity
in tradition. Indeed, the widespread occurrence of solar symbols in
different parts of Europe in the Bronze Age underlines the importance of sun-worship in the period.[146] Attention has often been
drawn in this context to the famous Trundholm figure – from the
Danish Bronze Age – of a disc drawn by a horse. This is considered to represent the chariot of the sun which crosses the heavens
and, if the Irish 'sun-discs' belong to the same basic tradition, they
too may be taken as evidence for homage paid to the sun which
returns each morning to give light and well-being to the world.[147]
The soil would be brought into the ambiance of such worship, for
a natural observation would be that the sun sinks into the earth
each night and sojourns there until the new dawning.

Treasure in the soil
The practice of burying valuables was further developed through
the Bronze Age – with evidence for more and more impressive

hoards of implements and art-work being deposited.[148] In view
of the fact that the hoards have often been found in situations
where retrieval would have been difficult, it is very likely that
these depositions had a magico-religious purpose and that a quite
elaborate ritual was involved. Especially notable in this regard
are the great Bronze Age hoards discovered in bogs, pools, and
lakes.[149] One explanation would be that these valuables were
hidden in time of war so as to prevent them from falling into the
hands of raiders, but the fact that they were not recovered by
either friend or foe would indicate otherwise. It is therefore logical to connect the deposition of such hoards in Ireland with a
similar custom, of more obvious ritual nature, observed in other
parts of Europe at this period.[150]

The likelihood that these were sacrificial offerings is further
strengthened by the find in an artificial pond in Co. Armagh – at
a short distance from Eamhain Mhacha (Navan Fort), which was
an inhabited site since neolithic times.[151] This pond contained
dog bones, and deer antlers, as well as fragments of clay mould.
Significantly, it also contained a cut human skull, which may be
an indication of human sacrifice at the site, but another possibility is that this was the venerated skull of some person already
dead which was offered in this way. That such man-made ritual
ponds had a wider provenance appears from a similar one –
though without any known deposits – immediately to the north
of Knowth and Newgrange.[152] A hoard found in wetland at
Mooghaun in Co. Clare had well over a hundred gold items,[153]
while over two hundred bronze artefacts were found in another
single hoard in a similar setting at Dowris in Co. Offaly. This latter included weapons, tools, cauldrons, and trumpets.[154] The
obvious interpretation for such votive deposits is that they were
offered to chthonic powers in the hope that these would provide
the community with crops and fruit and fill the land with game.

The practice of depositing hoards continued into the Iron Age.
In general, it can be said that the doubt in the minds of scholars,
as to whether these represent implements hidden for a practical
purpose or as sacrificial offerings, is paralleled by the questions
relating to many finds of casks of butter in Irish bogs in recent
centuries. Whereas it seems clear that the 'bog-butter' was

deposited for purposes of preservation, it has been suggested that this benefit was learned as a bye-product of the practice, and that the practice itself may have originated as a form of propitiation rite to the abstract force of fertility in the earth.[155] This opinion is supported by the common folk custom of deliberately spilling on the ground the first drops of milk taken from a cow, in order to obtain the good will of the fairies, and indeed by the parallel custom of throwing the first drops of liquor into the air for good luck by those engaged in illegal distilling![156] To placate with offerings the productive spirit of the landscape is so foreign to the attitudes of official culture that it is likely to have a long and hidden past behind it.

The crucial time

A major problem of Irish prehistory arises from the fact that the period which was crucial to the formation of the country's tradition as we know it is also the most difficult to specify by way of chronology. This is the first half of the 1st millennium BC, which witnessed a further refinement in metalwork, but also apparently a strong tendency towards more stratified and competitive power-structures. Although there is no archaeological evidence for important new groups of settlers in this period, there is no doubting the new influences which were at work. Most remarkable, perhaps, are the appearance of two distinctive types of dwelling at the beginning of the period. These were lakeside dwellings and the fortresses built on hill-tops. Both of these types are represented from the same period in Britain and on the Continent,[157] and therefore illustrate a spread – at the very least in cultural terms – from abroad into the country.

The lakeside dwelling – known later in Irish as *crannóg* – differed considerably from the ordinary undefended homesteads of the period. Stones, timber, and brushwood were heaped on top of each other to provide a platform on the marshy lakeside, and a circular dwelling-hut with wickerwork walls and thatched roof was constructed on this. The whole structure was then surrounded by a strong wickerwork fence, which would keep at bay marauding animals such as wolves and wild cats, as well, of course, as human enemies.[158] The situation of these dwellings had everyday practical purposes, they being so close to water and fishing; but it also served a defensive purpose, for the presence of the water more or less ruled out the approach of possible assailants from that side.

Some dwellings had been constructed on or near hill-tops since neolithic times, but at this period a much stronger and more elaborate type of structure developed. In this, the hill-fort, use was made of the strategic advantage of the hill-top, by encircling it with earthen banks or stone walls, often with the addition of ditches. The dwelling-huts were situated safely within these daunting enclosures.[159] In some cases, the enclosed space also contained remains of neolithic or early Bronze Age tombs, and this can hardly have been coincidental. The builders of the hill-forts obviously wished to dominate the landscape with their spacious and imposing structures. It is likely also that they wished to expropriate to themselves the prestige attaching to sacred burial sites from earlier epochs. Defence and dominance were the major functions of the hill-forts. Many of them must have been inhabited, but some were situated in such high and nigh-inaccessible terrain as to make this extremely unlikely. In these cases, it may be that the local population had recourse to them in time of war and raiding, and it seems very likely that they were used for assemblies. They probably had a ceremonial function, for which they would be very appropriate on account of their eminent positions and their imposing appearances.[160]

The rapid development of metallurgy in the later Bronze Age indicates the growth of more structured and organised societies, and indeed the great increase in weapon-artefacts at the same time demonstrates that such cohesion was the result of more centralised units of military power. This inevitably would have led to an increasingly violent tenor of life. By the 7th century BC, new types of bronze swords, longer and with divided tang-ends, began to appear. This design came from Britain, and is of the Hallstatt type which had spread from central Europe some time earlier.[161] The smelting of iron, which began in Britain at around the same time, must soon also have spread to Ireland. Compared to the skill in bronze, however, Irish ironwork remained very crude for a long time, and indeed iron does not appear to have become the metal in most demand for weapons until the 3rd or even the 2nd century BC.[162]

The ethnic background to this rapidly developing, and quite unstable, social life, is difficult to decipher, but the question of the hill-forts might help to provide an answer. In fact, a rather clear distinction between two types of hill-fort can be made – the univallate forts which predominate in the east and the multivallate forts which predominate in the west. Whether or not this distinction reflects two different population groups, it seems clear that some kind of internecine strife encouraged their construction. It is interesting to note that after some centuries the hill-forts seem to have undergone a change in function. Since evidence for actual habitation of them becomes very scarce from the 5th century BC onwards,[163] one can conclude that these fortresses had lost much of their military advantage, and perhaps even of their defensive purpose, by that time. This would in itself suggest a fundamental change in the general power situation.

One explanation for a change of this nature would be a general triumph of one group of people over the others. Such a group could be an indigenous one, or it could be of external origin – a problem which raises the vexed and probably related question of the origin of a Celtic language in Ireland. The question can perhaps be answered by suggesting that the predominant group in Ireland in or around the 5th century BC were proto-Celts, who had either been in the country for a considerable period or had been recent arrivals. The latter alternative seems to be the better one, but this brings us directly into the realm of Celtic culture itself.

-2-

Basic Tenets in the Iron Age

In a Greek text known as 'the Massaliote Periplus', there was a description of a voyage by sailors from Marseilles to the city of Tartessos (in the vicinity of the Gulf of Cadiz). There the Massaliotes had been told that the Tartessians had actually travelled north as far as the Oestrymnides (probably Brittany), whose inhabitants traded with two large islands, called 'Ierne' and 'Albion'.[1] These two placenames are easily recognisable from early Irish literature, namely 'Ériu' (from Celtic *Everiu*) for Ireland and 'Albu' (from Celtic *Albiu*) for Britain.[2] The voyage may have been undertaken as early as the 6th century BC, but there are some difficulties. Firstly, it is not altogether certain that these placenames were Celtic in origin and, even if they were, from the reference to them it would appear that the Tartessians got the names from Celts on the European mainland.[3] This reference does not therefore necessarily indicate that the two islands themselves were inhabited by Celts at that time. Secondly, the references to Ierne and Albion may not be as early as they seem, for the 'Periplus' account was rewritten in the 4th century BC and translated into Latin in the 1st century BC,[4] before it was fragmentarily put into the surviving Latin form.[5]

We can, however, be sure, that the names Ierne and Albion were current in Greek for the two islands by the 3rd century BC,

for they were thus referred to at that time by Eratosthenes.[6] Pytheas of Massalia, who visited Britain about 325 BC, may have
been acquainted with the same toponymics, but he collectively
calls the countries the 'Prettanik' islands.[7] This was derived from
the population name Pritani, which gave rise to the Latin 'Bri-
tannia' and the Welsh 'Prydein'.[8] The new name indicates that
much of Britain was at that time under the control of the people
who bore it, and there can hardly be any doubt but that these
Pritani were Celts. They had probably arrived in Britain from the
Continent at some time around 500 BC, bringing with them
weapons and tools of iron. The designation 'Pritani' would
appear to have been first applied to the inhabitants of the island
by Continental Celts.[9]

The Celts in Ireland
The possibility that an independent proto-Celtic people were
already in Ireland cannot be completely ruled out, but the likelihood is that the first Celts came to Ireland from Britain.
Although it is extremely difficult to correlate the archaeological
and linguistic data, the improvement of weaponry in bronze and
iron from the 5th century BC onwards suggests not only a technical influence from abroad, but also the coming of such a group
or groups of newcomers to settle here. This is more likely to have
been a gradual trickle of immigrants than a substantial invasion
force, although the very improvement in the weapons themselves
suggests that some military struggle took place.[10] Very probably,
the number of these immigrants gradually increased, and their
more advanced technology would have caused a corresponding
increase in their influence. The culmination of this process would
be reflected by the introduction, in or about the 2nd century BC,
of the more sophisticated Iron Age culture known as La Tène.[11]
By this time, the Celtic language must have already achieved a
dominant position in Ireland.

With the language, one would of course expect that many
beliefs and traditions from the Celtic world[12] would also have
reached the country, and would have become embedded in the
new context and environment. A question immediately arises
concerning older pre-Celtic peoples and the extent to which they

and their cultures survived or were assimilated into the newly dominant system of belief and practice. If, as seems very likely, most of the inhabitants of Iron Age Ireland were of other than Celtic stock, then they must have had some imput into the developing lore. The fact that this was so can be illustrated very clearly from the ritual importance which continued to be accorded to the impressive physical remains of antiquity.[13] As we shall see in Chapter 3, tumuli and other ritual sites came to be regarded as dwellings of great Celtic deities and heroes, and the mystique attached to them was rationalised in terms of the sacred otherworld of Celtic beliefs.

The issue of language is, of course, crucial to an understanding of the mythic and religious life of ancient Ireland. No traces of other indigenous languages can be clearly identified in Irish tradition, and from this it would appear that Celtic was already the general and unrivalled speech in pre-Christian times.[14] Much debate has, however, taken place as to its precise nature. Philologists are struck by the way in which an ancient Celtic consonant *qw- underwent little change in Ireland, appearing as a 'q' sound and later as 'c', whereas in British Celtic and in Gaulish the consonant was changed to a 'p' sound. On account of this, it has often been claimed that an antique form of Celtic was introduced into Ireland, whereas a more innovative form spread over most other Celtic areas of Europe. Occurences of the 'q' sound in placenames in some areas of Celtic Europe, especially in the Iberian peninsula, were thought to indicate that the Irish dialect had some special connection with these areas. More recently, however, scholars are inclined to regard the 'p'/'q' difference as less significant to the question of Celtic origins.[15] The real explanation would appear to be that there was a gradual replacement of the 'q' by the 'p' sound in Continental Europe, and that this penetrated into British Celtic but never affected Ireland.[16] On this premise, there would be no reason to regard the dialect or dialects of Celtic introduced into Ireland as having been of an exceptional nature.

If the language was not exceptional, neither does the material culture seem to have been so. The archaeological record, indeed, shows that the greatest innovation of the period, the adoption of iron, followed on its introduction to Britain. Similarly, items dating to the final centuries BC and the early centuries AD – such as horse-bits, riveted cauldrons, stone vessels with handles, tweezers, combs, mirrors, brooches, spoon-shaped objects, and a variety of pins – all follow the patterns found in Britain.[17] Although examples of weaponry are scarce from this period, several of those swords and parts of spears which have been found also show a similar relationship.[18] Nowhere is the connection more clear than in the case of art styles. Beginning in the 3rd or 2nd century BC, Irish ornamentation on metal and stone shows a marked dependence on the style known as La Tène. Although Gaulish sources seem likely for the earliest of the Irish examples, these may have been mediated through Britain, and many examples clearly originated in the sister-island.[19]

Votive deposits

The practice of depositing hoards is well-attested in the archaeology of the Celts abroad.[20] Diodorus Siculus, writing of Gaul in the 1st century BC, states that 'the Celts of the hinterland have a strange and peculiar custom in connection with the sanctuaries of the gods; for in the temples and sanctuaries which are dedicated throughout the country, a large amount of gold is openly placed as a dedication to the gods, and of the native inhabitants, none touch it because of religious veneration'.[21] His fellow Graeco-Roman writer, Strabo, mentions a tradition that a Celtic tribe, the Tectosages, took part in the sacking of Delphi in the 3rd century BC, and deposited the plundered riches in the city of Toulouse, 'adding to them from their own possessions by way of dedication in winning the favour of their god'.[22] Strabo, writing over two hundred years after these events, rejects the tradition, and instead favours the explanation given in the 1st century BC by Posidonius for the Toulouse hoard:

> The country being rich in gold, with inhabitants both god-fearing and of frugal life, possessed treasures in many parts of Celtica; and the lakes in particular provided inviolability for their treasures, into which they let down heavy masses of silver and gold ... In Toulouse,

moreover, the temple was a revered one, greatly esteemed
by the local inhabitants; and for this reason the treasures
there were unusually large, since many made dedications
and none would dare to profane them.[23]

It is noteworthy that, in both explanations cited by Strabo, the
votive purpose of the hoard is stressed. The lake at Toulouse was,
indeed, a centre of the cult of the god Belenus.[24] Obviously the
Celts were – in this case munificently – following the custom of
their predecessors of depositing hoards. This is further borne out
by the archaeology of Celtic regions – for instance, a fine hoard
of brooches and bracelets found in a bronze cauldron in a well at
Duchcov in Bohemia,[25] a splendid collection of wooden carvings
discovered at the source of the Seine near Dijon[26] and – most
notable of all – the finds at La Tène in Switzerland, which entailed
a great variety of weapons and woodwork in the eastern end of
the lake of Neuchâtel.[27] Often, it would appear, the purpose of
depositing such hoards was to give thanks for a victory in battle,
and in such cases the hoard would have consisted of the spoils
taken from the enemy. The Latin writer Orosius describes such an
action in the year 105 BC by the Cimbri, a Germanic tribe in Denmark who had close connections with the Celts:

> In accordance with a strange and unusual vow, they set
> about destroying everything which they had taken.
> Clothing was cut to pieces and cast away, gold and silver
> were thrown into the river, the breastplates of the men
> were hacked to pieces, the trappings of the horses were
> broken up, the horses themselves drowned in whirlpools,
> and men with nooses around their necks were hanged
> from trees.[28]

There is copious evidence for such practice in Britain also –
hoards of pottery, ornaments and weapons being thrown into
bogs, pools, and rivers from the late Bronze Age onwards.[29] The
most famous such deposit was at Llyn Cerrig Bach in Anglesey
where, in the period from the 2nd century BC to the 1st century
AD, over 150 such metal objects – including weapons, chariot-

fittings, and fragments of cauldrons and trumpets – were thrown into a pool from a high rock.[30] Gradually, swords were replaced by cauldrons as the favourite votive objects, and the tendency to leave them whole and unbroken increased.[31] As well as in water, votive offerings were often left in shafts or pits, and these could also include animal and even human remains.[32]

In Ireland, the custom of burying hoards was also, as we have seen, current since the Bronze Age. In the Celtic Iron Age, the general practice seems to have been to deposit valuable items in water. Although the majority of such hoards consisted of bridle-bits and horse pendants,[33] there are significant examples of more precious deposits. For instance, weapons and bronze bowls have been found in the river Bann, swords and fine brooches have been found in the river Shannon, while a magnificent bird-handled cup was discovered at Keshcarrigan in Co. Leitrim, in a tributary of that same river.[34] The most celebrated of all such finds was the Broighter hoard, discovered in the flood plain of the river Roe in Co. Derry. This consisted of elaborately wrought objects in gold, such as necklaces, a collar, a bowl, and a small model boat with mast and oars.[35] It can be compared to the find near Basle in Switzerland of gold objects, including also a collar, in the floodplain of the Rhine.[36]

A very unique deposit in a pool called – perhaps appropriately – Loch na Séad ('the Lake of the Jewels'), near Eamhain Mhacha, consisted of four bronze trumpets.[37] These instruments, of which a few others have been found at different locations in Ireland, seem to have been of some importance among the Celts, one being portrayed on the famous statue of the Dying Gaul from the 3rd century BC.[38] Diodorus Siculus described the Gaulish trumpets as being 'of a peculiar barbaric kind – they blow into them and produce a harsh sound which suits the tumult of war'.[39] The Irish bronze horns and trumpets could give a fair variation in sound,[40] and Irish literature mentions their use in war.[41] One early source, in fact, states that the trumpet (tob) 'has many sounds, and is different in each of them, to wit, it is different for battle, different for unyoking, or for marching, or for sleep, or for council'.[42] Since, in ancient societies, there was no clear distinction between 'sacred' and 'secular' ceremonies, we can accept the playing of trumpets as having had a religious function of some kind. In a text from the 8th century AD, horn-blowers are described as preceding, with wonderfully plaintive music, a warrior as he returns badly wounded after a great feat.[43]

Of undoubted religious significance were the large bronze cauldrons, which have been found in several Irish bogs as well as in votive deposits in other Celtic areas abroad.[44] The custom of depositing these dates from as early as the 7th century BC in Ireland, and those from Celtic times are of so fine and careful design as to suggest that, beyond their normal function in the preparation of food and drink, they must have also had a ritual purpose.[45] As a symbol of feasting, they would have been synonymous with material prosperity, and cauldrons have been found in several Celtic and Germanic burials from the pre-Christian period on the Continent.[46] Such vessels, as we shall see, were symbols of plenty with divine associations in early Irish literature; and the very elaborate Gundestrup cauldron discovered in a bog in Denmark, which is believed to have been of Celtic manufacture, had several ritual scenes depicted on it.[47]

In Ireland, as abroad, many of the votive offerings were broken, but this presents no real problem, as they were sacrificial. It would be natural to regard the offering as representing the essence of the object rather than the physical object itself, and this essence was the gift being proffered to the preternatural powers, who could put it to their own use in the otherworld.[48] It is interesting to note that a gradual tendency towards more realism is attested, as in Britain – that is, more and more objects came to be deposited in a quite complete form.[49] This would appear to suggest a variant attitude according to which the otherworld agencies required a fully functional gift.

Sacrifice
The burial customs in Iron Age Ireland were in themselves variable, the graves either being flat or covered by a mound. The fact that grave-goods – such as bronze and iron implements and bone and glass beads – have been found in some cases shows that a form of ceremonial accompanied the interments. Both cremation and inhumation were practised, and the bodies were variably

flexed and crouched.[50] Animal-bones often accompanied burials in Celtic Britain,[51] and there is some evidence that such was the case also in Ireland.[52] An intriguing example of burial was discovered at Knowth in Co. Meath, near the ancient megalithic burial mound. This – dating from the final century BC or the first century AD – consisted of two male skeletons, arranged head to toe in a pit, and accompanied by bone and glass beads, metal rings, and bone-dice with other apparent gaming pieces. Both skeletons were decapitated.[53] We can only guess at the circumstances of death and burial of these two individuals. Were they noted gamblers, buried together so as to continually contend with each other in the afterlife? Or, on the other hand, were they in fact sacrificed in the expectation that their posthumous gaming would ritually benefit some undertaking in the world of the living?

Other puzzling examples involve the burial of children, or even foetuses, along with adults, and archaeologists again see the possibility of such individuals having been deliberately killed and buried in this manner.[54] There is plenty of archaeological and literary evidence from abroad to suggest that the Celts practised, not only animal, but also human, sacrifice.[55] Ritual slaughter of people is referred to by Roman writers on the Gauls, who strongly condemned the practice, aware that it had become obsolete in other parts of the Empire. Many skeletons have been discovered from the Celtic period in Britain, placed underneath buildings in a manner which suggests that they were put there in order to guarantee the solidity and good fortune of the structures. The suggestion is strengthened by the fact that the skulls and other bones of animals, such as dogs, cattle, horses, and pigs have been found in pits and under ramparts, sometimes arranged in such a way as to make it clear that they were placed there ritually.[56]

Whether or not people were actually sacrificed in Celtic Britain is unclear, but at the very least the placing of human skeletons underneath buildings would mean that memory of such sacrifice persisted and that bodies of dead people were deposited with the same intended purpose. That such a custom existed in Celtic Ireland is apparent from a burial in the centre of an embanked enclosure – either a ritual or a dwelling-site – on the Curragh in Co. Kildare. This was of a woman who, to judge from her strained position, seems to have been buried alive.[57]

The ideas which must have lain behind such practices are well instanced from Irish folklore, and some of these ideas might even be survivals from the actual practices. For instance, there was a general folk belief that buried treasure was guarded by spirits of animals – those who went to dig up such a treasure might be frightened off by a ghostly cock, dog, bull, horse, or pig.[58] It was commonly believed that hidden treasure was guarded by a human spirit, and indeed several stories told of a person having been deliberately put to death upon the burial of a trove, so that his ghost would act as its guardian.[59] A less common, but nevertheless persistent, belief was that the blood of bullocks had been mixed in the cement of certain big houses or castles so as to make them more solid,[60] and a long-enduring custom was to bury the skull of an animal – usually that of a horse – underneath the floor of a new house.[61]

There are not many references to sacrifice in old Irish literature, but no doubt the Christian writers would have ignored such traditions except when they intended to vilify the archaic native customs. For instance, a speculative mediaeval tradition had it that the pagan Irish sacrificed one third of their children to idols in return for a good milk and corn yield.[62] This is surely an invention – echoing the child-sacrifice to Melech in the Old Testament – but a few other mediaeval sources may be based on a lingering memory of a real practice. One Irish text alludes to the custom of slaughtering hostages at the ritual centre of Tailtiu in order to remove the threat of plague.[63] Here we have a curious parallel to a Latin account from the 4th century AD, which claims that the Gauls at Marseille had formerly the custom of sacrificing a ritual victim in time of pestilence.[64]

There is reason to believe that, whether as sacrifice or not, hostages could be treated with great cruelty in early Ireland. One text, for instance, describes how the Munstermen refused to pay tribute to Criomhthann, king of Tara in the 5th century AD. This led to war, in which Criomhthann was successful but in which his nephew Fiachra was killed. As a result of this, 'the hostages who had been taken from the south were buried alive around the grave of Fiachra' at Tara.[65] Less impressive, however, is the statement in a mediaeval text that the ancient royal cult-site of Ulster, Eamhain Mhacha, was laid with a human victim – this is based on a fanciful derivation of Eamhain from *ema-uin*, which elements are, equally fancifully, taken to mean 'blood of one'.[66]

One very curious occurrence of the motif of sacrifice is in a late mediaeval romance, according to which the early but pseudo-historical king Conn Céadchathach took an otherworld woman as paramour and banished his son Art. As a result of the banishment, there was neither corn nor milk in Ireland for a whole year. When the druids were consulted, they advised that the situation could be corrected by the slaying of the son of a sinless couple. Such a youth was found, but when he was being prepared for sacrifice, a strange woman appeared and offered a cow as victim in his stead. The sacrifice had the desired effect.[67] This plot was borrowed from a 9th-century account in Nennius' *Historia Brittonum*, which describes how a Celtic king, Vortigern, is advised by his druids to sacrifice the mystically-conceived boy Ambrosius in order that the blood should consecrate a fortress.[68] This British Latin story is a version of a widespread folk legend,[69] and is therefore of little value here except for the possibility that the plot of that folk legend was superimposed onto an indigenous Celtic recollection of sacrifice.

Other mediaeval texts describe how a pseudo-historical race, the followers of Neimheadh, placated their oppressors by offering annually two-thirds of their children and of their corn and milk,[70] and how a druid offered himself as a victim to save his Déise sept (in the region of Waterford), but was transformed into a cow before sacrifice.[71] It is interesting to note the occurrence of milk and corn in several of these texts in connection with human sacrifice, and this may preserve a memory that a purpose of the custom in ancient times was to promote agricultural welfare. The corn and milk-yield, of vital importance in Irish life, was at the mercy of seasonal and other indeterminate factors, and it is apposite to mention that much superstition also attached to both in later Irish folklore.[72]

The cult of heads

The notion that the body or bones of a dead person continued to have some kind of power is illustrated by a very special type of motif. An instance occurs in a Latin text from the 7th century AD, which describes how Laoghaire, a Tara king of two centuries earlier, left instructions that he be buried on the ridges of that citadel, facing south against the royal graves of his Leinster foes at Mullaghmast as a token of undying hatred for them.[73] Later sources claim that Laoghaire gave this order as a deliberate rejection of Christian burial.[74]

A text which, although of later date, encompasses tradition from the early centuries AD, describes the warrior Mac Con raising a cairn of stones for each one of a group of fighting-men who were his allies. 'They were buried standing with their shields before them, each man in his own mound.'[75] Memory of this burial custom persisted, for in a mediaeval account, it is said that when Eoghan Béal, a fighting king of Connacht, lay mortally wounded after a battle in the year AD 543, he gave instructions that he was to be buried in the plain of his own Uí Fiachrach sept. He ordered that a red javelin be placed in his hand, and that he be standing upright and facing northwards against the Ulstermen, 'for they will not go to battle against Connacht while my grave faces them and while I myself am arranged in it in that manner'. His northern foes are reported to have later set aside this impediment by exhuming the body and burying him in another place, with his face downwards.[76] It would appear that the mediaeval writers did not always recognise this old tradition, for we read that one of the Ulster epical heroes, Cormac Connloingeas, had the appellation Nia an Chairn ('Champion of the Cairn'). It is explained that he protected his province at the 'White Cairn of the Lookout' on the Fews Mountains, but this is very likely a second-hand interpretation in the romantic literature.[77]

Inherent in this tradition of ghostly sentries was the idea that the spiritual part of the individual survived death, and that in this way the dead person could still be a force to be reckoned with. The idea is expressed very clearly in the lore concerning a Leinster champion of the 7th century AD called Maolodhrán. He had an extraordinary spear which, after his death, was manoeuvred by his spirit to avenge his slayer.[78] Again, we read that this spear was placed on a fork-stick in a gap called Bealach Duirghein (apparently the Glen of the Downs in Co. Wicklow) 'covered and pointing south', and that as long as it was there the Leinstermen could not prevail against their enemies to the north.[79] Sympathetic magic of this military nature may, indeed, have been practised since long before the time of the Celts. Recent archaeological discoveries indicate that many burial mounds of the Bronze Age were situated near river-banks, which are likely to have been territorial divisions.[80] It is reasonable to assume that dead leaders and warriors were buried at such locations so as to provide a sacred barrier which would discourage hostile but superstitious neighbours from intruding.

Parallels to the notion from mediaeval literature in Britain tell of how the Celtic prince Vortimer left instructions that he was to be buried on the strand and that the Anglo-Saxon invaders would not dare pass his body,[81] and of how his bones were interred at various sea-ports for the same purpose.[82] A later instance of the motif, in the Icelandic *Laxdaelasaga*, describes how a chieftain leaves instructions to be buried under the threshold of his house and his corpse later terrifies people until it is removed. This is probably based on British or Irish literature.[83] Most notable of all was the tradition, recounted in the *Mabinogi*, that the mythical Welsh king Bran had left instructions that his head be buried at 'White Hill' in London, with its face turned towards France so that no plague would cross the sea to Britain. This particular head was itself a great celebrity, for we read that when Bran was killed in Ireland his followers brought it back to Wales with them, and feasted joyously in its company for a long time while birds sang melodiously to them. This feasting became known as *Ysbydawt Urdaul Benn* ('the Hospitality of the Wondrous Head').[84]

That special properties were believed by the Iron Age Celts to reside in buried heads is clear from the archaeological record.[85] There was a common custom in Celtic Britain to behead bodies before interring them, and many skulls have been found under the foundations of buildings of the period.[86] The discovery of

some decapitated bodies, and of human skulls unaccompanied
by other bones, in burial sites in Ireland indicates that such practices were known here also.[87] There is strong confirmation of a
related rite in accounts of the Continental Celts, although the
Graeco-Roman writer Posidonius naturally tends to focus on the
military dimension:

> They cut off the heads of enemies slain in battle and
> attach them to the necks of their horses. The blood-
> stained spoils they hand over to their attendants and
> carry off as booty, while striking up a paean and singing
> a song of victory; and they nail up these first fruits upon
> their houses just as do those who lay low wild animals in
> certain kinds of hunting. They embalm in cedar-oil the
> heads of the most distinguished enemies and preserve
> them carefully in a chest, and display them with pride to
> strangers – saying that, for this head, one of their ances-
> tors, or his father, or the man himself, refused the offer
> of a large sum of money. They say that some of them
> boast that they refused the weight of the head in gold.[88]

The basis for this belief would have been that the individual-
ity, or even essence, of the person resides in his head. The head
of a dead leader was therefore a valuable possession to a community, and contrariwise, the loss of such a head to the enemy
was a singular defeat. This is graphically illustrated in the report
of a skirmish fought in the year 54 BC, in which the Roman cavalry beheaded the Gaulish leader Indutiomarus, and brought it
back to their camp. Even though their war against the Romans
had been very successful up to that point, Caesar reports that the
army of Indutiomarus disbanded on hearing this news.[89] This
behaviour, incidentally, is paralleled by the reputed Irish custom
of retiring from battle when the leader fell, for 'one does not
wage war after the loss of a lord'.[90]

Early Irish literature has several accounts of warriors being
beheaded in battle and their heads being kept as trophies. Curiously, however, the victorious enemies tend in these accounts to
have a quite friendly and respectful attitude to the gruesome

prizes. Most of these Irish accounts concern the seer-warrior Fionn mac Cumhaill and, as will be clear, the decapitated head as described in them has a mantic function. The earliest reference is in an 8th-century text, which has a rival warrior, Fothadh Canainne, being reconciled to Fionn. The latter invites Fothadh to an ale-feast, but Fothadh declares: 'I may not drink ale unless it be drunk in the company of white faces!' Accordingly, Fionn goes forth to kill a man but, ironically, the victim is a brother-in-law of Fothadh.[91] Thus Fothadh is punished for his ferocity but, significantly, the writer does not have Fionn question his savage request, and we can consider this to result from the motif of feasting in the presence of the dead being too well founded in antique lore. In fact, another text has the severed head of Fothadh himself, after his death, chanting a poem.[92]

A text from a century or so later repeats the motif, but in a more specifically mantic context. According to this, a rival called Cairbre lay with Fionn's mistress. The tryst was observed by Lomhna, the jester of Fionn, who told his master of it, but Cairbre in turn beheaded Lomhna. Fionn set out to seek revenge, and came upon Cairbre in his hunting-booth cooking fish on a heated stone. The head of Lomhna was on a spike by the fire. When Cairbre began to divide the food among his companions, he put no morsel into the mouth of the head. Then the head spoke a rhetoric to Fionn in complaint. Again Cairbre served the food, but neglected the head, and it spoke and threatened that Cairbre's sept, the Luaighne, would have enemies on this account:

> 'Put out the head,' said Cairbre, 'though it be wrong of me to say it!'
> And something was heard from the head outside:
> 'The stake relates that a champion was running with his battle-spear at their [i.e. your parents'] first coupling. Ye will be like several pieces or many fragments. Fionn will light the Luaighne with much fire!'
> At that, Fionn approached Cairbre and slew him.[93]

Doubtlessly under the influence of the foregoing account, another mediaeval story told of how, after Fionn himself was slain and decapitated, he spoke and demanded a piece of fish from his feasting murderers.[94] The fact that the speeches made by such heads are in the form of obscure rhetoric would lead us to consider that there was a belief in some sort of hidden knowledge which could be gained from them. Mediaeval Norse literature has several similar accounts of speaking heads, and some scholars believe that the motif was borrowed into that context from Irish sources.[95] The best known Norse example is in the *Ynglinga Saga*, where we read that Mímir, the wisest of men, was killed by his enemies, but his head was restored to Odin and his own people. 'Odin took the head, smeared it with such herbs that it could not rot, chanted spells over it and worked such charms that it talked with him and told him many hidden things.'[96]

That such rituals concerning dead heads may have survived into historical times in Ireland is suggested by a 10th-century story concerning the battle of Allen, which took place in AD 722 between the High-King, Fearghal mac Maoldúin, and the Leinstermen. We read that among Fearghal's defeated forces in that battle was a young man called Donn Bó, who was a great storyteller and entertainer. A soldier found his body on the battlefield, cut off the head, and brought it into the victory feast. It was placed on a pillar and, when asked to sing, it turned to the wall so as to be in darkness and then commenced. It asked to be replaced on its body, and in this way Donn Bó returned to life. The High-King Fearghal was also slain, and when the king of Munster, Cathal mac Fionghuine, heard this he was incensed. In order to placate Cathal, the Leinstermen brought the head of the High-King to him. Cathal had it washed and combed and arrayed in satin, and held a feast in its honour. The head blushed and spoke piously, after which it was returned to its own people.[97]

It is clear from these sources that the custom of keeping heads as trophies had become assimilated to a different kind of belief – namely, that the head of a person who possessed knowledge could in certain circumstances still impart that knowledge after death.[98] This latter seems to have been a belief held by the Celts generally, for the example cited above of the wonderful head of Bran would indicate that it was familiar in Wales also. In this

regard, reference can be made to the many representations of
heads in art and in sculpture from Celtic areas of Britain and the
Continent. Several of these representations of heads can be taken
to refer to deities, which naturally indicates that divine wisdom
was incorporated in that part of the anatomy.[99]

Mediaeval Irish literature describes the first of the Gaelic people to set foot on the soil of Ireland, Amhairghin (literally 'the
wonderfully conceived') reciting a chant on the occasion in
which he claims to be the essence of all things – including inspiration itself, 'the god who gives sense to the head'.[100] Moreover,
a celebrated mythical Irish king – to whom prophecies were
attributed – had the name Conn, which meant 'intelligence' or
'head' in the sense of a leader;[101] while Welsh literature features
the hero Pwyll, whose name meant 'reason' and who was
described as *penn* (literally, 'head') of *Annwvn* (a term for the
spiritual realm).[102] The literal meaning of this term Annwvn was
'underworld',[103] and it would thus parallel the region of darkness, where the dead reside. That those who have departed this
life, due to their experience and no doubt antiquity, are possessed
of special knowledge, is a natural proposition. It is curious to
note that in the Irish story of Donn Bó the head turns to the darkness before it speaks to the company. Indeed, longstanding Irish
tradition of the mystical knowledge possessed by the poet (*file*,
literally 'seer'), stresses the communion of that profession with
the otherworld and the custom of composing in darkness.[104]

Images of heads among the Continental Celts were variously
sculpted in stone and represented on vases. Some of these are
given three faces, and these may have been intended to represent
an 'all-knowing god' who sees all dimensions of reality
together.[105] The three-faced head, cut in sandstone, from Cor-
leck in Co. Cavan is a celebrated Irish example of the type.[106]

The god of the dead

Drawing on the parallel of a three-headed rider of the heavens in
Thracian myth, as well as on a more speculative counting of
heads in lieu of days of the week on Gaulish vases, Pettazzoni
identifies this three-headed image with the sun and with a divine
ancestor. The complex of ideas is intriguing, for it connects a

number of important basic themes in early Irish literature. It should first of all be noted that the divine ancestor seems to have been primarily associated in archaic Irish tradition with the world of the dead.[107] This also may have been the case with the Continental Celts, if we accept what Julius Caesar says in this regard in referring to the ancestral deity, whom he calls by the Roman name of Dis Pater:

> The Gauls all assert their descent from Dis Pater and say that it is the druidic belief. For this reason they count periods of time not by the number of days but by the number of nights; and in reckoning birthdays and the new moon and new year their unit of reckoning is the night followed by the day.[108]

This system of counting of nights before days was known to other early European people also,[109] and terminology reflecting it survives still in Irish and other Celtic languages.[110] It is clear that Caesar saw a connection between the darkness of night and the lord of the dead ancestors, but the functional link between this and the computing of time raises a question. The sun, which brings the light of day, is of course the basic determiner of time, but for Caesar's Gauls, time was computed by the sun's absence. We can explain this by the proposition that knowledge of time, as other abstract knowledge, came from the realm inhabited by the ancestors, the realm into which the sun descends each night. There is, in fact, strong evidence of the belief in ancient Europe that the sun, when sinking in the west, entered the underworld each night to abide there with the dead.[111]

We have discussed several indications of a similar belief in pre-Celtic Ireland in Chapter 1, and there are other more direct examples from the records of antiquity. In ancient Greek litera-ture, for instance, Hesiod described the western Mediterranean as the entrance to an underworld in which the Titans were con-fined – 'a dank place where the ends of the huge earth are' and 'where night and day draw near and greet each other as they pass the great threshold of bronze'.[112] This area of the setting sun was not only associated with the dreary aspect of the otherworld, however, but also with the more attractive aspect. Homer refers to 'the Elysian plain at the world's end' to which some go after death and where all is pleasant and where 'day after day the west wind's tuneful breeze comes in from the ocean to refresh its folk'.[113] Hence the idea that a wonderful otherworld island called Elysion was in the western world.[114]

The earliest Greek myth concerning the straits at the western extremity of the Mediterranean was that the sky was upheld by Atlas there.[115] In time, however, a different explanation grew up, according to which the rocks of Gibraltar and Almina were raised by Heracles as the columns of the gate to the Atlantic Ocean. This allowed for the fancy that the sun went away through a great topographical archway, and what lay beyond was the subject of much speculation. It was claimed that it was in this vicinity that Heracles overcame the triple-headed or triple-bodied Geryon, and took away his herd of cattle.[116] The abode of Geryon was on Erytheia ('red island'), another derivative of the sun setting in the west. The exact location of the island was disputed. Some identified it with the marshy site of Cadiz or with an island close by, others considered it to be off the coast of Lusitania and – most significantly of all – yet others thought it to be far out in the western Ocean.[117]

Some of these Greek writers claimed that earlier designations of the straits were 'the pillars of Cronus' and 'the pillars of Briareus'. They also report that a temple was in fact dedicated to Cronus on the western cape of Cadiz,[118] and this may have been suggested to them by reports of the great megaliths in that area.[119] Another writer, Scymnius of Chius, claimed that the pillars were situated in the western extremity of Gaul,[120] which claim represents an extension of the notion into the Celtic area. It would, indeed, appear that Celtic beliefs in the otherworld as a western island owe much to the Greeks. The probable source of this influence was the Greek colony at Marseilles, which was established as early as the 6th century BC and continued to thrive. Navigators passed through this port on their way to the western regions and it was, moreover, an important contact-point in trade and other matters with the Gauls. It has been suggested that the Gaulish learned class came under the influence of

Greek philosophy through this very colony,[121] and the spread of popular or quasi-popular fancies concerning the otherworld would have been a much easier process.

These ideas would soon have spread to the Celts in Britain, who were much influenced by the culture of the Celts of Gaul. That the ideas were adopted there also, and became traditional there, appears from a description given in the 1st century AD by Plutarch. Using information which he had from a traveller called Demetrius, Plutarch claims that 'the inhabitants of Britain located the land of the dead in adjacent small islands' and 'there is one island where Cronus is prisoner, being guarded in his sleep by Briareus, for sleep has been devised as a chain to bind him, and there are many deities about him as satellites and attendants'.[122] 'Cronus' and 'Briareus' were underworld deities whom, as we have seen, were associated by some Greek writers with the area of the setting sun,[123] and Plutarch would therefore have borrowed their names in this context from the literature known to him. Behind the Greek dressing, however, there must have been some worthy and established British data, for the account given by Plutarch is a startlingly concrete one:

> On the ocean strand opposite Britain dwell certain fishermen; they hear a voice calling them and a knock at the door. Rising from their beds they find at the shore unfamiliar boats heavily laden. They grasp the oars, and in an hour are across, although their own boats would require one and a half days. When they arrive, although they see nobody, they hear a voice calling out the names of those who disembark.[124]

One is struck here by the resemblance to the Greek lore of Pluto and the ferrying of souls across the river Styx. The similarity may be explained as a common ancient tradition concerning the dead which had come down to both Greeks and Celts but, in view of what we have said, it seems more sensible to regard it as having originated in general Greek influence. Since the emphasis in these death-beliefs was on the imagery of the west, it is not surprising that the lore was further extended to the westernmost island of Celtdom, Ireland itself. Irish tradition does, indeed, have plenty of material in a similar vein, and particularly the motif of an offshore island presided over by a lord of the dead. He is Donn, which name is derived from Celtic *dhuosno-, meaning the 'dark' or 'black' one,[125] and he is described as inhabiting a small island off the southwest coast of Ireland.[126] That island, known as *Tech Duinn* ('the House of Donn'), is in fact nothing more than a rock, but has an unusual formation, being in effect a natural archway under which the sea flows with tremendous force. It is known in English as Bull Rock, and lies some miles off the shore of the Beare peninsula, being the most westerly piece of land in all that area.

Mediaeval Irish texts describe the 'belief of the heathen' to the effect that souls go there to Donn,[127] and in the pseudo-history Donn is euhemerised as one of the leaders of the Gaelic people when they came to Ireland. We read of this pseudo-historical Donn, however, that he was not destined to reach the shore of Ireland, but was drowned near the rock which bears his name.[128] A poem written on the theme of this story in the 9th century AD claims that the rock itself was raised by Donn's followers as a memorial-cairn to him, but seems to depart from the elaborate fiction by quoting a final statement uttered by him to these followers: *'Cucum dom thig tíssaid uili íar bar n-écaib!'* ('to me, to my house, you shall all come after your deaths!').[129] Although the word-forms used in the phrase are of the historical period, the author seems to be giving a genuine echo of a statement of belief in the afterlife from pagan Ireland.

The general cult of Donn as god of the dead must have been widely known in Ireland. Varied references in the literature as early as the 8th century AD show that the belief had been long established. One such allusion, from Ulster, is to a departed warrior returning from the realm of the dead in the House of Donn in the southwest.[130] In another text of the same period, with Leinster provenance, a prophecy is given concerning a group of heroes to the effect that 'death will defeat them on the morning ebb towards the House of Donn'. In the same text, three red horsemen appear as an omen of death, and they announce: 'We ride the horses of toothless Donn from the tumuli, although we

are alive we are dead!'[131] Donn is here a personification of the
elders buried in the tumuli, which illustrates the physical aspect
of funerary practice.

The general imagery, however, refers to the spiritual destina-
tion of the dead, for the colour red and the triplicated horsemen
accord well with the ancient ideas concerning the sun which we
have already mentioned. In its most symbolic form, it would
appear that the departure of the spirits of the dead was envisaged
as following the course of the sun as it passed under the archway
of Donn's dwelling into the sea and from thence to the nether
world. This has the marks of a survival in Ireland of the idea of
otherworld portals borrowed by the Continental Celts from the
Greeks many centuries before. The dolmen-shaped Bull Rock
would have been an obvious identification for such an entrance
to the world of the dead.

Nor is the image of the Greeks' 'red island' contradicted by
the darkness inherent in the name of Donn, for we have seen that
an early Irish text has red horsemen conducting the slain to the
House of Donn. In fact, the heroes in that same text met their
death in a house which belongs to a personage called Dearg
('red'), and he is also referred to as Da Dearga (which seems to
be a corruption of Dia Dearg, 'the red god').[132] The writer of this
text was no doubt making use, for dramatic effect, of the black
imagery of death and the red imagery of slaughter, but in view of
what we have said, the original import of these contrasting
colours must have been the symbolism of the sun, which is dark
by night and flaming by day.

The deity as provider

We have noted the report of Julius Caesar that the Gauls considered themselves to be all descended from one ancestor, an
ancestor with whom he connected their counting of nights and
days. The name which Caesar gave to that divine being was 'Dis
Pater', a Roman designation which meant 'the god who is
father'. One figure in early Irish literature who is readily identifiable with both solar and ancestral themes is *an Daghdha*. This
name is derived from a primitive Celtic form *dago-devos*,
meaning 'good god'[133] and the personage to whom it is applied

is represented as the possessor of a 'cauldron of plenty' and the father of several other divine beings.[134]

The sun-god of the Continental Celts was sometimes repre-sented as riding a great horse, and in one inscription he is even referred to as 'Atepomarus' – the *epomarus* here meaning 'great horse'.[135] So it comes as no surprise that the Daghdha had an alternative designation *Eochaidh* (which meant 'horseman'), and under this name was given the soubriquet *Ollathair* (literally 'father of all').[136] Furthermore, early Irish literature refers to other characters called Eochaidh who can be taken as derivatives of him – these have soubriquets such as *Áncheann* and *Aonsúla* ('glowing head' and 'one-eyed').[137] Sources referring directly to the Daghdha give him the nicknames *Aedh Álainn* and *Rúadh Ró-fhessa* ('beautiful fire' and 'ruddy one of much wisdom'),[138] which immediately call to mind the bright sun which sees all on earth. We have seen in Chapter 1 that a similar belief in the sun as a life-giving ancestor may have been current among some of the megalithic people of Ireland, and it is no surprise to find that Celticised Irish culture made the Daghdha into an inhabitant of the Newgrange tumulus (known as *Brugh na Bóinne*). One source, indeed, claims that he died there.[139]

Linguistically, the name of the Indo-European sky-god would have been *Deiwos or *Dyeus, from which are derived the Indic Dyâus, the Greek Zeus, the Roman Jupiter, and the Germanic Tyr.[140] The Daghdha ('the good *Devos*') was the Irish version of this same ultimate personage. A certain tendency to stress the solar aspect of the sky is apparent from some of the European personages, and this probably took place under the influence of a surviving Bronze-Age sun-cult; but it is notable that in the case of the Daghdha, the deity has become much more fully trans-formed into a personification of the sun. The explanation for this would lie in the influence of the much older and pre-Celtic Irish stratum of sun-lore, and specifically such lore in the context of Newgrange.[141]

The European and Celtic origin of the Daghdha himself is, however, quite clear. Caesar described the Gaulish cult of Dis Pater as 'the druidic belief', and the Daghdha is referred to in Irish literature in strikingly similar terms. One reference states of the divine race, Tuatha Dé Danann, that 'they themselves had a god of druidry, Eochaidh Ollathair, i.e., the great Daghdha, for he was a good god'.[142] Another text, in claiming that he was the father of all the divine race, goes on to describe him under his designation Rúadh Ró-Fheasa as having 'the perfection of the heathen science' and as having 'the multiform triads'.[143] As we shall see in Chapter 3, the druidic teaching was often expressed in triadic form. It is obvious that this principal deity of the Irish Celts was envisaged, not just in the role of Donn presiding over the world of the dead, but also as an abundant life-giving force in the world of the living.

That the goodness of the Daghdha did not have a specifically moral import, but rather one of competence and largesse, is clear from a mediaeval text on the mythical battle of Magh Tuireadh ('the Plain of the Pillars'). In that text, he is a leading member of the divine race, the Tuatha Dé Danann, and promises to assist them against their enemies by shaking the mountains, draining the lakes, and bringing showers of fire. As a result of this promise, the Tuatha Dé give him his title of 'good god'.[144] By his prodigious strength, he builds a fortress without assistance and places a circular rampart around it.[145] He receives a heifer as reward for his work, and later uses this heifer to attract the whole herd which their Fomhoire enemies have taken from the Tuatha Dé, thereby restoring the cattle to their rightful owners.[146] In the actual battle, he smites multitudes with his great club.[147]

The text also represents him as being of massive size and having a voracious appetite. In an episode which has him visiting the Fomhoire camp, these enemies mock him by inviting him to partake of a meal. The fare consists of huge amounts of gruel, milk, and lean and fat meat. All of this is cooked together in a cauldron, into which goats and sheep and pigs are also thrown. Taking his huge ladle, 'big enough for a married couple to lie in its middle', he consumes all of the food with zest, so that his stomach was swollen 'as big as a house-boiler'. After this, he meets a girl and, following on lively physical contact, he copulates with her.[148] This description, of course, had a humorous purpose, but the mediaeval writer was burlesquing original themes such as abundance and reproduction.

Other mediaeval texts testify to the tradition concerning his huge size and ability, and much stress is laid on his cauldron and great club. We read that the cauldron (*coire an Daghdha*) was 'a huge mighty treasure' and that 'an assembly used not to go unsatisfied from it'.[149] This can be connected with the importance of cauldrons in the votive deposits of the Celts, referred to above, and no doubt such gifts were given to the deities in the hope of reciprocation. Mediaeval Welsh literature tells of magical cauldrons in Ireland, particularly that taken by Bran, in which the bodies of dead warriors are cooked and thereby restored to life.[150] The great club (*lorg an Daghdha*) was said to have a similar miraculous effect, as is clear from a 9th-century Irish description of the Daghdha himself:

> A very big and tall man, with remarkable eyes, thighs and shoulders, and a fine grey cloak about him . . . nine men on either side of him, a dreadful iron club in his hand, one rough end on it and one gentle end. This is his trick and his feat – he lays the rough end on the heads of the nine men so that he kills them immediately; he lays the gentle end on them so that he revives them in the same instant.[151]

The dialectic of rough and smooth would appear to be of druidic origin, for the druid-poets of early Ireland used the same contrast to describe their words of magical power (see Chapter 3). Fascination with the image of the club caused later writers to invent further details concerning it, such as how the Daghdha had received it as a gift from three strangers on his travels in the eastern world,[152] and how he used it to repel a sea-monster and cause the sea itself to recede.[153] It might well be that these accounts owe something to sun-symbolism in the image of the deity himself. It is clear, at any rate, that an old tradition portrayed him as a kind of technician of the environment. For one of his daughters, for instance, he fashioned a tub which used to drip when the sea was in flood and to stabilise when the sea subsided.[154] We read that his countenance was 'broader than half a plain',[155] and that he cleared twelve actual plains in one night.

On another night, he cut the paths of twelve rivers and, as further proof of his importance to agriculture, he controlled the weather and the crops for the Tuatha Dé.[156]

Although it is difficult to identify the Daghdha with any specific personage among the Celtic pantheon abroad, certain parallels have been adduced by scholars. Various Continental Celtic dedications to their deity whom the Romans in Gaul identified with 'Jupiter', for example, represent that deity as a solar horseman and as a patron of mountains. Especially interesting in this regard are the 'columns' dedicated to the personage – they consist of a pillar, decorated to suggest a tree, standing on a stone plinth and surmounted by the sculpted figure of a heavenly horseman overcoming a monster.[157] Another possible parallel is furnished by reliefs and statues from Britain and the Continent of a mature male deity with a pot in one hand and a mallet in the other. In a few cases, this deity is given the title Sucellos (literally 'the good striker'). He is usually portrayed in ordinary peasant clothing, but is sometimes accompanied by solar motifs. Scholars have opined that his hammer may have symbolised the striking of the earth so as to make it fruitful and that the pot may have symbolised the fruits of labour.[158] As such – in function as well as in imagery – he resembles the Irish Daghdha with his club and cauldron.

This hammer-god of the Celts is often accompanied on reliefs by a female companion, and she may be holding a jar, a pot, or some other apparent symbol of agricultural fertility. In several cases where the hammer-god himself is called Sucellos, this lady-companion of his is given the name Nantosuelta. The first element 'nant-' indicates water and the full meaning may be 'stream-flowing' or the like.[159] It is probably best to consider her as a river-goddess who fertilises the soil, and the coupling of these two personages together would accordingly have an agricultural function.[160] An account in the Irish text on the battle of Magh Tuireadh would appear to exemplify the same type of lore:

The Daghdha had a tryst arranged within a year at the Samhain [November-feast] of the battle, at Gleann Éadain, and the (river) Uineas of the Connachta roars to

the south of it. He saw the woman at a weir in the
Uineas, washing, with her second foot at Alladh Eacha
at the south of the water and the other (foot) at Lios
Conduibh at the north of the water. Nine loosened tresses
were on her head. The Daghdha addressed her, and they
copulated. The name of the place since then is 'the Lying
of the Couple'. The woman mentioned here is the Mor-
Ríoghain.[161]

Notwithstanding its burlesque flavour, this account can be
taken to be a residue of an old tradition which had the Daghdha
uniting with a water-goddess to fertilise the land. Curiously, the
Welsh story of Bran referred to above has the cauldron of life
emerging from a lake in Ireland while being borne on the back
of a huge man, who is accompanied by a huge woman,[162] and
this may be a reflection of the Daghdha tradition. The productive coupling of the male and female divinities was, of course,
especially apt to the locus of the Newgrange tumulus on the
banks of the river Boyne. As if to underline the ancient mythic
format, one mediaeval poem claims that Brugh na Bóinne was
built by the Daghdha and that, after a hunt, he paid court there
to the Mor-Ríoghain – hence the tumulus is referred to as *imdai
nDagdai deirg* ('the bed of the red Daghdha').[163]

The mother-goddess
Almost all Irish rivers have female names, and the mediaeval literature described how several of these were names of otherworld
women to whom the rivers belonged. This is obviously an indication that the water which irrigated the soil was understood as
a female force. A notable example is the lady Bóinn, eponym of
the Boyne river, who – as we shall see in Chapter 4 – was another
consort of the Daghdha in his Newgrange tumulus. That the concept of river-goddess was important in other Celtic parts of
Europe is clear from many appellations – for instance, the goddess Sequana who presided over the river Seine, Souconna over
the Saône, Sabrina over the Severn, and Verbeia over the river
Wharfe.[164] A direct identification of a river with the maternal
principle is found in the case of the Marne in northeastern

France, which derives its name from Matrona ('divine mother').[165] A derivative of this appellation occurs in mediaeval Welsh literature as Modron, the mother of a mythical hero.[166] This illustrates the integrity of Celtic tradition and – as we shall see in Chapter 4 – several examples from Irish tradition are equally compelling. These examples show how various titles of the mother-goddess were converted into personages such as Bóinn, Brighid, Sionainn, etc., in the lore of early Ireland. It will suffice to say here that they usually functioned as the sources of such essentials as water, milk, and corn.

Most notable is the designation Danu.[167] An aquatic goddess called Dánu occurs in Sanskrit literature,[168] and the Irish goddess seems to be a cognate, even though the 'a' is shortened in her name. This shortening may be due to the influence of the word *anae* (see below), and the lengthened form does indeed appear in the frequent mention in Irish literature of *trí dée Dána* (understood as 'three gods of craftmanship'), which parallels the designation *trí dée Danann* ('three gods of Danu') which also occurs.[169] It therefore appears that the Irish Danu (from a Celtic **Dánuv*) was an Indo-European goddess in origin. This Indo-European goddess, whose own name would have meant 'the flowing one',[170] is considered to have given rise to the names of many rivers, most notably the Danube.[171] Figures with similar designations in Greek mythology may also be related – for instance the mythical women called Danaë, founders of the three cities of Rhodes; and the mythical king Danaus who had fifty daughters, called the Danaides, one of whom discovered for the Greeks a river which never dries up.[172] In Irish literature, Danu is described as being the mother of many of the deities, and indeed the whole race of divinities was known as Tuatha Dé Danann, meaning 'people of the goddess Danu'.[173] A parallel in mediaeval Welsh literature is Dôn, mother of a family of mythical warriors;[174] and, since Celtic was the first and only Indo-European language to reach Ireland in the Iron Age, the cult of Danu must have been brought here as part of the basic stratum of Celtic lore.

Strictly speaking, the appellation in its nominative form is not attested from Ireland. The mediaeval literature was drawing on

the well-known group name Tuatha Dé Danann, and therefore
proposed a later form 'Danainn' as nominative for the personage
herself. The nominative of 'Danann' in earlier Irish would, however, have been 'Danu', and this form is evidenced in an indirect
way by references to a patroness called Anu, described as 'the
mother of the Irish gods' and a great food-provider to whom the
province of Munster owes its special prosperity.[175] That this
'Anu' was an earth-goddess is without doubt. An early text
describes Ireland as *iath nAnann* ('the land of Anu');[176] and two
mountain-tops southeast of Killarney on the Kerry-Cork border,
the shape of which are remarkably suggestive of a woman's
breasts, were known as *Dá Chích nAnann* ('the two paps of
Anu').[177] These two designations would, in fact, have since early
mediaeval times been pronounced identically with *iath nDanann*
and *Dá Chích nDanann*, and therefore one suspects that the original reference was to Danu. It would appear from this that Danu,
a river-goddess in origin, had in Ireland taken over the function
of land-goddess in general. This would have caused the mediaeval writers to speculate on a connection with an Old Irish word
'anae', which meant wealth,[178] and would accordingly have led
to the alternative designation 'Anu' for the goddess.[179]

The goddess 'Anu' was claimed in some sources to have been
one with the Mor-Ríoghain,[180] whom we have encountered as the
paramour of the Daghdha. This Mor-Ríoghain is, in fact, identified in the exact same way with the landscape in sources which
described two hillocks near Newgrange as *dá chích na Mórrígna*
('the two paps of the Mór-Ríoghain').[181] Manuscripts vary as to
the spelling of the first element in her name, and for that reason
it is unclear whether she was originally the Mor-Ríoghain ('phantom queen') or the Mór-Ríoghain ('great queen').[182] At any rate,
it is clear that a goddess, representing the soil and its irrigation,
and variously called Danu and Ríoghain, was taken to be the
partner of the ancestral sun-deity. One mediaeval text puts the tradition in microscopic form by telling us that a particular field was
known as *Gort na Mór-Ríoghna* because the Daghdha had given
it to her and she had afterwards tended to it.[183] It is also thought
that such a pairing lies behind the confused memories in Wales
which gave rise to the mediaeval romance in that country of Pwyll

and Rhiannon.[184] Pwyll, as we have seen, can be taken to emanate from an ancestral figure of great wisdom, whereas Rhiannon is a late form of the Celtic *Rigantona*, meaning divine or great queen.[185]

Under her title of Mor-Ríoghain, this primal goddess, in addition to agricultural prosperity, is given other functions in connection with the landscape. For instance, the remains of ancient cooking-sites were associated with her. Such sites – attested since the Bronze Age and continuing in use into historical times[186] – consisted of pits in which cooking was done by means of stones heated in water. The designation *fulacht na Mór-Ríoghna* ('hearth of the Great Queen') was used for such a structure.[187] A major function attributed to her in the mediaeval literature is that of patroness of war, and in this context she is sometimes triplicated – for example into the personages Neamhain, Fea, and Badhbh. This goddess gives warning of battles, incites her favoured side, and screeches over the battlefield during the actual fighting.[188] We can therefore suppose that this is an inclusion, within the role of the Mor-Ríoghain Danu, of the function of political or military protection of those who possess the land. A parallel is afforded by the Greek tradition of the three Danaë – referred to above – who were foundresses of the cities of Rhodes, and who had the attributes of unavoidable destiny (similar to the three fateful women called Moerae).[189] That Danu herself could be cited in triplicate form appears from the Welsh river-name Trydonwy,[190] and from groups of three associated with her in Irish sources.[191]

Especially dramatic is the figure of Badhbh, who is 'red-mouthed' and appears in the form of a carrion-crow. She is accordingly known as Badhbh Chatha ('the scaldcrow of battle'), a designation which has a direct parallel in the Gaulish inscription 'Cathubodvae'.[192] The fact that she echoes Continental Celtic tradition is significant. Ravens are found in some Continental reliefs in the company of female deities who are otherwise represented as providers of food and nourishment.[193] Moreover, the triplication of the Mor-Ríoghain parallels the frequent triplication of the Matronae and other 'mother-goddesses' in British and Continental iconography.[194] All of this suggests that the imagery of goddesses in Irish lore derives from a complex of beliefs once current among the Celts overseas.

Names given to leading goddesses in different Indo-European cultures do not synchronise together as does the name of the sky-god, and from this we can gather that the cult of the European earth-goddess was a later development than was his.[195] Her outline is, however, quite distinctive in characters such as the Germanic Jordh,[196] the Latin Tellus,[197] and the Greek Demeter.[198] Each of these was described as the wife or mistress of an ancient deity and the mother thereby of other deities or heroes – the archaic Indic earth-goddess Prthivî, in fact, was the consort of the sky-god Dyâus, and by him mother of all gods and men.[199] It is therefore no surprise to find that the earth-goddess – under the name of Danu or Mor-Ríoghain – was the partner of the Daghdha, 'the father of all', in Ireland.

−3−

The Druids and Their Practices

ALTHOUGH BELIEF IN spiritual or otherworld forces is a general tendency in human culture, ancient and primitive peoples have generally relied on a small number of individuals to act as intermediaries between themselves and these powers. Such special individuals are marked out from their fellows by some extraordinary traits or abilities, and particularly by their mental powers. The selection of them to mediate on behalf of their community is a rather spontaneous process, and is studied by modern scholars under the heading 'shamanism'. There is abundant evidence for shamanism among the ancient Indo-European peoples,[1] and the early Celts doubtlessly had such select personages among them also.

A distinction can be made as to the degree to which such religious practice is institutionalised – for instance, societies with more general and structured organisation would tend to regularise the role of the shaman with standardised training and with more systematic dogma. Such a development among the Celts is instanced by the phenomenon of druidism.

The Continental background
We cannot be sure that all the Celtic-speaking people of antiquity had druids as a learned and priestly caste. Most of the evidence for

them is from the western part of the Celtic world, especially from
Gaul. The only real indication that the institution may have been
known further east is given by the Greek writer Diogenes Laertius
who, drawing on a source from the 2nd century BC, states that
'the Celts and the Galatians had seers called *druidaei* and *semnotheoi*'.[2] This might be taken to mean that the Celts of that eastern area (Galatia is in present-day Turkey) had a type of druids
known as 'semnotheoi', but the meaning of this latter word is
unclear. It may indeed not be a Celtic, or even Indo-European,
word at all, but rather a borrowing of the word 'shaman' itself, a
Tungu term which is believed by scholars to derive from Turko-
Mongolian languages spoken in central Asia. The word may therefore have been heard by the Greek writers and wrongly associated
with the Celts of the eastern Mediterranean. In fact, a later writer
associates the learned caste of *samanaei* with the Bactrians.[3]

Diogenes Laertius gives his reference to 'druidaei' and 'semnotheoi' in a list of priestly castes of eastern peoples – such as
the 'magi' of the Persians, the 'chaldeans' of the Babylonians and
Assyrians, and the 'gymnosophists' of the Hindus. It would
therefore appear that he had heard of some institutionalised caste
of seers among the Galatians, whether or not they were actually
known as druids. Later Greek writers refer to the Galatians as
having druids, but these are all based either on Diogenes or his
source. The argument for druids in Galatia is weakened by the
fact that the Greek writers often referred to Gaul itself as 'Galatia'. On the other hand, Strabo describes how the Galatian judicial council assembled at a place called Drunemeton ('great
sanctuary') and – since 'nemeton' was the word commonly used
by the western Celts for a sacred centre[4] – this might be taken to
indicate that broadly similar types of institutions were found
throughout the Celtic world. The likelihood is that, already by
the 3rd century BC when the Celts reached Galatia in the east, a
formalised socio-religious system had begun to develop.[5]

Several places in the western Celtic world were referred to by
this word 'nemeton', indicating that these were sacred centres.
Instances are Nemetodurum (Nanterre in France), Nemetobriga
in Spain (now Puente-de-Navéa), Medionemeton in Scotland
(now Kirkintilloch), and Vernemeton between Lincoln and

Leicester in England. The word 'nemeton' is based on the element *nem- ('sky'), indicating the divine status of the firmament, and many such shrines are thought to have been situated in forest clearings.[6] This tendency towards arboreal settings appears also from the Greek *némos* for a wood and the Latin *nemus* for a forest sanctuary.[7] A related word in Irish is 'neimheadh', and this is a designation used for several sites – for instance, one in the Fews Mountains in Co. Armagh, one at Downpatrick, and one apparently near Newgrange in Co. Meath.[8] The word was sometimes prefixed with *fiodh* ('tree') to indicate such a location, and a sacred tree itself could be referred to by this word. An Irish poem from the 7th century AD states a prohibition against cutting down such trees,[9] and an Old Irish glossary states that it was in the *fiodhneimhidh* 'that the seers used to perform their rituals'.[10] We can, accordingly, relate the imagery of sacred sanctuaries in Ireland to those of the Celts abroad.

Practitioners of the sacred

Early and mediaeval Irish literature insists that those who officiated at sacred rites were the *druíd*, and the designation in its nominative singular was *druí*. Caesar gives the plural form *druides* for the usage among the Gauls,[11] and the singular form in Gaulish would accordingly have been *druis*. Taking into account the loss of the Celtic endings in Irish, which took place in the early centuries AD, this means that the prehistoric forms of the word in Irish would have been identical with those in Gaulish. Clearly, then, our Irish druids represented Celtic society and culture.

The word itself is derived from a compound of *dru* ('strong' or 'great') and *wid-* ('knowledge').[12] Several of the Classical writers regarded the Gaulish druids as philosophers, but this is based on a confusion with learning as understood by their own Classical culture – enriched as it was by the tradition of Greek philosophy. Many of their comments are of a speculative nature, but certain basic aspects of the life and work of a druid can be deciphered from them. The most reliable descriptions of Celtic ethnography are broadly based on a lost work of Posidonius, written between the years 125 and 121 BC. Selections from this work are quoted

and paraphrased by later Greek and Latin writers, particularly by
Strabo, Diodorus Siculus, Athenaeus, and Julius Caesar.[13] Writing
in Greek, Strabo has the following to say:

> Among all the tribes, generally speaking, there are three
> classes of men held in special honour; the *bárdoi*, the
> *ováteis*, and the *druídai*. The *bárdoi* are singers and
> poets; the *ováteis* interpreters of sacrifice and natural
> philosophers; while the *druídai*, in addition to the science
> of nature, study also moral philosophy.[14]

Celtic scholars are agreed that the proper forms of these three
words are *bardi*, *vátes*, and *druides*, and in their nominative singular forms *bardos*, *vátis*, and *druis*.[15] In Irish they are well
attested as *bard* (a term for a minor poet or reciter), *fáidh* (a
prophet) and *druí* (a druid or magician). All three words are to
a large extent interchangeable, although the *bard* is not generally
accorded equal status with the others. Instead, Irish sources have
fili (later, *file*) as a member of the exalted triad, and it is most
plausible to regard this as having been the situation among the
Continental Celts also. This word (nominative plural, *filid*)
would come from a Celtic **velitos*. It occurs in the form *velitas*
in an early Irish ogham inscription,[16] and the historian Tacitus
refers to an honoured prophetess among the Germanic Bructeri
called Veleda,[17] which name or title is considered to have been a
Celtic borrowing. The element **vel-* had the meaning 'to see',
and the survival of this root in verbal form in Old Irish[18] shows
that *file* (which is the usual Irish word for a poet), had the original literal meaning of 'seer'.[19] In Irish tradition, indeed, the poet
had mystical knowledge, and his compositions were often
thought of as having magical power.[20]

Given their similarity in function abroad, and their inter-
changeability in Ireland, it seems best to regard these three terms
druis, *velitos*, and *vátis* as indicating the functions of the wise
man among the ancient Celts. In the world of antiquity, we
should not look for a clear distinction between great wisdom in
its practical and sacred senses. The recognised 'great wisdom
possessor' (**dru-wid-es*) would have been understood by the

Celts, not just as one who had practical or technical knowledge, but also as an intermediary between the society and the mysterious powers of destiny. In other words, he would have inherited the shamanic function from a more primitive stage of culture.

The Classical authors tell us a good deal about the practices of the Continental druids. Caesar, for instance, states that they were concerned with divine worship, the performance of sacrifice, and the interpretation of ritual matters. Other writers refer to prophecies uttered by them,[21] and some connected this with the practice of human sacrifice. On this latter issue, the Classical writers were no doubt exaggerating in order to denigrate the Celts, giving dramatic and shocking accounts so as to justify the Roman conquest of them. We have seen in Chapter 2 that there is other evidence for the practice of such sacrifice among the Celts, however, and it would not be surprising – given their ritual functions – that the druids would have played a central role in it. Behind the lurid language of Caesar, the rationale for these human sacrifices can be detected:

> The whole Gaulish people is exceedingly given to religious superstition. Therefore those who are suffering from serious illness or are in the midst of the dangers of battle, either put to death human beings as sacrificial victims or take a vow to do so, and the druids take part in these sacrifices; for they believe that, unless one human life is given in exchange for another human life, the power of the almighty gods cannot be appeased. Sacrifices of this kind are also traditionally offered for the needs of the state.

He goes on to claim that some Gaulish tribes sacrificed large amounts of men by burning, and that they considered that the gods preferred thieves and robbers to innocent people for this purpose. Diodorus Siculus makes a direct connection between human sacrifice and divination in the practices of the druids. According to him, they told the future by watching the flights of birds and by observation of the entrails of victims. When attempting divination upon important matters, they had an old tradition of killing a man by stabbing him above the midriff, and then foretelling the future by the convulsion of his limbs and the pouring of his blood. The Gauls held that no sacrifice should be made to the gods without a druid, 'for they say that thanks should be offered to the gods by those skilled in the divine nature, as though they were people who can speak their language; and through them also they hold that benefits should be asked'.[22]

Human sacrifice was banned by the Romans,[23] who – we may add – by their own practices showed that they did not themselves have much qualms about cruelty and inhumanity.[24] The druids did not change their general tradition on this account, however, as is clear from the statement of Pomponius Mela that in the middle of the 1st century AD, they were refraining from outright slaughter, but nevertheless still drew blood from people as a substitute for sacrifice.[25] Although he also accused the druids of performing hideous human sacrifices, Strabo was willing to look on them in a more positive light:

> They are believed to be the most just of men, and are therefore entrusted with the decision of cases affecting either individuals or the public; indeed in former times they arbitrated in war and brought to a standstill the opponents when about to draw up in a line of battle; and murder cases have mostly been entrusted to their decision.[26]

Caesar also stresses the function of arbitration, and in so doing, represents the druid as a sacred person. He claims that, when an individual or a tribe disobeyed the ruling of a druid, the offenders were banned from attending at sacrifices. This, says Caesar, was considered the harshest penalty, for 'men placed under this ban are treated as impious wretches – all avoid them, fleeing their company and conversation'.[27]

There are no contemporaneous accounts of the druids in Ireland, but several centuries later the Irish literature is expansive on the topic. Although many of these Irish descriptions are fanciful, there is reason to believe that they contain some genuine strands of tradition. In them, the wise man – variously called *druí, file,* and *fáidh* – is claimed to have possessed an arcane and magical kind of knowledge called *fiss* or *imbas* (from *im-fhiss,* meaning 'complete *fiss*'). The wise man himself is frequently referred to in the literature as *fisidh* (another derivative of the word), and his knowledge was portrayed as antiquarian, clairvoyant, and prophetic.[28] It is in these three levels of knowledge, indeed, that occult wisdom specifically operates in Irish tradition, and the possession of such knowledge was considered by the writers to be a sufficiently impressive quality for the druid.

The occult knowledge
Prophecy and divination are the accomplishments most frequently attributed to druids in Irish literature. For instance, in the pseudo-history the druid Caicher is claimed to have prophesied to the original Gaelic people that they would successfully take Ireland,[29] and in the hero-lore the druid Cathbhadh declares a particular day to be an auspicious one for the champion Cú Chulainn to take arms,[30] while his druid-grandfather instructs Cormac mac Airt as to the auspicious day for him to go and seek the kingship of Tara.[31] This was an old tradition among the Celts, as is clear from the marking of some days as *mat* ('good') and others as *anm-* ('not good') in the Gaulish calendar from the 1st century AD found at Coligny.[32] In relation to birds, there is a long tradition in Irish literature and folklore of drawing omens from several of them – especially the raven, who has generally been regarded as portending misfortune.[33] One mediaeval text gives a list of interpretations to be gleaned from different types of croaking of the raven,[34] and this may have had some basis in earlier divinatory practice. Since the 9th century AD, at least, the wren has been thought to have a special connection with druids. This springs from a fanciful etymology of the bird's name *drean* as *druí-én* ('druid-bird'), which one glossarian explains as 'a bird who makes prophecies'.[35] A mediaeval text gives detailed prognistications from the directions from which the wren is heard to call.[36]

Much of this, however, has the mark of fanciful invention. The reality was that, due to the Christianisation of Ireland in the 5th-6th centuries AD, the mediaeval writers knew little of what ancient pagan ritual would have been like. The concept of druidic knowledge was so general that they considered mere reference to it sufficient to cover for their lack of information. Thus we have several accounts of druids and poets relaying the history of past events, making penetrating comments on the present, and foretelling the future. However, there was in Irish a wide range of terminology which referred to different grades of such knowledgeable skill and of its practitioners[37] and, although reshaped according to Latin literary patterns, this reflects a rich native tradition. That this tradition had to do with the supernatural powers of druids can hardly be doubted.

The more imaginative texts in which the druids figure often group them into triads. The mediaeval pseudo-histories, for instance, allot three specific druids to several of the fictional races who are claimed to have come to Ireland in antiquity, as if this was an expected convention when speaking of members of the mysterious profession.[38] This reflects the frequent grouping of deities in a similar way,[39] thereby underlining the supernatural nature of druidry. Another wondrous aspect of Irish druidry is its association with water, an association which is not clearly stated in the sources dealing with their Continental counterparts. However, we have already mentioned the hoards found in water in Celtic areas abroad, and it is assumed that these were offerings to deities. It would therefore appear that Irish literature provides the only conscious illustration of the attitudes of the Celts to the notion of divinity residing in water.

A text from the 8th or 9th-century AD, which reflects several ancient ideas, describes how the poet (*file*) Néidhe mac Adhna, when a young student, resorted to the sea-shore one day in order to find inspiration, 'for the poets regarded the edge of water as a usual place for the revelation of wisdom':

> He heard a sound in the wave, that is, a chant of wailing and sadness, and he thought it strange. So the lad cast a spell upon the wave, so that the matter might be revealed to him. And then it was declared to him that the wave was bewailing his father who had died.[40]

Other texts, as we shall see in Chapter 4, claimed that *imbas* could be gained from the waters of the river Boyne. In the fictional literature and in the folklore, the druid-poets are represented as having the power by their incantations to cause rivers and lakes to dry up, or to raise storms at sea, and this can be regarded as a reflex of their special relationship with water.[41]

Since there is an intimate connection between water and the land, one would expect similar traditions also in respect of the latter. We have seen (Chapter 2) that the archaeological evidence indicates hoards being deposited to land-deities also. What Strabo says of the Gauls may be of relevance in this regard: 'When there are many such cases [i.e., sacrifice of criminals condemned by the druids] they believe that there will be a fruitful yield from their fields.'[42] Although definite memory of human sacrifice had disappeared in Ireland by mediaeval times, the power of the druid-poets to lay waste the land or to make it fruitful had not, and several fanciful examples of such are mentioned in the literature.[43] So it was believed that the power of the druids could be so great as to influence the attitudes of the father and mother deities of sun and land towards the community.

The social role
The functions of *druí*, *file* and *fáidh* seem to have been interchangeable in archaic Irish with that for a judge (written *brithem*, later *breitheamh*),[44] and from the frequent mention of kings seeking counsel from them, we can be sure that arbitration was also one of the functions of these wise men in Ireland. Literary sources describe the welfare of the land – in terms of health, agriculture, and crops – as depending on the judgement given by a *breitheamh*,[45] and this parallels the magical power which we have described for the *file*. Furthermore, if a member of this profession gave a false judgement, the ill-effects of it could fall on himself.[46]

One account tells of how, as a result of such a judgement, blotches appeared on the cheeks of the *breitheamh* – this is paralleled in references to blisters coming on the face of a *file* if he satirised a person in the wrong.[47] It should also be noted that the term 'true' (*fíor*) was repeatedly used to denote the mystical gift

of wisdom possessed by the able *breitheamh* and the able *file*
alike;[48] and that the legal texts represent several famous poets as
giving judgements.[49] Indeed, the celebrated Amhairghin
Glúngheal, one of the leaders of the Gaelic invasion of Ireland in
the pseudo-histories, was simultaneously a poet and a judge.[50]
One source claims that, since this fictional Amhairghin gave the
first judgement in Ireland, 'judicature belonged to the poets
alone'[51]; and thus was rationalised the descent of the judicial
profession from that of the druids.

The ability of the druid-poets to counteract criminal activity is
stressed in one text. The text is an 11th-century compilation, but
this and some other portions would seem to have belonged to a
period some centuries earlier. In it we read that in the final years
of the training of the *file*, he was taught how to recite spells,
including one to regain stolen cattle. This was in rhetorical language, and it was chanted three times through the fist of the right
hand over the track of the animal or its thief, after which the identity of the thief would be revealed in a dream. Other spells cited
in the text include one for a new house and one for a long life, but
no actual ritual is described to accompany these. The hand is used
in one other case, however, according to which a spell was recited
into the right palm, and when the palm was then rubbed onto the
rump of a stallion, that animal became tame.[52]

Charms and magical power

The symbolic use of the hand seems to have been common in
such rituals. In one source, perhaps as early as the 7th century
AD, some charms against diseases and ailments are cited. They
contain a mixture of Christian and pagan material, for instance
both Christ and the smith-god Goibhniu are invoked in a charm
to remove a thorn. Another, against multifarious ailments,
invokes only the native patron of leech-craft, Dian Cécht: 'I put
my trust in the salve which Dian Cécht left with his family that
whatever on which it goes be whole!' The instructions for the
application of the salve are as follows: 'This is laid always in
your palm full of water when washing, and you put it into your
mouth, and you insert the two fingers that are next to the little
finger into your mouth, each of them apart.'[53]

Some other mentions survive in the earliest Irish literature of what appear to have been actual rituals of the druids. For instance, from around the year 900 AD, we have an account of *imbas forosnaí* ('knowledge of enlightening') by which the druid-poet discovers anything which he wishes. The writer here, being a devout Christian, is very much a hostile witness, but the description is nevertheless of value:

> The poet (*file*) chews a piece of the flesh of a red pig, or of a dog or cat, and places it afterwards on the flagstone behind the door, and sings an incantation on it, and offers it to the idol-gods, and afterwards calls his idols to him. And if he does not receive (the knowledge) next day, he then sings incantations on his two palms, and calls again unto him his idol-gods that his sleep may not be disturbed. And he lays his two palms on his two cheeks and falls asleep. And he is watched so that nobody may interrupt or disturb him. And what he seeks is then revealed to him after a minute or two or three, or as long as he was estimated to be at the offering.[54]

This resembles the other early Irish accounts with regard to hand-rituals and to the dream of revelation, and it is therefore very likely that these were genuine memories of old druidic practice. The writer here, indeed, claims that the rite of *imbas forosnaí*, along with another called *teinm laída*, were abolished by St Patrick. The saint, he says, allowed the poets to perform another rite because, in its case, 'it is not necessary to make an offering to demons, but there is revelation at once from the ends of his bones'.[55] The term used for this latter rite is *díchetal do chennaibh* (literally 'incantation from heads'), and the likelihood is that it originally referred to the practice (discussed in Chapter 2) of seeking inspiration from the heads of slain friends or foes. If so, the writer here misunderstood it to mean a pronouncement 'from the ends of his bones', probably in the sense 'from the tips of his fingers'.

Here again we find the imagery of hands, although the literal sense which the writer intended to convey may have been simply that of extempore composition. Such composition 'without thinking' was regarded in Irish tradition as being the test of the *fíorfhile* ('true poet'), and no doubt it echoes an ancient emphasis on the divine source of the druid-poet's power.[56] The same text in another place gives a good illustration of function, although its etymology is mistaken, when the word *druí* is explained as *dorua ái* – 'that is, recitation, for it is through a poem that he does his spells'.[57]

The other rite mentioned above, *teinm laída*, is more difficult to interpret. It is variously spelt in the literature, an indication in itself that the writers were not sure of its meaning. One early story tells of how a poet called Moen mac Etnae identified the skull of a lap-dog through recourse to his *teinm laoido* – it was, the text claims, the first lap-dog ever in Ireland, and had been brought from Britain.[58] That this represents a special type of anecdote associated with druidic knowledge is clear from a variant which has another poet, Lughaidh 'Dall-éces' (literally 'blind seer') to whom a skull is brought. 'Place the poet's wand on it', orders Lughaidh, and then he identifies it as belonging to a lap-dog which was on board a boat which sank with all its crew on the sea between Ireland and Scotland.[59] Elsewhere in the literature, the seer-warrior, Fionn mac Cumhaill, several times finds inspiration through his *teinm laega* or *teinm laída* by placing his thumb in his mouth and chewing it.[60] The term may derive from an ancient divinatory practice and may have originally meant 'chewing of the pith',[61] but other interpretations are possible.[62]

The early literary sources stress that knowledge of these three skills – *imbas forosnaí*, *teinm laída*, and *díchetal do chennaibh* – was essential to an *ollamh* (chief-poet),[63] and in this we again notice the survival of the druidic tradition under the guise of the poet. The original ritual meanings of terms such as these were gradually lost, and they were transformed into more mundane terms to describe technical aspects of composing verse. Yet an aura of magic continued to surround the poet in fanciful literature and in folk legend down to recent times.[64] The simplest, and yet the most telling, evidence for the supernatural skills of the druids in ancient Ireland is furnished by the word for druidry itself, *druídecht*. This (in modern spelling *draíocht*) has always been the ordinary term in Irish for magic.

Help and harm

Continental accounts show that the druids there were not only held in highest regard, but their words were also feared. The celebrated orator Dion Chrysostom, writing around 100 AD, gives his impression of what the situation was:

> The Celts have men called *druides*, who concern themselves with divination and all branches of wisdom. And without their advice even kings dared not resolve upon nor execute any plan, so that in truth it was they who ruled, while the kings . . . became mere ministers of their will.[65]

Such a situation was bound to vary from one instance to another, but there is no doubting that impressive social power was generally wielded by druids. In referring to the bards, Diodorus Siculus states that 'they sing to the accompaniment of instruments resembling lyres, sometimes an eulogy and sometimes a satire'.[66] As the succeeding account shows, Diodorus was alluding to a custom shared by the druids in general:

> It is not only in the needs of peace, but in war also, that they (the Gauls) carefully obey these men and their song-loving poets, and this is true not only of their friends but also of their enemies. For oftentimes, as armies approach each other in line of battle with their swords drawn and their spears raised for the charge, these men come forth between them and stop the conflict, as though they had spell-bound some kinds of wild animals.[67]

This power attaching to the pronouncements of the druids is expressed very clearly also in Irish sources. The heroic literature of the Ulster Cycle refers, for instance, to a prohibition on the king to speak in the assembly before his druids did.[68] The same Cycle describes how the judge Seancha arbitrates among the

Ulstermen and how, when the warriors come to blows at a feast, he calls them to order with a few words or by shaking his 'peace-making branch'.[69] There apparently was a tradition also that druids could build a kind of barrier between armies. For instance, later accounts of a battle fought in the year 560 AD refer to how a certain Tuathán mac Diomain placed a druid's *erbe* (probably a 'command') over the heads of an army in battle, and to how the only combatant who stepped outside of it was slain.[70]

There were, of course, charms which could be used for the opposite effect, as is clear from one early Irish source which states that 'a defeat against odds, and setting territories at war, confer status on a druid'.[71] A 9th-century text describes an operation in which the *file* 'squeezes the lobe of the ear between his two fingers, and the person on whom this skill is practised dies – that is reasonable, for this member is external to the person, and thus this person is placed outside of the community, as if sick; and this member is weak compared to other members, and thus also this man'.[72] A variant of the description, again focusing on the ear-lobe, states that 'just as there is no bone there, so also the person whom the *file* constrains has neither honour nor strength'.[73]

The title of this ritual is given as *briamon smethraige*, the first element (*bria-mon*) of which is explained to mean 'word-trick'. Because of its lack of clarity, *smethraige* was taken by the mediaeval scholars to be a compound of *smit* ('ear-lobe') and thus to signify 'lobe-manipulation'. All of this seems quite fanciful. Perhaps the original phrase was *bria-mon is meth righe* ('word-trick which constitutes the decline of reign'), which would be a natural way of describing the satirising of a king. The rather quaint manner in which the scholars concretised the phrase into a rite is typical of the long-established fanciful attitude towards druidic practice, and it is significant that the emphasis is placed on the social alienation of those who earned the displeasure of the *file*.

The belief that the druid could, by his words, bring good or bad fortune, is well attested in Ireland, especially in the case of the *file*. The literature and folklore of Ireland, down through the ages, have understood poetry in terms of *moladh agus aoir* ('praise and satire').[74] In order to emphasise this, indeed, medi-aeval texts picturesquely claim that the *file* had two little com-partments in his tongue, one for honey and the other for poison.[75] The same dialectic of eulogy and vituperation is found in other early European traditions,[76] and it is therefore clear that in this we are dealing with the survival in Ireland of a very ancient idea. The Irish sources place the greater emphasis on the blaming, and it was believed that – if the satire were justified – its object would fall ill and might even die.[77] In the heroic liter-ature, the bitter poet Aithirne threatens his foes in the following manner: 'Fierce hounds will be sent by Aithirne against ye – satire and insult and reddening, howling and burning and bitter word!'[78]

The belief was dramatised by many anecdotes which por-trayed the satire as a kind of dart shot from the mouth of the *file*.[79] Of the many examples of such anecdotes from Irish tradi-tion, it will suffice to quote one from a text which dates from the 9th century AD or perhaps earlier. According to this the poet Néidhe mac Adhna was asked to satirise his uncle Caier, king of Connacht, by Caier's wife. Néidhe protested that his uncle was so generous that he could not find an excuse to satirise him, but the woman told him to ask the king for his dagger. There was a magical prohibition on Caier to part with the dagger, and so he refused:

> Néidhe made a *glam díchend* ('decapitating howl') on him, so that three blisters came on his cheek. This was the satire: 'A curse, death, short life to Caier! May spears of battle slay Caier! The reject of every territory, of every land be Caier! Beneath mounds and rocks be Caier!' Caier got up early in the morning to go to the well. He placed his hand on his face. He found three blisters on his face from the cutting of the satire – a disgrace and a blemish and a defect, red and green and white.

Fearful lest anyone should see his disfigurement, Caier vacated the kingship and later, when Néidhe came to visit him, he died from shame in the presence of the poet.[80] This idea, that the face would break out in embarrassment due to a satire is no doubt connected to the psychosomatic effect of blushing, but tradition has it as a dramatic extension of abstract feeling into the concrete world. There is no reason to doubt that the imagination of the prehistoric Celts, and particularly the propaganda of their druids, had a similar tendency to dramatise events. In actual life, indeed, the isolation of a person following on condemnation by the druids would have been a social reality. We may also assume that, to add to its psychological effect, the ancient druids would resort to symbolical actions in delivering their condemnation.

A survival of such may be instanced by a strange posture which is mentioned in the literature. This was known as *corrghuinecht*, and one glossary describes it as 'to use one foot and one hand and one eye while making the *glam díchend*'.[81] The posture is attributed, for instance, to the deity Lugh, who encircles his foes in battle while adopting it. At the same time he chants a spell, calling on 'the strong druidic skills' to destroy the foe through the forces of sky and soil, sun and moon.[82] In the Ulster Cycle, the hero Cú Chulainn uses the same posture while writing a spell on a sapling and placing it on a pillar, and by this means delays a hostile army.[83] In another text, a female satirist puts a cursing spell on warriors and 'on one leg and in one breath she chanted all that against them'.[84]

There are several accounts in Irish literature of druids using their skill in battle and, although the details derive from the fancy of the mediaeval writers, they reflect the ancient belief that such destructive magic could have real effect. The accounts include druids causing fires and storms and thunderbolts to confound and destroy the enemy.[85] In the remote background to this fictional tradition, also, lies the belief that the druids had special knowledge of, and thus control over, the elements. Pomponius Mela wrote of the Gaulish druids: 'They profess to know the size and shape of the world, the movements of the heavens and of the stars, and the will of the gods.'[86] One text states that the Irish druids went even further, claiming that they themselves created 'heaven and earth, sea, sun and moon',[87] but this must be propaganda of the early Christian missionaries. A more accurate assessment is given in another text, which states that destiny was believed by the pagan Irish to have been administered by 'sun, wind and the other elements'.[88] The indirect control of these elements, claimed by the druids, would have been couched in terms of the proper time and method for undertakings.[89] When we read, for instance, that the grandfather of Cormac mac Airt, who was a druid, advised him to go to Tara on a certain day so as to gain the kingship, the term used is *lá sobais*, literally 'a day of good knowledge', and behind it must lie the idea that certain days accord with fate and others do not.[90]

There is no doubting either that the druids claimed to be able to influence the world by their speech, or that they would when feasible claim that this influence was magical. Their role in preserving mythical and historical narratives must have been of great importance to their status, and this survived into historical times in the tradition that the recitation of certain stories brought good fortune to those who heard them.[91] The basic role of the druid was as mediator between this world and the otherworld, and it is therefore not surprising that his pronouncements were held to be efficacious. This is presented in appropriately symbolic form in an Irish story, which has an otherworld lady coming to seduce the son of the ancient king Conn Céadchathach. The druid of Conn, called Corán, intervenes, and chants a spell against the woman, with the result that the young man can neither hear nor see her.[92] There probably were druids who claimed such dramatic powers. The resourceful druid would, however, tend to display his magical knowledge in a more circumspect way, as in the account of the celebrated Seancha mac Ailealla. This druid may in fact have been an historical personage, though accounts of him are fictional. One such account has it that – in adjudicating a case – he would take a piece of timber from the fire and hand it to the accused. He would then chant a spell, which would cause the timber to stick to the palm of the guilty or fall from the palm of the innocent.[93]

Mystical healing
It is clear from the Classical accounts that not only hostile action, but also healing was one of the druidic tasks. Pliny, in his

Naturalis Historia,[94] gives a description of the Gaulish druids which is limited in its scope to herbalism, but from it we may infer a broader scheme of practice. First he speaks of a plant which he calls *selago* and which was gathered without using iron and 'by passing the right hand through the left sleeve of the tunic, as though in the act of committing a theft. The clothing must be white, the feet washed and bare, and an offering of wine and bread made before the gathering.' These Gaulish druids recommended that the plant be carried as a charm against every kind of evil, and they claimed that the smoke from its burning was good for eye-diseases. Pliny then speaks of a marsh-plant 'which they call *samulos*', and which must be gathered with the left hand, when fasting. It was a charm against diseases in cattle, but the gatherer, Pliny says, 'must not look behind him, nor lay the plant anywhere except in the drinking-troughs'.

Finally, Pliny refers to 'a kind of egg of much renown in the Gaulish provinces' called *anguinum*, but the description which he gives of this is quite fantastic. It is, he says, derived from serpents, being combined of a secretion from their bodies and from their spittle. The druids claimed that one of these 'eggs' can only be taken on a certain day of the moon, and that when the serpents throw it up into the air it must be caught in a cloak before it touches the ground. One must instantly take to flight then on horseback, as the serpents will pursue until cut off by a stream. Pliny was further told that such a ball could be tested by placing it in a river where, if it was the proper item, it would float against the current. Well may he remark that 'it is the way of magicians to cast a cunning veil about their frauds'.

The performance of cures in traditional cultures is, indeed, often surrounded by charlatanism and deliberate attempts to mislead the witness and, given that healing was one of their functions, the druids would naturally have used a number of such ruses. It is interesting to note that several of the notions reported to Pliny are instanced from folklore in Ireland and elsewhere – for example, the claim of exotic sources for healing materials, the taboos to be observed when gathering herbs, the belief that evil spirits and other pests had difficulty in crossing running water and that certain talismans could flow upstream.[95]

Much attention is given in Irish literature to the magical powers of mythical leeches, and their portrayal is quite similar to that of the druids. Most dramatic in his skill was the mythical patron of leechcraft, Dian Cécht, whose name we have already referred to as occurring in an early Irish charm for healing. He is described as attended by three other leeches, which can probably be taken as an indication of his divine status presiding over a druidic triad. To him are attributed the words: 'Any man who is wounded, unless his head be cut off or the membrane of his brain or his spinal cord be severed, will be fully healed by me.' In the same mythical text, he and his trio make a well, into which they cast the battle-wounded while singing incantations of healing.[96] In the heroic Ulster Cycle, the principal healer is Fínghein, who has the soubriquet *fáithliaig* ('prophetic leech'). His skills are also impressive, it being claimed that by one glance at a wound he could tell how it had been inflicted and by whom.[97] More dramatically, he could tell the nature of a person's illness by observing the smoke which came from the patient's house or by hearing his moan.[98]

The literature indicates also that the druids were able practitioners of psychiatry. In a tale of the hero Cú Chulainn, his wife wishes him to be cured of his maniacal passion for the otherworld woman Fand, and the Ulster king sends poets and druids to find and restrain him: 'Cú Chulainn tried to kill the skilled men. They sang spells of druidry against him until they caught his hands and feet, and he came to his senses in a while. He was asking for a drink then. The druids brought a drink of oblivion. When he drank the drink he did not remember Fand.'[99] On the other hand, several literary sources attribute to the druids the ability to cause insanity. This they did by chanting over a wisp of grass or straw, and then throwing it in the face of the victim. One text regards this as a form of sympathetic magic, the fluttering of the wisp causing a fluttering of the senses.[100] Whether or not these details are reliable, it need hardly be doubted that the ancient druids – like their counterparts in other cultures – did really employ some psychological devices in order to impress their authority on individuals and society.

The preparation of a druid
The status enjoyed by the druids depended to a large extent on
their success in stressing the importance of their craft and in convincing the populace of it. Cicero, who knew the Gaulish druid
Divitiacus, described how that man 'claimed to have that knowledge of nature which the Greeks call *physiologia*, and he used to
make predictions, sometimes by means of augury and sometimes
by means of conjecture'.[101] Commenting on them as eloquent
teachers of wisdom, Pomponius Mela states:

> They teach many things to the nobles of Gaul in a course
> of instruction lasting as long as twenty years, meeting in
> secret either in a cave or in secluded dales.[102]

Mela got this information from the lost text of Posidonius.
Using the same source, Caesar states that the druids were
excused by the Gauls from military service and exempt from
taxes and all liabilities, and for that reason their profession was
very attractive to the sons of nobles. He also mentions the teaching methods of the druids, saying that 'a large number of young
men flock to them for training and hold them in high honour'.
Irish sources give a similar picture of druidic education. In the
Ulster Cycle, for instance, the leading druid Cathbhadh is represented as having with him 'a hundred active men learning the
druid's art',[103] while in general the seer-poets are described as
instructing their students in learned courses which lasted for
twelve years.[104] Caesar elaborates further on the druidic educa-
tional system, saying that the students in these schools learned a
great number of verses by heart and did not commit this material to writing. He considers that there were two reasons for this
– one, so as to train the memory, and the other that the druids
were unwilling to have 'their system of training bruited abroad
among the common people'. Concerning the range of their
knowledge:

> They also have much knowledge of the stars and their
> motion, of the size of the world and of the earth, of nat-
> ural philosophy, and of the powers and spheres of action

of the immortal gods, which they discuss and hand down
to their young students.[105]

Further indication of the care taken by the druids to guard the
secrets of their profession is given by Diogenes Laertius, whose
information was based on a source from the 2nd century BC. He
states that the druids 'make their pronouncements by means of
riddles and dark sayings, teaching that the gods must be worshipped and no evil done and manly behaviour maintained'.[106]
There is a ring of truth about this statement, for it is in triadic
form, and in the Irish and Welsh literary sources similar triads
were a favourite method of imparting knowledge.[107]

The deliberate use of enigmatic speech, too, is very well
attested. In early Irish literature, the poetic rhetoric is described
as having the qualities *duibhe* ('blackness' in the sense of obscurity), *dorchatu* ('darkness' in the sense of being mysterious), and
dlúithe ('compactness').[108] The 'darkness' of the poets' language
is particularly stressed, and one early text poses the question
'where is poetry?' and then gives the answer 'in darkness' (*i ndor-
chaidhéta*).[109] There are several descriptions from Irish tradition
which show that a concrete ritual was employed in accordance
with this imagery, namely that poets sought out dark surroundings when composing in order to improve the quality of their
work.[110]

The teaching situation, involving students being introduced to
obscure phraseology, is well instanced by an Irish anecdote which
features such phraseology and which may date to as early as the
8th century AD. According to it, the poet Cruitíne, accompanied
by one of his students, set out on a visit to a fellow-poet. Arriving at the house, Cruitíne did not enter, but sent the student in
ahead of him to meet the poet:

> When the pot was boiled, the poet said in the presence of
> the student '*dofotha tairr tein*', and this was so that he
> might know what answer the student would give him
> . . . And he did not respond to those words. Then the stu-
> dent arose and came to where Cruitíne was and related
> the news to him and said the phrase which the poet had

spoken. 'Good', said Cruitíne, 'when he says it again, say
to him '*tóe lethaig foen fris, adaind in dlis!*' – that is 'put
a kneading-trough under it, and light a candle to see if
the pot be boiled!' When the student, on his return, sat
down inside the house, the poet said the same, and the
student spoke accordingly. 'That is good,' said the poet,
'it is not the mouth of a student which has answered thus.
Cruitíne is nigh. Call him in from outside!' Cruitíne was
then called, and a welcome was extended to him.[111]

Obscure phrases such as these were termed *bélra na filed*
('language of the poets'), and are cited in many early Irish texts.
The function of such convoluted speech must originally have
been to impress the public with the mysterious knowledge possessed by the druid-poets. It was a type of 'divine language'
which – as Diodorus Siculus noted of the Gaulish druids[112] –
could be used by those who mediated between human society
and the otherworld.[113] It should be stated, however, that these
poetic rhetorics in early Irish literature all belong to the historic
period. None of them exhibit the original Celtic word-forms,
which only became obsolete in Ireland in or around the 4th century AD. It is therefore best to consider the rhetorics which are
cited as inventions by the manuscript-writers in order to illustrate the arcane nature of the poetic tradition. These writers
would, however, be echoing an older tradition by which the
druids were celebrated, and caused themselves to be celebrated,
in rumour and anecdote.

The learned class of early literary Ireland, like their druidic
predecessors, were determined to keep their prestige at a pre-
mium. Irish texts state that there were various grades of poetry,
and that the teaching of these grades could take many years. A
chief-poet (*ollamh*) would preside over their schools.[114] The special schools persisted in Ireland down to the 17th century, and
there is evidence also for similar institutions dealing with legal
and medical matters.[115] The students were of adult age, and the
schools were usually situated in quiet parts of the countryside,
where the students would not have many distractions during
their terms of study.[116] It can hardly be doubted that this system

of education had its remote origin in the druidic system of ancient times.

Being the wise men of prehistoric Ireland, it would be natural for druids to have some sacramental function also, even if rudimentary. There may, for instance, have been some form of druidic baptism, for several Irish sources have druids declaring that a child will be known by a particular name. This is found most clearly in the case of the druid Cathbhad who – in the epical Ulster Cycle – is described as giving their names to leading worthies such as Conchobhar, Cú Chulainn, and Deirdre.[117] In the other major heroic cycle – that of the Fianna – the boy Demne, when he is seven years old, is renamed Fionn and sets out on his career as the most celebrated hero of Irish narrative tradition. Significantly, the renaming is done by a seer, and that with the statement 'you are the Fionn surely'.[118] As we shall see in Chapter 4, the name has connotations of illumination, brightness, and wisdom – all in keeping with the fame of the hero.

The understanding in all these cases is that the name was especially apt for the child, placing him or her in a predestined social or mythical role. There are indications that such a system prevailed also among Gaulish druids, with reference to the naming of persons and places alike.[119] This type of 'baptism' accords with the tradition of augury discussed above – both practices echoing a system whereby the druid's pronouncements entailed a knowledge of destiny. That some kind of druidic benediction was considered necessary when a king or other leading functionary was undertaking some important task is clear from mentions of auguries given by druids on such occasions.[120] Although there is little direct evidence from Ireland of druidic involvement in funerary rites, we may presume that the druids played a leading part in burial scenes of the type frequently mentioned in early Irish literature, which entail digging a grave, raising a pillar-stone over it, chanting laments, and – in some cases – writing a dedication in *ogham*-script.[121] We also may assume that such druidic warranties were a luxury available only to individuals who had a high social status, and that in all other cases the procedures were of a more informal type.

Deliberate mystification

The practice of the Gaulish druids of seeking seclusion, mentioned by Mela, is again referred to by Lucan, in sarcastic verses which he addressed to the druids: 'To you alone it is given to know the truth about the gods and deities of the sky, or else you alone are ignorant of this truth; the innermost groves of far-off forests are your abodes.'[122] On this issue of groves, Pliny gives an account which is well-known both for its speculation as to the meaning of the word druid and for its reference to a rare plant:

> They choose groves formed of oaks for the sake of the tree alone, and they never perform any of their rites except in the presence of a branch of it; so that it seems probable that the priests themselves may derive their name from the Greek word for that tree. In fact, they think that everything that grows on it has been sent from heaven and is a proof that the tree was chosen by the god himself. The mistletoe, however, is found but rarely upon the oak and, when found, is gathered with due religious ceremony, if possible on the sixth day of the moon (for it is by the moon that they measure their months and years, and also their ages of thirty years). They choose this day because the moon, though not yet in the middle of her course, has already considerable influence. They call the mistletoe by a name meaning, in their language, the all-healing. Having made preparation for sacrifice and a banquet beneath the trees, they bring thither two white bulls, whose horns are bound then for the first time. Clad in a white robe, the priest ascends the tree and cuts the mistletoe with a golden sickle, and it is received by the others in a white cloak. Then they kill the victims, praying that the god will render this gift of his propitious to those to whom he has granted it. They believe that the mistletoe, taken in drink, imparts fecundity to barren animals, and that it is the antidote for all poisons.[123]

This account is an intriguing one, not least for its rich combination of different images. On the question of the derivation of the term druid, it should be noted that this interpretation has remained popular with some scholars to the present time. It is based on the supposition that the initial element in *drui(d)s* was the word for the oak-tree (Gaulish *dervo-*, Irish *dair*). This would therefore give an original sense *dervo-wid-es* ('oak-wisdom possessor') for druid. However, a special connection with trees is much more likely to have developed through a homonyme by which the element denoting wisdom (*wid-*) became confused with the term for a wood (*vidu-*).[124] Given this, the oak in particular would have come to be associated with the druids, for it was regarded since paleolithic times as a sacred life-giving tree.[125]

The mistletoe, a parasitic shrub which feeds off trees, was thought by different ancient European peoples to have magical properties – it was evergreen, and therefore could be thought of as a life-preserving force which came to the tree from the skies. If Pliny's account is based on reliable sources, it would indicate that the druids had adopted the mistletoe lore into their own cultus. The use of this shrub as a panacea for ailments, whether on its own or as an ingredient in concoctions, was common in various parts of Europe,[126] though not in Ireland – where the mistletoe was unknown. The term *uile-íoc* ('all-healer') for it in the Irish language is a learned post-mediaeval invention based upon the Pliny text.

The reference to the waxing of the moon as a propitious time to undertake a task illustrates the druidic use of widespread superstitious lore.[127] In his allusion to the counting of time by the moon, and in periods of thirty years, however, Pliny may have been instancing a special tradition of the druids themselves;[128] and this may also be the case with the sacrifice of the bulls, for such a sacrifice is depicted on the Gundestrup cauldron, which was manufactured – apparently for Celtic leaders – in the 4th or 3rd century BC.[129] Irish literature mentions a ritual sacrifice of a white bull by the druids (see Chapter 6), and we note that Pliny also describes the victims as white. Although the Romans themselves sacrificed cattle of this colour to the gods,[130] it is very likely that the Celts had an old tradition of considering white cattle to have a special connection with the otherworld. The name of the river Boyne (originally *Bou-vinda*) had the meaning 'white cow', and this was also the name of the goddess who presided over the river.[131] White red-eared cows occur in Irish sources as cattle from the otherworld.[132] It is doubtful if cattle with this colouring were ever in Ireland, but they were in Britain, where a variety still survives in the wild state.[133] The likelihood is that the early Irish inherited reverence for white cattle from Celtic culture, and that they rationalised this by reference to the white red-eared breed which they knew to exist in Britain.

Wisdom from the east

Britain being the nearest Celtic country, it is easy to understand why the early Irish should regard it as a repository of antique lore. But there may also have been a realistic source for this notion, for Caesar gives the credit to that island for the origin of druidic lore: 'It is thought that this system of training was invented in Britain and taken over from there to Gaul, and at the present time diligent students of the matter mostly travel there to study it.'[134] We can take this to mean that in Caesar's time, the 1st century BC, the institution of druidism was particularly strong in Britain, so strong indeed that the island could be taken to be its headquarters. Pliny, a century later, does not share Caesar's view as to the origin of druidism, but he does testify to its healthy state in Britain:

> It flourished in the Gaulish provinces, too, even down to a period within our memory; for it was in the time of the Emperor Tiberius that a decree was issued against their druids and the whole tribe of diviners and physicians. But why mention all this about a practice that has even crossed the ocean and penetrated to the utmost parts of the earth? At the present day, Britain is still fascinated by magic, and performs its rites with so much ceremony . . .[135]

A little later still, Tacitus compared the Britons to the Gauls, stating that 'in both countries the same ritual and religious beliefs are found', and adds 'there is no great difference in language'.[136] To the Irish of the time, therefore, Britain would have been the most obvious external source of Celtic ritual. Since druidism was a basic, and therefore very impressive, element in such ritual, it is not surprising to find echoes in early Irish literature of a special regard for Britain, the whole of which island was in early Irish referred to as *Albu*. In a mediaeval story, an *ollamh* ('high-poet') of the 6th century AD, Seanchán Toirpéist, is said to have travelled in Albu and to have met there with the spirit of poetry, who 'profited him' by speaking in very obscure rhetoric.[137] This account may contain a vestige of the idea that druidic art was taught especially well in Britain. An account of the less historical poet Néidhe mac Adhna agrees with this by claiming that he went 'to learn *écsi* (seer-craft) in Albu'.[138] Again, in the heroic literature, we encounter a prophetess called Feidhilm, who has just returned to Ireland from Albu having learned *filidhecht*.[139]

Women, wisdom, and war
There is an amount of curious detail in the ruthless description given by Tacitus of how the Roman general Agricola destroyed one of the last great sanctuaries of British druidism, on the island of Anglesey:

> On the shore stood the opposing army with its dense array of armed warriors, while between the ranks dashed women in black attire like the Furies, with hair dishevelled, waving brands. All around, the druids, lifting up their hands to heaven and pouring forth dreadful imprecations, scared our soldiers by the unfamiliar sight, so that, as if their limbs were paralysed, they stood motionless and exposed to wounds. Then urged by their general's appeal and mutual encouragements not to quail before a troop of frenzied women, they bore the standards onwards, smote all resistance, and wrapped the foe in the flames of his own brands. A force was next set over the conquered; and their groves, devoted to inhuman superstitions, were destroyed.[140]

The effect which the druids intended to have on the foe in that account calls to mind a passage in an Irish mythical text.

According to it, the goddess Mor-Ríoghain weakens a hostile
king by magically taking from him 'the blood of his heart and
the kidneys of his valour'. She then gives these parts of him to
the poets of Ireland so that they can chant spells against his
army.[141] In the same text a druid boasts of what he will do to
the enemy: 'I will take out of them two-thirds of their courage
and of their martial skill and of their strength, and I will bind
the urine in their own bodies and in the bodies of their
horses.'[142] In another Irish text, three goddesses go to a hill during a battle and from there pour forth on the enemy 'magic
showers of druidry and compact clouds of mist and a furious
rain of fire, with a downpour of dark blood'.[143] There are several other Irish references to poets and druids chanting satires
against enemies in military confrontations,[144] and we can therefore conclude that such a practice was part of battle strategy in
Celtic Ireland.

The role played by women in these passages is noteworthy. We
have already met with the druidic poetess Feidhilm, who was
said to have learned her skill in Britain. She it was who, in the
Ulster Cycle, foretold ferocious battles with the cryptic but
graphic words: 'I see crimson, I see red!'[145] We read that, as she
made this prophecy, she carried a weaver's beam and was weaving with it. This parallels the actions of the Moerae (or 'Fates')
in ancient Greek tradition;[146] and all indications are that the
practice of weaving, as a concrete way of expressing magical for-
mulae, is very old in European tradition.[147] There is evidence
from the Continental Celts that, just as *druis* was a male-druid,
the word *dryas* was used for the female counterpart.[148] One such
dryas, prophesying in Gaulish, is reported to have foretold defeat
to the Roman Emperor at the start of a military expedition in the
early 3rd century AD.[149]

Whereas the Celtic name of a Continental prophetess Veleda
bears witness to a feminine form of the word *file* (< *velitos*,
meaning 'seer'), in Irish the gender of such personages is indicated by the female prefix *ban*. Thus *banfhile* was the term used
for a seeress or poetess, *bandruí* for a druidess, and a female
satirist was described by such terms as *bancháinte*, *banlicerd*,
and *banrindile*. The frequent and casual mention of several such

women in early Irish literature shows that they were not unusual in society[150] and, like male druids, they were even described as operating in groups of three.[151] Irish tradition, however, shows some reticence about poetesses, and generally stresses their satiric tendencies and accordingly the special danger which attaches to them.[152] It may be that this way of thinking prevailed also in the druidic culture, and if so it would reflect the male fear, frequently encountered in anthropology, of female magical power. Accordingly, when a woman became particularly notable as a seer, the magical power in her case would have been thought of as duplicated. Female practitioners of druidry may have had a separate institutional structure – corresponding to priestesses in other ancient traditions.[153]

The feeling that a druid was a sacred personage is expressed in different ways by the early Irish literature. Stories tell of them being used as ambassadors between warring camps[154] and, indeed, Irish culture has at all times regarded the poets as people who had the right to travel unhindered from territory to territory.[155] The word *nemeton*, used by the Celts abroad for a sacred place where the druids performed their rites, occurs with an additional meaning in its Irish form *neimheadh* – as well as the sacred place, it can refer to the actual sacred person himself.[156] To further underline the high degree of continuation of this ancient Celtic system in Ireland, we can add that in the territory of the Carnutes, which was regarded as the centre of all Gaul, the druids are reported to have convened at a given time every year to pass judgements and settle disputes.[157] This is paralleled by the Irish tradition that Uisneach (in Co. Westmeath), site of an important ancient festival at the feast of *Bealtaine* (May),[158] was a focus of druidic ceremony[159] and was the centre-point of Ireland.[160] The meaning of the festival's name (in earlier form, *Bel-tine*) was 'bright fire' and the tradition was that at this festival 'the druids used to make two fires with great incantations, and they used to drive the cattle through them so as to protect them against the diseases of each year'.[161]

–4–

The Teachings of the Druids

IT IS APPARENT that confusion between the mythical realm and the community of the dead was a major factor in Celtic religious thought. This confusion survived into late Irish folklore, in which the *sidh*-beings (or 'fairies') were variously understood to be ruled over by gods and goddesses and to number among them recently departed people.[1] In the early Irish literary sources, the dead were described as going to *Tech Duinn* (the 'House of Donn') off the southwest coast, but this did not exclude other ideas. We have seen in Chapter 2 that this Irish Donn can be identified with the father-god of the Celts, and this would of course provide a synthesis between the deities and the afterlife of humans.

There is no clear indication, however, of the way in which the Celts understood the actual connection between their deities and the afterlife. From Caesar's account of the Gauls' belief in Dis Pater as their general ancestor, and from what he wrote in the same context concerning their custom of placing the night before the day in their computing of time, it would appear that they believed in the realm of the dead as a kind of otherworld which presided over the affairs of the living. Caesar further states that this cult of the divine ancestor and this system of computing time was the teaching of the druids, from which we can gather that the druids had a reasonably consistent dogma with regard to the otherworld. Although most of the mythological figures of early Irish tradition had a cultic significance which related more to the preoccupations of ordinary human living, some of these figures were put into the context of the afterlife which people expected to be their lot.

The continuance of life

The Classical writers attribute to the Celts a quite definite understanding of the afterlife. Strabo, for instance, states that the druids 'have pronounced that men's souls and the universe are indestructible, although at times fire or water may prevail'.[2] Pomponius Mela is more specific in his reference to druidic teaching:

> One of their dogmas has come to common knowledge, namely, that souls are eternal and that there is another life in the infernal regions, and this has been permitted manifestly because it makes the multitude readier for war. And it is for this reason too that they burn or bury, with their dead, things appropriate to them in life; and that in times past they even used to defer the completion of business and the payment of debts until their arrival in another world. Indeed, there were some of them who flung themselves willingly on the funeral piles of their relatives in order to share the new life with them.[3]

From this account it would appear that the afterlife was not generally understood as a sad and dreary place, but rather as a kind of new and valuable sphere of existence. This is borne out by Lucan, in his hostile poem addressed to the druids, when he claims: 'It is you who say that the shades of the dead seek not the silent land of Erebus and the pale halls of Pluto; rather, you tell us that the same spirit has a body again elsewhere, and that death – if what you sing is true – is but the mid-point of long life!' Lucan is here lampooning the druids for what he considers their unjustified pretension in claiming that the afterlife is a more pleasant state than that described in Greek literature. Significantly, also, he suggests that the druids theorised that the body after death is not the same as the natural one.

Apart from transformation in the body itself, however, the reported attitude of the Gauls to the afterlife is a distinctly concrete one, and apparently very similar to social life as experienced in the physical world. It is clear that the Classical writers were quite amazed by this, and were struck in particular by the pursuit of commerce in the afterlife. For instance, Valerius Maximus – writing, like Mela and Lucan, in the 1st century AD – mentions what he calls 'an old custom of the Gauls' and then elaborates:

> It is said that they lend to each other sums that are repayable in the next world, so firmly are they convinced that the souls of men are immortal.[4]

There is abundant evidence that a similar, or identical, attitude to the otherworld was current in Celtic Ireland and that it survived for a long time. Perhaps the clearest example of this is in a text from the 9th century AD. This is from a culture to which paganism was part of the dim and distant past, and the context is thoroughly Christianised, but it nevertheless displays aspects of belief which are quite obviously pagan. It relates an adventure of the high-king Diarmaid mac Aodha Sláine (who reigned from 642 to 664 AD) – a fictional adventure we may add, but one set within a genuine traditional framework.

We read of how Diarmaid met with a beautiful woman, who returned with him to his capital Tara and became his paramour. Because Diarmaid had given her a small brooch as token, his druids named her Beagfhola ('little wealth'). She fell in love with Diarmaid's foster son, however, and made a tryst with him. Accordingly, she left Diarmaid's bed at the break of day but, on her way to the meeting-place with her lover, she was attacked by wolves and had to flee into a tree from them. She was not long in the tree when she saw a fire in the wood, tended by a young and very handsome warrior. He was roasting a pig. He did not speak to her, but ate the pig, washed his hands, and then went from the fire towards a nearby lake. She followed him into his boat, and they came to a fine island. They entered a beautiful but deserted palace there, and after eating sumptuously went to bed, but still he paid no heed to her. Then some startling things began to happen:

Early in the morning they heard a call from the jetty of the island: 'Come out, Flann, the men are here!' He arose then and put his armour on and went out. She went to look at him to the door of the house, and saw three men on the jetty of the same appearance and same age and same figure as him. She also saw four men on the jetty of the island with their shields held erect in their hands. Then his four went against them. They smote one another until each was red with the blood of the other. Then each went his way, wounded.

He went to his island again. 'A glorious victory for you,' she said, 'that is a champion's deed!' 'It would be good,' said he, 'if it were against enemies!' 'Who are the warriors?' said she. 'Sons of my father's brother,' he said, 'the others are my three brothers!' 'What were you fighting about?' said she. 'This island,' said he. 'What is the name of the island?' said she. 'The Island of Fedach son of the Blind Man,' said he. 'And what is your name?' said she. 'Flann, grandson of Fedach,' he said. 'It is the grandsons of Fedach who are in contention. The island is indeed good – a meal for a hundred men, with food and ale, is its provision every evening without human attendance. Should there be only two people on it, they receive only what suffices them.' 'A question,' said she, 'why may I not stay with you?' 'It is indeed a bad union for you,' he said, 'to stay with me and to leave the king of Ireland, and to be following me in soldiering and exile.' 'Why do we not make love?' said she. 'Not on this occasion,' he said. 'If, however, the island becomes mine and if we are alive, I shall go for you, and you are the woman who will be with me always.'

He then brought her to Tara, and Diarmaid was just awakening when she arrived, as if no time had passed. One morning, exactly a year later, she and Diarmaid were awakening when they saw a wounded man pass by the door of their dwelling. The man was Flann, and Beagfhola got up and followed him. Diarmaid ordered that she not be stopped, 'for it is not known where she is going nor whence she came'. Soon a group of four clerical students, sent by St Molaise, arrived and reported that a farmer on their monastic island of Damh-Inis had seen eight warriors fighting early in the morning, and that one man only had survived. The saint had buried the other seven. Diarmaid told them to use the gold and silver of these warriors' accoutrements in order to make a shrine and crozier for the monastery.[5]

This story represents the rendezvous of the two worlds – that of Christianity and the earlier pagan one. The claim that 'druids' officiated at the court of a 7th-century Christian king is an anachronism, but it provides a hint of the strength of the ancient type of lore which is at work within the narrative. We note also the change of name which is claimed for the island, from the pagan Island of *Fedach* ('tree-man') to the ordinary designation Damh-Inis (Devenish on Lough Erne, where the celebrated monastery of St Molaise was).[6] This, like the change in use of the gold and silver, is meant to illustrate how one system of sacred values displaces the other. Clearly, then, the writer of this text regarded Flann and his associates as representatives of pagan belief. Although for some reason she is not quite au fait with the affairs of Flann, it is clear that Beagfhola herself belongs to the pagan otherworld and she returns to it. And this brings us to the basic notion of the interfacing of two worlds, which suggested the secondary juxtaposition of pagan-Christian to the writer.

This is the intermingling of the living and the dead, which we can take to have been an essential part of actual pre-Christian belief in Ireland. Beagfhola is a woman who moves between two worlds – the ordinary one in which she has a relationship with Diarmaid, and the timeless otherworld in which Flann is her lover. Flann is in many ways typical of the otherworld. His name means 'scarlet', thus instancing the imagery of red associated with the dead, and he exists in the environment of the island in its earlier phase. This environment of his is also a socially remote one, of woodland and water, which was – as we shall see – considered appropriate to the otherworld. The most striking thing about him, however, is that he moves back and forward between both worlds, and indeed that his way of living in the otherworld is a

mirror-image of this world. Thus he has to contend for possession of family property, just as people do in the ordinary world.
The parallel is clear to the Classical accounts of Continental
druidic teaching on issues such as the body being similar, but not
quite the same, in the afterlife, and the continuance of commercial transactions in that life.

The elements which provide the setting for this fictional
adventure are well attested in other accounts in Irish literature.
The hero Cú Chulainn, for instance, is said in a story from the
8th century to have fallen in love with a woman called Fand,
who is married in the otherworld to the mythical Manannán. At
the feast of Samhain, Cú Chulainn fails to shoot down two
strange birds, after which he is overcome by fatigue and falls
asleep by a rock. In a vision two strange women, Fand and Lí
Ban, come to him and strike him, leaving him in a delirious sick-
ness for a year. At the feast of Samhain again, a strange man
comes to him with a message in verse that he is required in a
place called Magh Cruaich. Cú Chulainn gets up and goes to the
rock where he had fallen asleep, and there Lí Ban comes to him
and tells him that he will be cured on condition that he fight a
battle on behalf of her husband, the king of that land, after
which he shall have the love of Fand. She further explains that
the real name of their clime is Magh Meall.

After some prevarication, Cú Chulainn consents, and goes to
Magh Meall – which is reached by rowing across a lake to an
island – and by his tremendous fighting secures victory in the
battle. He then dallies with Fand for a month. There is a palace
there, beautifully adorned with gold, as well as trees bearing
wonderful fruit, a never-ending supply of mead, the accompaniment of sweet music, and fine horses. On his return home,
however, Cú Chulainn is upbraided by his wife Eimhear, and
cannot decide what to do. In the end, Fand returns to her husband, and Cú Chulainn is recovered – through the assistance of
druids – by his wife.[7]

We note here that – as in several stories in the old literature –
the festival of Samhain is the time at which the two worlds meet.
Samhain, as the beginning of winter, was, and remains still in
folklore, the principal date with which Celtic culture in Ireland

associated the otherworld.[8] This gives a clue as to the ultimate
origin of such lore, namely that the idea of mortals engaging in
supernatural adventures grew out of the performance of special
rituals and ceremonies. Many other cultures also have this idea
of festivals as sacred time, when the mythical and ancestral
beings are recalled.[9]

The nature of the otherworld
The portrayal of the otherworld as a bright and beautiful place,
and situated on a strange island across the water, is found in several Irish sources. A 9th-century text, for instance, describes travellers coming to such an island surrounded by a revolving wall
of fire, with one open doorway in the wall. Through the doorway, glimpses are caught of the life within – handsome people
dressed in beautiful clothes, drinking ale from goblets of gold,
and with wonderful music being played for them.[10] This reminds
one of the great ale-feast of the divine race, the Tuatha Dé, which
in another text is said to be presided over by the wonderful smith
Goibhniu, and the partakers of which are preserved from age and
decay.[11] In other sources, the wonderful realm is variously called
Magh Meall ('the enticing plain'), Eamhain Abhlach ('the sacred
place of apples'), and Tír na nÓg ('the land of the young').[12]
From these designations we gather that it was a pleasant place,
with delectable food, and where time stood still. Mediaeval Irish
texts, indeed, describe the mysterious beauty of this otherworld,
have mortals brought away there by handsome young people
carrying magical apples, and represent pork as the most favoured
diet there.[13]

There is, however, some ambiguity concerning the location of
this other existence. Although it is at a geographical distance in
the story of Cú Chulainn and Fand, that same text describes the
otherworld as being in a *sídh*. Another text from the same period
describes how a well-dressed stranger visits the Connacht assembly early one morning through a mist. The stranger explains that
he is of the people of the *sídh*, and seeks help for a battle. A young
prince called Laoghaire mac Criomhthainn agrees to assist, and
with fifty companions dives into the nearby lake and they thus
reach Magh Meall, which is here described as a fortress. Having

won the battle, and got wives in Magh Meall for himself and his men, Laoghaire returns to Connacht for a short visit. 'After that he went from them into the *sídh* again.'[14]

So the otherworld was conceived of variously as a fortress and as an island. The storytellers could, of course, rationalise this by describing it as an island with a royal palace as its focus, but the relatively easy access to it betrays its mystical rather than geographical nature. It was in effect a wondrous existence side by side with the ordinary mundane world, a realm for which the term *sídh* sufficed to indicate its supernatural atmosphere. This is significant, for in origin the word *sídh* meant an abode, referring to the abode of the dead within a mound or tumulus.[15] It was through a process of development that its meaning came to be applied to a strange world within the tumulus and, indeed, to those who resided there. Those residents were the dead who had been interred in the tumulus, and it is therefore clear that the otherworld was thought of as the place to which deceased individuals went.

Archaeology shows that this idea was a very ancient one among the Celts. The earliest artefacts from a definitely Celtic culture date from the 7th to the 5th centuries BC, and cover a wide area of central Europe from present-day Hungary to eastern France. This is known as the Hallstatt culture, from a small lakeside town in upper Austria where great burial grounds were situated. Throughout the large area covered by this culture, chamber-graves have been discovered within tumuli. In several cases there have been impressive grave-goods, such as splendid four-wheeled carts, harness-fittings, and beautifully decorated vessels, weapons and clothing. There are numerous examples also of food, for instance joints of boar with knives as if the individuals buried there would require feasting within the tumulus. It is obvious that the more magnificent of these graves were those of chieftains and their relatives, and that no such pomp and ceremony attended the burials of ordinary people, of which there are numerous examples also in that area.[16]

The custom of burying members of ruling castes with grave-goods, and with food and drink, was continued in the next phase of Continental Celtic culture (5th to 4th centuries BC), known as

La Tène. Again, some mode of transport in the afterlife was considered necessary by those who constructed the tumuli, but in
this phase the smaller two-wheeled war-chariot was buried with
the dead.[17] From this archaeological evidence, we can assume
that a journey was considered imminent after death, and that
accoutrements and sustenance would be required for that journey. It is difficult to say when such a journey was actually
thought to take place, and what interval of time was thought to
elapse between the interment and it. What does seem clear, however, is that the nobility were believed to go to the afterlife in a
very special and ornate way, and that the voyage hence of the
commonality was not quite the same.

The likelihood is that the tumulus was considered to be inhabited by the spirit of the noble dead for a definite period, and that
there was a supernatural passage-way from it to the otherworld.
This would mean that the inside of the tumulus was a very sacred
place, the focus of relations with the spiritual otherworld. That
the ancient Celts had great respect for such tumuli, where the
dead resided and with which the otherworld beings communed,
is clear. Referring to the seeking of knowledge from oracles, Tertullian states that the Celts 'spend the night near the tombs of
their famous men, as Nicander affirms'. This Nicander was a
Greek writer from the 2nd century BC.[18]

Similar respect for the dead as sources of otherworld knowledge is found in Irish sources. The best-known instance is the
mediaeval tradition that the poet Seanchán Toirpéist went to the
burial-mound of Fearghus mac Róich seeking to learn a lost epic
from that dead hero.[19] The antiquity of this tradition is indicated
by an independent occurrence in mediaeval Welsh literature,
which has the hero Pwyll (whose name symbolised wisdom), sitting on a mound in order to make contact with the otherworld.[20]
Since the night and darkness was associated with the realm of
the dead, the imagery of darkness in the lore of the druid-poets
(see Chapter 3) would therefore appear to have derived from this
belief in inspiration from the otherworld.[21]

Another strong indication of the centrality of the connection
of druid-poets with the dead is the special skill in antiquarian-
ism attributed to them. Several texts tell of ancient Irish poets

relaying the history of mounds and naming the mythical and semi-historical worthies who have been buried there.[22] The idea, indeed, survived with impressive vigour down to modern times, though in a modified form, for Irish folklore represents many poets as gaining inspiration from the otherworld, especially when sojourning in the vicinity of ancient mounds.[23] In effect, this reflected the central role in their society claimed by the druid-poets, for burial-mounds and related enclosures were the locations ordinarily used for public assemblies.[24] The Celtic druid-poets of Ireland, therefore, were very willing to continue the respect which from time immemorial had been accorded to the outstanding funerary monuments. Centres such as Newgrange, Tara, Knockaulin, Navan Fort were given in Celtic culture the same celebrated status which they had enjoyed since tumuli were first erected at them by Stone and Bronze Age inhabitants.[25]

The otherworld community
The motif, which frequently occurs in Irish literature, of a living person being enticed away by an otherworld lover, does not seem to have been a basic element in the tradition of the *sídh*. It may have sprung from the very old convention of the ruler being the symbolic spouse of the goddess of sovereignty (see Chapter 6). Once the original meaning of intercourse with the dead ancestors had been blurred, the romantic appeal of this motif would have guaranteed its adoption into storytelling. In speculating on the very archaic elements in the *sídh*-traditions, a much more fundamental problem lies in the relationship between the afterlife and the divine beings. As we have seen, there was some sense in which the dead – especially the aristocratic dead – graduated on to the realm which was inhabited by divinities.

This can be illustrated by a very basic layer of pagan lore in Ireland – the situating of the deities within the landscape. Regardless of the precise manner in which Celtic culture came to permeate Irish life, there can be no doubt that aspects of earlier cultures were expropriated by it. We have referred to the adoption of far earlier burial sites into the Celtic system of belief. The clearest instance of this is the great passage-tomb at Newgrange, for it was here that the Celtic religion located its greatest mythical ancestor or father-god, the Daghdha. It was claimed that he and his immediate family lived within this conspicuous mound and that the surrounding area was their special territory. The inherent connection in his case between the divine realm and the burial site is of the greatest significance.

Since, according to Caesar, the father-god was especially the patron-divinity of the Gaulish druids, one is inclined to look for elements within the portrayal of the Daghdha which would indicate a druidic rationale. In Chapter 2, we have discussed the importance attached to male and female symbolism in Celtic religion, and have assigned this to the Daghdha and Danu as a primordial couple of Irish mythology. This and other mythical ideas must have been a heritage shared by the population in general, but there are indications that several aspects of that mythology were rationalised and developed by a learned caste such as the druids. Since their function was largely a sacred one, we need not doubt but that the teachings of this caste were responsible for solidifying the connection between the realm of the dead and the realm of divinity. We can also suspect that they reworked much of the common mythological lore into something in the nature of a theogony. The raw material of popular lore available to the druidic class must have been very rich. From his origin, the Daghdha was identified with the sky or sun, the one-eyed horseman of the heavens, and the descent from one father was probably a common belief also. But it is clear from early Irish literature that such themes had been set within a framework which was quite systematic. That the sun-deity was male and fertilised the female earth was an old concept, but the intricate details and imagery connected with the Daghdha and his female consort bear the marks of design.

The portrayals of this major deity have been correlated in a manner which is very adept and consistent. He is solar, provident and life-producing; he regulates time and agriculture; he exists in the world of the living by day but in that of the dead by night, yet unites these two worlds. This latter he does according to a pattern which gives pre-eminence to the more mysterious of the two, the realm of the dead. Such a pattern would, of course, have been to the advantage of a special caste who involved themselves in mantic practices, such as the druids did. Most pertinent of all to the issue of druidic influence is the Daghdha's special designation Aedh Ruadh Ró-fhessa ('red fire of all knowledge'),[26] which focuses the special area of interest of a learned caste.

As if to illustrate the Celtic belief that the night comes before the day, the Daghdha as divine ancestor had pre-eminence in the Irish pantheon. This view of time was expressed also in the division of the year, which was understood as consisting of two parts – from Samhain (November) to Bealtaine (May), and from Bealtaine to Samhain. The winter half (representing darkness) was primary, whereas the summer half (representing light) was secondary.[27] It is not surprising, therefore, to find a two-part division of time expressed in lore of the Daghdha himself. He is described as 'a famous king over Ireland'[28] and it is claimed that 'over him did the men of Ireland make *Sídh an Bhrogha*'. This designation, literally, meant 'the Mound of the Hostel', and it was – like *Brugh na Bóinne* ('the Hostel of the Boyne') – an ordinary term in use for the Newgrange tumulus.[29] A story was found in various forms in the mediaeval literature, according to which the Daghdha was the first resident in that tumulus. His son Aonghus asked for permission to occupy the *sídh* for one day and one night, and then he claimed it for himself forever 'for there is only day and night from the beginning of the world until the end, and that is the tenure which you have given to me'.[30] An interesting – and perhaps more appropriate – inversion is found in one text of the story, which states the eternal unit of time as *adaig is lá co lí* ('night and day with colour').[31] The import is that the light of day succeeds the darkness of night in taking possession of the world, and that this order is eternally ordained.

This indicates that in early Irish belief the dead did not predominate over the living, but that in effect the benefits of life could be without end. And it was so with the consent of the ancestors who, in the continuation of their existence in the afterlife, were in fact benefitting from this order. The beginning of that same story has the Daghdha deliberately planning for the conception of Aonghus. He gains access to Bóinn (the eponymous goddess of the Boyne river) by sending her husband away

on an errand for one day. He then causes the sun to stand still
for nine months, so as to make it appear that but one day has
passed, and in this way he manages to have the baby Aonghus
taken away to be adopted before the husband of Bóinn returns.
His control of the sun illustrates the solar nature of the
Daghdha; while the unsuspecting cuckold can be taken as a hint
at those men who do not understand the mystic teaching of
druidism.[32]

As we have seen in Chapter 1, it is tempting to regard the
Daghdha/Aonghus relationship as a continuation of the ancient
pre-Celtic symbolism of the new sun replacing the old one at midwinter in the tumulus, and to speculate that the Celtic culture at
the site had encountered some such idea from earlier inhabitants.
This is possible, and may even be likely. We know that the different peoples who inhabited Ireland, down to and including the
Celts, tended to use the same sites for burial;[33] and that very tendency is reflected in the above story, where it is stated that it was
the Daghdha 'who apportioned out the tumuli to the divine
race'.[34] Furthermore, it has been suggested from calendar-read-
ings that – even in the Celtic period – the Irish continued for some
centuries to celebrate the midwinter festival;[35] and, if this was so,
it would also indicate a Newgrange tradition with some continuity from the Stone Age to the Iron Age. Be that as it may, the
Daghdha in his role of provider is represented as responsible for
what are repeatedly referred to in early Irish literature as the two
basic food commodities, *ith ocus blicht* ('corn and milk').[36] These
commodities are even more intimately attached to the land-goddess, and so we encounter again the combination of male and
female deity which creates well-being for the populace. We note
that the area of the Boyne valley is especially stressed in this lore,
thus underlining the duality of ideas in yet another way – that
area being notable for its burials and also for its agricultural fertility. It is accordingly easy to understand why the ancestral
Daghdha was said to have begotten Aonghus on the lady Bóinn.

The name of the river Boyne must be very old – it is attested
as 'Buvinda' by Claudius Ptolemaeus in the early 2nd century
AD. Its proper Celtic form would have been *Bou-vinda*, meaning 'the white lady with bovine attributes'.[37] In mediaeval Irish

it was *Boand* and in later form is *Bóinn*. It referred to the river-goddess who was bright in appearance and who could be envisaged as a cow.[38] Being thus a descriptive appellation, it seems sensible to regard it as a pseudonym for the land and river goddess in general, for whom Danu was a more basic name. Bóinn is said to have had her residence in a *sídh* at the source of the river, which is described in several texts as a mystical place. There was a well there, surrounded by nine hazel-trees, from which nuts fell into the water. These nuts contained *imbas*, the special all-encompassing knowledge claimed by the seers.[39] The river thereby became pregnant with wisdom, and we read that, because of this *imbas* being in it, a person who drank from the river in June would become a poet.[40] This claim is hardly to be taken literally, but rather as an echo of some special ritual. The mention of June (*Meitheamh*, literally 'the heat-time') suggests the involvement of the sun in the process.

The same symbolism is expressed in another way. According to this, a special source of wisdom was *imbas gréine* ('*imbas* of sun'), defined in the early literature as 'bubbles which the sun impregnates on herbs, and whoever consumes them gains poet-craft'.[41] This is a reference to dew. Elsewhere, there are highly significant references to *druchtu Déa* ('dew of a goddess'), which in early poetic rhetoric was a kenning for the all-important *ith ocus blicht* ('corn and milk').[42] The impregnation of the land-goddess by the sun, and her production of corn and milk as dew from her body, constitutes a statement of essential agricultural fact. It is, however, a somewhat embellished and rhetorical statement, and it is surely not without a purpose that the symbols employed are identical with those used for the wisdom of the learned caste. In other words, the druid-poets were determined to portray their profession as intimately connected with the actual well-being of the community.

In several of the texts which tell of visits to and from the otherworld, the druids act as spokesmen for the living community and they advise mortals on how to behave in the unknown realm.[43] In this way, their control of the boundaries between the two worlds gave them a central position in the whole of life. This reworking of general lore in order to claim centrality for

themselves is much in keeping with the overall influence of the
druids on Irish tradition. Their wisdom was presented as being
the same in its source and its function as providence itself, and
the antiquity of this assertion is evidenced by the special claim
made by the Gaulish druids on the ancestral deity. The overall
claim on the goddess is of equal or perhaps of even greater
antiquity. There are, indeed, indications that it may predate
Celtic culture and be Indo-European in origin. The ancient Sanskrit collection of hymns, the *Rig Veda*, uses the cow repeatedly
as a metaphor for the river-goddess, the streams of the river
being synonymous with the milk flowing from her in her shape
as otherworld-cow. Just as the irrigating waters of the river
make the countryside productive, so does the divine liquid give
mystical inspiration to the Vedic poets.[44] Other Sanskrit references were to how cows drink the otherworld liquid 'soma' and
how the knowledge therefore became mixed in with their milk
and was consumed with it by the seers.[45]

Early Irish literature provides direct connections between such
imagery and the role of the goddess vis-à-vis the 'filidh'. A mythical lady called Edar is referred to in one text as *muime na filed*
('the nurse of the seer-poets' – that is, she who suckles them).[46]
The goddess, under the designation Brighid, was *bé n-éxe, ban-
deá no adratis filid* – that is 'the woman of poetry, the goddess
whom the seer-poets adored'.[47] A quite early tract on poetry
describes that art as 'a noble woman' who is 'multiformed mul-
tifaceted multimagical', and claims that she mystically appears
to the poet when he is composing.[48] It is not surprising that,
given the druids' use of Danu and Bóinn, they would also connect the land-goddess under this other designation Brighid to
their craft. In the case of Brighid, the designation seems to have
had an original meaning of 'the exalted one'[49] and was in existence since the common Celtic period, for it occurs as *Briganti* in
place and population names on the Continent and in Britain.[50]
It is well-known that many of the functions of the goddess
Brighid were later applied to the Christian saint of the same
name, and it is significant that in popular culture St Brighid is
especially a patroness of milk-cows and that dew and herbs are
believed to be sacred to her.[51]

Since Celtic forms of the compound 'Bou-vinda' are not attested from outside Ireland, it may be that this particular designation for her was not converted into a river-name abroad. The image-parallels in Sanskrit literature are, nevertheless, warranty enough that such imagery must have been widespread in Celtic culture. A divine cow called Damona is featured in dedications in Gaul, some of which have her in the company of the deity Bormo or Borvo, whose name and cult represented bubbling springs and thermal waters.[52] The convergence here again of water and heat is very significant. In Ireland, traces of the cow-goddess can be observed in the lore of other female figures. One such is Flidais, whose name derives from flowing liquid, in particular milk, and who is represented as milking the wild deer and in being in possession of a great herd of cattle.[53] We also may note the old and widespread Irish folk tradition of a wondrous milking-cow called the Glas Goibhneann, 'the grey of Goibhniu'.[54]

Of particular relevance is the story – told in a mediaeval text – of the west Munster ancestor hero Corc Duibhne. The name of this hero reflects that of a goddess Dovinia, who features in several inscriptions from the same area. The story of Corc Duibhne has him being reared by a druid and a mythological woman called Boí on her island, and being bathed by her each morning in the sea on the back of a white red-eared cow.[55] There are some elements in this description which are worthy of attention. The woman Boí was otherwise known as the Cailleach Bhéarra, a personage who represented several aspects of the land-goddess.[56] Boí's name is itself a variant of 'bó', a cow, a factor underlined by her special cow in the story. The cow is white, as we might expect, but she also has the red ears which mark her otherworld nature.[57]

The skills of mediation

In describing the druidic attitudes among the Gauls, Diodorus Siculus refers to belief in the continuance of life after death and states that 'this is the reason given why some people at the burial of the dead cast upon the pyre letters written to their dead relatives, thinking that the dead will be able to read them'.[58] This is of special interest, for according to Caesar the druids deliberately

refrained from writing down their traditions. There are survivals
of many short and non-doctrinal inscriptions in Gaulish – including dedications to deities, phrases and verses from ordinary life,
and the celebrated Coligny calendar.[59] These inscriptions variously use the Greek and Latin alphabets, and the 'letters' referred
to by Diodorus may of course have been written not in Gaulish
at all but in either of these two Classical languages. It is likely that
Diodorus was referring to a rather localised innovation, by which
writing was substituted for druidic rhetoric as a means of communicating with those in the afterlife.

The Classical system of writing was borrowed also into Ireland,
though at a later date. From the 4th to the 8th centuries AD
inscriptions were written on standing stones in a script called
ogham, in a more antique form of Irish than that evidenced by the
literature. Each inscription consisted of only a few words. These
words were in Celtic, or partly Celtic, form, and it is clear that the
inscribers were deliberately archaising their language. Interestingly,
such Celtic archaisation is not evidenced by Irish literature, which
was contemporaneous with the final centuries of ogham-writing,
and we can therefore surmise that this script was considered to be
particularly sacred. Most of the inscriptions in it were memorials
to dead individuals, and a few were dedications to deities.[60]

The ogham-script was a combination of notches and grooves,
representing the letters of the Latin alphabet. The vast majority
of the known examples of it are on stone, with a few instances
on metal, but the literature refers to the writing of this script on
wood by the poets of old, and there may be some truth in this.
Mediaeval writers – who themselves understood something of
the script – regarded its writing and interpretation as a kind of
arcane skill in prehistory. Thus, for example, we read of a fictional poet of old, Fearadhach, reading an ogham inscription and
deliberately changing its meaning for his listeners. The inscription's import is described as fortgithe ('hidden'), the same word
which is used for the rhetorical language of the poets.[61] In the
Táin epic, the hero Cú Chulainn cuts an enigmatic verse in
ogham on a sapling of oak in order to delay a hostile army, and
a druid examines the sapling and deduces its 'secret', i.e., the sort
of man who wrote it.[62] A reference in a later text is even more

explicit as to the druids' skill with *ogham*. According to this, the druid Dallán ('blind man') was sent to search for an abducted lady, but he met with no success for a whole year. Then, coming to a hill one night, 'he made four rods of yew, and marked an *ogham* in them, and it was revealed to him through his keys of seercraft and through his *ogham*' that the lady was concealed in an otherworld dwelling.[63]

The designation of the script is related to Oghma, which was given as the name of one of the divine race, the Tuatha Dé Danann. This Oghma is described as *mac ealadha* ('son of art') and as 'a man most knowledgeable in speech and in poetry'.[64] Even more significantly, in view of what we have said concerning solar symbolism, he was given soubriquets such as *grian-aineach* ('sun-faced') and *grian-éces* ('sun-poet').[65] The Gauls had a deity of eloquence called Ogmios, according to the Greek writer Lucian in the 2nd century AD. Lucian describes a portrait, which he had seen, of this Ogmios leading a group of followers by little chains of gold and amber which attached their ears to his tongue.[66] The name may originally have been a Greek translation of a Gaulish word denoting rhetoric, and it would appear that – in the form 'Ogma' – it was brought to Ireland by Gaulish mercenaries in the early centuries AD.[67] It may therefore evince a similar view on the adoption of rhetoric into writing, and of the attribution of mystical power to both in certain circumstances.

The way in which Diodorus describes the Celtic belief in survival after death does, however, have a puzzling aspect to it. This is a claim that the druids taught some form of the doctrine of reincarnation, which Diodorus even goes so far as to link to a Greek school of philosophy. In writing of the banquets of the Gauls, he says:

> At dinner they are wont to be moved by chance remarks toward disputes and, after a challenge, to fight in single combat, regarding their lives as naught. For the belief of Pythagoras is strong among them, that the souls of men are immortal, and that after a definite number of years they live a second life when the soul passes into another body.[68]

Diodorus does not, however, state what kind of body he had in mind. He had his information from Posidonius, who wrote in the 2nd century BC, a few generations before his own time, and on this matter does not appear to have a specific understanding of the belief in question. His contemporary Caesar, drawing also on Posidonius, describes the teaching of the druids:

> They are chiefly anxious to have men believe the following: that souls do not suffer death, but after death pass from one body to another; and they regard this as the strongest incentive to valour, since the fear of death is disregarded.[69]

Here there is no confusion with the doctrine of the Greek philosopher Pythagoras, but a simple statement to the effect that a person lives on in a new body after death. Lucan, a hundred years later, accords well with this, when he says to the druids that 'you tell us that the same spirit has a body again elsewhere'.[70] To discover what kind of body, these writers would presumably have had to consult the druids themselves, for the evidence shows that these practictioners tried to keep knowledge of abstract and spiritual matters within their own profession.

The point is illustrated very well by what Irish literature tells of the connections supposedly made with the otherworld. When a being comes from that realm to encounter mortals, we usually read of a supernatural mist enveloping those present. This mist is an otherworld device in order to allow the two realms to interface. In such situations, the druid is described as explaining the meaning of the fog and communicating with the beings who have caused it.[71] For their own part, the druids can themselves create a supernatural mist. This, known as *ceo druidechta* ('fog of druidry'), is described as a device to confuse foes,[72] but there can be little doubt that originally it had the ritual function of opening the portals of the otherworld.

Certainly the druids did not hesitate to employ techniques of illusion. There are several mentions of one such technique, which again they shared with spiritual beings. This was the *féth fiadha*, an obscure term which is variously spelt in the literature but which seems to have had an original meaning such as 'art of semblance'.[73] This was a special skill possessed by the deities or otherworld community. Thus, the Tuatha Dé Danann are described as employing it so that they cannot be seen by mortals,[74] and heroes of this world are rendered invisible through having it put around them by the community of the *sídh*,[75] or can have the skill taught to them by that community.[76] Its function resembled that of the 'tarnkappe' in Germanic tradition, and there is every reason to consider it of some antiquity in general mantic lore. An early Irish legal text stipulates that the druids by profession 'perform the *féth fiadha* or the divination'.[77] A related power attributed to Irish druids is that of shapeshifting. In one mediaeval Irish text, a blind druid called Dil is described as prophesying to his Osraighe sept that they will defeat a hostile sept, the Déise, in a forthcoming battle. A prelude to this defeat will be the slaughter by the Déise of a hornless red cow which will stray onto the battlefield. Being informed of this, a druid of the Déise puts himself into the semblance of such a cow. Dil then realises that the prophecy is being turned against his own sept, and he orders his Osraighe men not to kill the cow. Some servants do so, however, and as a result the Osraighe are routed in the battle.[78]

The variety of names given to the Daghdha indicates that he was a shapeshifter, and one text expressly states that through his perfection of knowledge he had 'multiform triads'.[79] Other divine figures are also represented in the mediaeval literature as changing into different forms during their adventures. These include Aonghus and his lover Caer, who take on bird form periodically; the beautiful princess Éadaoin who lives for a long time in the form of a butterfly; and god-like personages such as Manannán and Cú Roí who enter the ordinary world in a variety of disguises.[80] Such stories are best considered as a reflex from ancient belief in metamorphoses of deities. The fact that supposed actions of the druids follow the divine pattern of illusion and transformation underlines the sacred nature of the druidic profession, but it also suggests that the druids actually had mantic practices with the purpose of impressing their audiences.

The personification of wisdom

The imagery of brightness is often associated with true poetry in Irish tradition, and there is a tendency in the literature to describe druids and poets as fair-haired or dressed in white.[81] It is therefore quite impressive to find that the most famous possessor of occult knowledge was the mythical hero Fionn, whose name means fair-haired. This Fionn, celebrated in Irish story-telling down to the present day, is traditionally taken to be the leader of a warrior-band called the Fianna and he is not regarded as being particularly druidic. However, tradition perennially has him as a seer-warrior, and his most typical action is a mantic one – to gain hidden knowledge, he places his thumb in his mouth and sucks or chews it. In the early centuries of Irish literature, as we have seen (Chapter 3), this knowledge of his is identified with the skill of the druids. It is therefore logical to regard Fionn as having had a special connection with the druidic profession in ancient lore.

His name is very significant – in Old Irish it was Find, which derived from Celtic 'Vindos'. This in itself may involve the idea of wisdom. The present-stem of an Indo-European verb which indicated the gaining of knowledge was *weid-, which survived in various Indo-European languages and in Irish as fet- (a verbal stem for 'knowing') and fiss (the word for knowledge itself, of which imbas was a compound). This Indo-European verb had a less influential present-stem *wind-, which became *vind- in Celtic, and from which in turn the Irish verbs ro-finnadar and findad ('to discover') and Welsh gwn ('to know') were derived.[82] It has been suggested that this could connect the personage of Fionn very intimately to his quality of fiss. The semantic process in such a case would have a Celtic verb giving rise to an adjective, based on the sense that knowledge clarifies and brightens the understanding. The adjective for brightness or whiteness would then give rise to a name for a person with hair of bright colour.[83]

Other etymologies have been argued for the Celtic adjective and noun vind-, especially one which claims that they should be derived from an aspirated form of *sweid, which had the meaning of 'shine'.[84] But even if this is so, the imagery of shining could easily be assimilated to the illumination of wisdom. There are several examples in early Irish texts of the adjective *find* being used to describe the speech of poets.[85] In these cases it has connotations of mystical knowledge, and indeed *find* has been glossed from a very early period to mean 'true'.[86]

The personal names Vindos (for a man) and Vinda (for a woman) are attested among the Continental Celts, and various tribal names both in Britain and on the Continent began with the element *vind-*.[87] The word in these cases may refer only to brightness in colour, but an indication that it could be used as more than just a physical description is provided by the appellation Vindonnus given to deities at Celtic sites in southern Germany, in France, and in England. It may be relevant that at Essarois in Burgundy a Vindonnus is associated with both sun and water, and votive offerings to him there include bronze eye-models, as if he were a patron of sight.[88] The name Vindonnus signified something like 'divine Vindos'. There was a strong tendency among the Celts to have individual deities as personifications of definite aspects of life,[89] and so we might expect that the seers would have had a special deity to characterise their own craft. It would not be surprising if the element *vind-* were to be found in the name of such a personage. The Celtic placename Vindobona (the original form of Vienna, among other places) could be of relevance, for it meant 'the settlement of Vindos'. It can be inferred from Romanised Celtic toponymics like Juliobona and Augustobona that this Vindos was – like the Roman emperors Julius and Augustus – a personage of high importance.[90]

Celtic *Vindos* developed in Irish through *Find* into *Fionn* in the modern language. A number of characters mentioned in the early literature have names which derive from *find*, among them an unhistorical Leinster king Find Fili, the wise but fictional judge Morfhind, and the long-living and shape-shifting Fintan mac Bóchna.[91] By far the most celebrated, however, is the hero of many Irish literary and oral tales Find (later, Fionn) mac Cumhaill, who was claimed to have got the gift of wisdom from eating a salmon from the river Boyne. At all stages of Irish tradition, this hero demonstrates an extraordinary method of gaining knowledge of past, present, and future – that is, of gaining types of knowledge appropriate to the *file*. He places his thumb in his mouth and chews it, and then the inspiration comes to him.[92] The process of chewing may once have been associated with breaking open the pith of the wisdom-filled nuts of the Boyne,[93] and therefore is of obvious relevance. But it does not seem to have been the original and basic idea in the motif – a more natural explanation would be that it represents the image of an inspired child, who in common with many children sucks his thumb.

The idea of a divinity in the form of a child is attested in many ways in ancient cultures. A parallel to the imagery in question is, in fact, found in an unrelated culture – the iconography from ancient Egypt of the child-god Horus sucking his finger.[94] The figure of the divine child has been studied in depth for the ancient Minoan civilisation,[95] and the notion of such children is much developed in Greek and Roman literature.[96] Wise speeches made by a baby after birth are also featured in early Irish literature. Morfhind (literally 'great' or 'phantom' Find) is born with a caul and, since this was considered a monstrous birth, he was flung into the sea. The baby surfaced, however, and spoke to the men who had thrown him in. They took him out again, and when brought to his parents he continued to speak.[97] One text has him surfacing at the ninth wave from the shore and immediately pronouncing nine wise judgements.[98] Another relevant character is the child Noíne, of whom only a birth-story is told. This Noíne seems to have been in origin a double of Find, his name being a confusion of the word 'noídhiu' ('a child') and 'noí' (the number 'nine'). One text, in fact, gives his father's name as Umhall, thus paralleling texts of the 6th to 7th century AD which called the famous seer-warrior 'Find mac Umhaill'.[99] We read that Noíne was conceived after his mother was impregnated by a sea-spirit. She was pregnant for nine years, and when the child Noíne was born he immediately uttered nine statements. Another wondrous aspect of this child was that at his birth he had long locks and a curly beard.[100]

All of this is made clearer by the birth-story of Mongán mac Fiachnai, a historical prince of the Dál nAraidhe in east Ulster

who was slain in battle against the Britons in the year 624 AD.
A variety of amazing stories came to be told concerning this historical Mongán, and the 8th-century compiler of these stories
states rather bluntly that Mongán was a reincarnation of Fionn
mac Cumhaill.[101] The only possible explanation for these
accounts of Mongán is that they are an echo of a poetic eulogy
which made comparisons between that local historical character and Fionn. We can therefore take it that the stories contain
elements of some early lore concerning the seer Find. They state
that Mongán was born the son of a sea-deity, that he was a wonder-child, and that he showed amazing knowledge of past, present, and future. The name Mongán means 'hairy fellow', and
it may be that the historical prince was so called from having
some hair at his birth. At any rate, the parallels between the
births of Morfhind, Noíne, and Mongán – all in their own ways
avatars of Find – leave us in little doubt regarding the basic features of the original lore of Find as a wonder-child. These features are – his birth in some way associated with water, his
wisdom and symbolical sucking of the thumb, his maturity at
the beginning as evident from the wise statements and perhaps
also from the fully-grown hair. We find all of these features
reflected in the mediaeval literature concerning Fionn mac
Cumhaill.[102]

The fully-developed Fionn mac Cumhaill of tradition can be
explained as a martialised version of the seer Find, which was
developed by the Leinstermen in the 5th and 6th centuries AD
during their struggles to regain the Boyne valley from the ascendant Connachta, or Uí Néill, sept.[103] As such, Fionn mac
Cumhaill was said to have had his fortress in the frontline area,
at Almhu (the hill of Allen, in Co. Kildare), just as Find File was
said to have had his at Aillind (the hill-fort Knockaulin, also in
Co. Kildare). Both of these may have been locations of a cultus
based on Vindos. Furthermore, as a symbol of military struggle,
Fionn mac Cumhaill was invested with a band of young hunter-
warriors or *fianna*. This martialised Fionn has not, however, lost
all of the original lore, for – as well as being a hunter and warrior – the famous character of Irish literature and folklore is still
a great seer.

The mediaeval literature featuring Fionn mac Cumhaill does not expressly connect his birth with water, but the number nine – which we have encountered in the context of the nine hazel trees at the source of the Boyne and in the other birth-stories – does occur in that we read that Fionn was conceived nine hours before his father's death.[104] It is apparent that the number nine was important in the druidic learning. With regard to the water it is significant that he is said by some sources to have been called Find from birth, whereas his mediaeval biography has him being so named when he is a young boy and after he overcomes nine other boys at wrestling in water.[105] A later story, which has his hair change its colour after he dives into a lake, is well known.[106] The kernel of these traditions is that he gained his bright hair-colour, and concomitantly his name, from the water. Folk tradition, indeed, has him falling into water, or being thrown into it, immediately after his birth. He does not drown, but emerges holding an eel in his hand.[107] This is obviously related to what we have seen in the birth-stories of Morfhind and Noíne.

Such ideas reflect the pre-natal state, and their dramatic development in mythic thought to stress the birth of a wondrous child must be very old. For instance, the Greek god Dionysus was described as rising from the deep or being washed ashore as a child;[108] and Scyld, the mythical ancestor of the Danes, came as a child over the sea in a treasure-laden ship.[109] Most striking of all was the Hindu deity Vishnu, who came from the world-ocean as fish and child at once and was 'radiant with the lustre of wisdom'.[110] In brief, we can speculate that the basic idea of the child-seer Find was that he was born of the goddess Bóinn and that he emerged from her, out of the river,[111] bringing with him the *imbas*, that all-embracing wisdom. The *imbas* would thus be paradoxical – living fire within water. This arcane idea is found in the Indic and Iranian traditions concerning Apam Nápat, a 'descendant of the waters' who illuminates his followers;[112] and also in an ancient Armenian poem on the fire-god Vahagn who comes as a child from the water.[113] The Slavic Svarozhich, who personified fire and was the son of the sun-god,[114] may also be related. There is therefore every reason to regard this as archaic lore among the peoples of Europe and western Asia, and such an arcane motif would be regarded by the Celtic druids as suitable material for the mystification of their own skills. The question arises, of course, who was the father?

In considering the notion of poetry or wisdom as contained in dew impregnated by the sun, one is tempted to regard the sun as in some sense the father of Find. This likelihood is enhanced by one mediaeval text, which imaginatively has the river Boyne coursing around the world before returning to its source.[115] Indeed, the illuminative imagery of Find himself might suggest an understanding of him as a little sun, a reflection of the larger sun upon the water. This tentative theory gains some support from a Leinster genealogy, dated as early as the 6th century AD. Here Find File is claimed to have been son of an enigmatic figure called Ross Ruadh, viz. *Find Fili mac Rossa Rúaidh*. The patronymic here is no more than a learned inversion of the name of a personage who occurs elsewhere as *Aedh Rúadh Ró-fhessa* – this was, as we have seen in Chapter 2, the Daghdha himself, radiant with sunlight.[116]

The same basic formulation can therefore be deciphered behind the lore of the seer Fionn. The sun-father Daghdha is here represented under the guise of wisdom, impregnating the goddess who represents the fertility of the land, especially envisaged as a river-patroness. As we have suggested, the druids were using the basic religious beliefs and putting these into the context of the primary social importance of their own profession. It therefore seems likely that it was the druids who in this context caused the name of the Daghdha's consort to be changed from Danu to Bou-vinda. This may, indeed, have been how the river first came to be called by that bovine name. We note that *Bou-vinda employs the same element as does the name Vindos (> Fionn) itself. Traces of this goddess-name Vinda can be found in other ways in Irish literature.[117] The word *mong* ('mane' or 'hair' was a metaphor for crested waves in early Irish literature and, significantly, the Mor-Ríoghain is described in an early text as inhabiting the water and as having white hair (*mong fhind*).[118] The name Mongfhind, indeed, survived into later tradition as that of a goddess and a tutelary nurse.[119]

Most striking is the obscure tradition of the *trí Find Emna*. These three warriors, who figure in the heroic literature,[120] are an example of triplication of the ancient Vindos. The second part of their name is the genitive of *emon* ('twin', from the Indo-European **yem-os*), and so their origin can be linked to divine twins of ancient Hindu, Greek, Roman, and Germanic traditions.[121] All of this suggests that the lore in question is of a quite archaic type. It is clear that the seers saw the main purpose of the Find personage as being a representative of their own interests. In this context, it is well to recall the idea of maturity which we have mentioned – the imagery of fullness in the beginning. This reflects the concept of wisdom in many ancient societies, a concept well attested from Irish traditions of poets – true wisdom which is not learned, which is not piecemeal, not so as to speak 'profane', but is a mystical quality or genius which is full and entire and undivided from start to finish.[122] In other words, the divine seer-child is already old in wisdom.

This would call forth a certain duality in imagery, and it is clear that the seers of early Ireland developed a conceptual framework to facilitate it. We find traces in many ways of a duplicated Find, a youth and an elder who – in tune with actual rituals – is a wisdom-giving ancestor. This repeats the pattern which we have already encountered in the case of the Daghdha and his son Aonghus. The literature of Fionn has him gaining knowledge at the Boyne from an old man called *Find-éces* (literally 'Find the Seer'), obviously a double of himself. The existence of this concept of the older, or progenitor, Find, seems also to be attested by the name Fintan in mediaeval literature. The character called Fintan is described in an imaginative text as having lived from time immemorial and having gained great knowledge as a result. His name can best be explained as a derivative of Celtic **vindo-senos* – that is, 'Find the old one' – a designation attested also in mediaeval Welsh in the forms 'Gwyn hen' and 'Henwen'.[123]

The text on Fintan – who is called 'mac Bóchna' – 'son of the Sea' – gives a further insight into the seer lore, for we are told that the personage has lived his long life while going through transformations. He has been in the shapes of a fish, an eagle, and a falcon; while another character modelled from him in the literature has been a salmon, a stag, a boar, and an eagle for long periods.[124] One suspects a shamanic type of belief here – the idea that the seer can take the form of different creatures in order to gain his full knowledge by way of different perspectives on the world. That such an idea was part of the seer lore of Find is indicated by other sources, particularly by the texts on Mongán. There we are told that this avatar of Find had the ability to travel in the form of a wolf, a deer, a salmon, a seal, and a swan.[125] A late echo of the antique lore is found in a 12th-century poem, which describes how Fionn once found a cape in a sun-bright stream. It was of otherworld manufacture, being decorated with gold and silver, and had been for thirty years in Magh Meall. By donning this cape and turning it, Fionn 'could be a hound, a person, a deer'.[126]

It is clear that the druid-poets of early times were quite flamboyant in their dress. One account states that 'it is of skins of white and multicoloured birds that the poet's toga is made from the girdle downwards, and of necks of mallards and of their crests from the girdle upwards to the neck'.[127] The 8th-century text on the rhetorical contest between Ferchertne and Néidhe mac Adhna had these two seers contend for the chief-poet's robe. The robe was purple, and adorned with gold and silver. It had 'a colouring of bright bird-feathers in the middle, a showery speckling of bronze on the lower part outside, and a golden colour on the upper part'.[128] The younger Néidhe chants a spell to make it appear that he has a beard,[129] and in their contest they utter enigmatic speeches which hint at mystical experiences in different shapes.[130]

A clear signal that this was ideology emanating from the seers themselves is given by another preternatural ability attributed to Mongán. He is described as visiting tumuli (*sídhe*) and gaining knowledge of secret things in these.[131] There are many instances of stories dealing with visits to such otherworld dwellings by Fionn mac Cumhaill. One of the earliest, dating from the 8th century AD, tells of how Fionn tried to enter the cairn on top of Slievenamon in order to quaff a drink from a fair-haired lady there, but the door was slammed against him as he entered. His thumb was caught between the door and the jamb, it thus being the only part of his body to gain entrance, and so is rationalised the strange motif of his thumb of knowledge.[132] All of which again enhances the rituals of the druid-seers themselves, by having them enacted by a bright figure who personalises the craft.

This brings into focus the question of the whole relationship between the brightness of the otherworld, which is so often met with in Irish sources, and the darkness of the nocturnal world of the dead. The existence in darkness is symbolised by Donn, with whom – as we have seen in Chapter 2 – everybody was thought to finally depart. There are indications that this duality was reflected in a mythic corpus which contrasted the colours represented by Fionn ('white') and Donn ('black', from Celtic *Dhuosnos).[133] This most clearly emerges from the contrast of the two bulls bearing these actual names in the Ulster epic, where it is said that the bulls fought each other for a long time while assuming the forms of different creatures.[134] Mediaeval Welsh literature furnishes other echoes of such an ancient mythic corpus. We read there, for instance, of how two characters, Gwynn and Gwythyr, are destined to fight against each other on every May Day until the end of the world.[135] The name Gwythyr (from Latin 'Victor')[136] is an obvious intrusion; but Gwynn is the exact Welsh equivalent of the name Fionn. Gwynn is, however, said to have the assistance of the spirits of Annwfn ('the underworld'),[137] which would encompass the role of Donn, and so it would appear that both roles had incidentally fallen together in his personality. In another mediaeval Welsh story, the hero Pwyll substitutes for the King of Annwfn, who is dressed in grey-brown clothes and must fight an annual duel with a character called Hafgan ('summer white').[138]

In this dualistic formula may lie the roots of the contest – described variously in mediaeval Irish stories – between Fionn and an otherworld warrior at the festival of Samhain.[139] Furthermore, while drawing its force from pre-Celtic lore at Newgrange concerning the revival of the sun in midwinter, the Celtic tradition of Aonghus replacing the Daghdha would also seem to have been influenced by the same formula. Behind these accounts must lie a mythical portrayal of time, whether annually or daily, alternating between the triumphs of Dhuosnos and Vindos. Yet we can gather that, just as light follows darkness and as the living benefit from the influence of the dead, there was no absolute dualism involved in pagan Celtic belief. The druids rationalised the issue by claiming that their profession was a balance between the world of the dead and that of the living. They may also have claimed that the wisdom which was safeguarded by their profession held the key to bring light out of darkness in the afterlife.

−5−

The Society of the Gods

ON THEIR ARRIVAL or on the arrival of their culture in Ireland, the Celts noticed that there were particular sites which were held in reverence by the indigenous inhabitants. The prestige attaching to these places was obvious to the newcomers, who soon – from a combination of strategic and numinous reasons – incorporated them into their spiritual worldview. The sacred value of the sites was due variously to matters such as elevated position, sepulchral remains, and probably also the survival of rites connected with them among the earlier population.[1] There is room for debate whether the Celts came as conquering bands or as a gradual but increasing cultural strain, but the dominance which they had achieved by the Iron Age is undoubted. As a result, the whole landscape, with its sacred aspects, was redefined in terms which accorded with the new culture. Celtic deities became associated with the revered sites, and Celtic rites and customs mingled with the earlier practices.

The rituals would have been concerned generally with social well-being and specifically with the power and prestige of particular groups. The archaeological record has some light to shed on such matters. For instance, the systems of parallel banks, facing towards the foci at Tara (in Co. Meath) and Rathcroghan (in Co. Roscommon), appear to have had to do with rules of assembly at

these sites. Of interest also is the resemblance between these parallel structures and the rectangular or square enclosures found at
sacred sites of the Celts abroad. Such Continental and British
structures enclose cremations, burials, post-holes, and stone monuments, and were obviously sanctuaries of great importance to
their Celtic designers.[2] It is therefore not surprising that similar
features should be found at locations expropriated by Celtic culture in Ireland.

Tara and its cult
The most famous and prestigious site in Celtic Ireland was the
hill of Tara (*Teamhair*) in Co. Meath. The meaning of this placename seems to have been 'spectacle'. There is a wide view from
there over a large area of Ireland, and it was doubtlessly for this
reason that it was a celebrated and revered place for a very long
time.[3] There are signs of habitation at Tara dating from around
4,000 BC.[4] A small passage tomb was constructed there at the
end of the 3rd millennium BC, and it continued in use as a burial mound through the Bronze Age.[5] It is now known as the
'Mound of the Hostages', a designation which comes from a fanciful account in mediaeval literature of hostages being kept
there.[6] As if to underline the ceremonial importance of Tara from
remote antiquity, two magnificent gold torcs have been found
there, dating to the end of the 2nd millennium BC.[7]

The evidence shows that there was an increase in the importance attributed to the site in the early Iron Age, and most of the
structures there are considered to have had their origin at that
time. Some of the more notable of these are now known by speculative names applied to them since mediaeval times. They
include two circular earthworks, the 'Royal Seat' and 'Cormac's
House', the latter of which encloses an earlier burial mound.[8]
Both of these earthworks, together with the earlier passage-tomb,
are surrounded by a large oval enclosure which consists of a single bank and an internal ditch. This is known as the 'Rath of the
Kings' and was once topped by a timber palisade. To the south
of it is another and smaller enclosure, and to the north is the so-
called 'Rath of the Synods', which seems to have been inhabited
and which once contained a burial mound. North of this again

are the remains of yet more burial mounds, and the so-called
'Banqueting Hall' – a long rectangular structure which has the
appearance of a ritual enclosure.[9]

The most intriguing artefact at Tara is the upright carved stone
of phallic shape called the *Lia Fáil* ('stone of Fál'), which now
stands on the main rath but was originally on the raised surface
within the structure known as 'Cormac's House'.[10] The word *fál*
seems to derive from an Indo-European root **ual-* meaning 'to
be strong', and accordingly would be related to the other Irish
word *flaith*, meaning 'sovereignty'.[11] The original meaning of Lia
Fáil would thus have been something akin to 'the stone of prosperity'[12] and, since Fál was also used as a rhetorical term for Ireland, this indicates that it was regarded as the most important
ritual stone in the whole country. The structure known as 'Cormac's House' may, however, have been a ritual enclosure, and if
so the term *fál* could have been taken in the sense of 'enclosure'
(from the Indo-European **uel-*),[13] thus bolstering the sacred
importance of the actual site where it stood. The mediaeval literature describes it as one of the four great treasures brought to
Ireland by the divine race, Tuatha Dé Danann[14] and, as we shall
see, it was considered to have had a unique importance as a fetish
in the inauguration of kings. Its presence at Tara, in the immediate vicinity of so many burial mounds, ritually illustrates the continuity of life. It must have symbolised the springing of new
social vigour from the realms of the dead.

Of special importance in this regard are the repeated connections made in the literature between Tara and the festival of
Samhain (the beginning of winter),[15] which as we have seen in
Chapter 4 was the principal time of the year for the ancestors to
intervene and to guarantee good fortune. There may indeed have
been a special rite practiced there at that time of year, although
the mediaeval writers were wrong in assuming that such a rite
was the *feis Temro* ('feast of Tara'). This actual *feis* was only held
once in the reign of a king, and its purpose was to sacralise and
proclaim his right to the kingship.[16] The residue of this early
Tara cult had a huge effect on Irish tradition. All the literary
sources, in their backward look onto the prehistoric era, portray
it as a sacred and consequently a royal centre. It was there and

in its vicinity of the Boyne valley that they locate the most crucial decisions governing the culture, as well as many of the most
important mythical events.

The divine kings

It was in the natural order of things for the divine community
themselves, Tuatha Dé Danann, to be described as having their
principal kingship at Tara. One very important narrative illustrates how mythical characters, to whom other landmarks were
assigned, were brought within this ambit. The narrative, in the
form which has come down to us, dates from the 10th century
AD, but it is clearly based on much earlier tradition.

It tells of how Aonghus was visited in his dwelling in the Newgrange tumulus by his foster-father Midhir and, during his stay,
Midhir had an eye knocked out as he tried to separate two
youths who were fighting. He demanded as compensation from
Aonghus the most beautiful maiden in Ireland, called Étaín
Echraidhe, daughter of the Ulster king. Her father demanded
that twelve plains be cleared for him and twelve rivers made, all
of which was done by Aonghus' father, the Daghdha. In this way,
Étaín was got for Midhir. When he brought her home with him
to his own tumulus at Brí Léith (near Ardagh in Co. Longford),
Midhir's wife was jealous of her and turned her into a pool of
water. The pool turned into a worm and then into a butterfly. In
this form Étaín was blown away and, after long misery, she flew
to Newgrange, where Aonghus kept the butterfly in a sun-bower.
She was blown away again, however, and fell into the drink of a
woman in Ulster. In this way, the woman conceived, and Étaín
was born for a second time.

When Eochaidh Aireamh became king at Tara, he decided to
hold the *feis* of Tara, but his subjects would not allow him to do
so without a queen. He therefore sought out the most beautiful
bride in Ireland, and found the reborn Étaín. Midhir, who knew
who she was, planned to take her back, and accordingly came to
play chess with Eochaidh at Tara. Eochaidh won many games,
and demanded as prizes horses, pigs, cows, sheep, swords, and
cloaks. Then he won more games, and demanded that Midhir
perform massive tasks for him. These included the clearing of the

plain in lower Meath of stones, the covering of the plain at
Tethbha with rushes, and the construction of a forest in Breifne.
The actual performance of only one of the tasks is described, and
this is the building of a causeway over a marsh called Móin
Lámhraighe. We read that Midhir gathered a huge number of
men together in the marsh:

> They all made one mound of their clothes, and Midhir
> went onto that mound. A forest with its trunks and roots,
> they placed that at the bottom of the causeway. Midhir
> was standing up and encouraging the multitude on every
> side. You would think that below him all the men of the
> world were raising a tumult. After that, clay and gravel
> and stones are placed on the marsh.

Finally, Midhir won a game, and demanded as his prize one
kiss from Étaín. It was agreed that he would have this a month
hence. Fearing that Midhir might snatch her away, when the
time came Eochaidh had his palace surrounded with warriors,
but Midhir suddenly appeared among them and took Étaín out
through the skylight. They flew away in the form of swans to
the cairn on top of Slievenamon in Co. Tipperary. Eochaidh
and his men went there and dug up the cairn, but the couple
had departed. Then they went to attack Midhir's own dwelling
at Brí Léith, and to prevent this the kidnapper promised that he
would send the lady to Tara. Accordingly, fifty women arrived
at Tara, but all had the appearance of Étaín. Eochaidh, knowing that his wife was the best woman at serving drink in Ireland, asked them to perform that service. He chose the lady
whom he thought best at it, but he was wrong, and thus Étaín
stayed with Midhir.[17]

The characters in this story, and the parts they play, are highly
significant. The king Eochaidh bears the same name as the
Daghdha or father-deity, and his soubriquet Aireamh meant
'ploughman'. It is notable that most of the forfeits which he
demands from Midhir are farm-animals. In tradition he had a
brother, also a Tara king, with the same name but with the
soubriquet Feidhleach, meaning 'herdsman'. One text in fact

makes this Eochaidh Feidhleach the husband of Étaín, and it is clear that each Eochaidh is a double of the other. This duplicated Tara king is connected with the Daghdha not only in name, but also in his role of food-provider. Étaín is well-suited as a partner for such a personage. Her name (in later form Éadaoin), probably meant 'she who evokes jealousy'.[18] Like her husband, she has equine associations, since her soubriquet Echraidhe meant 'horse-riding'. This further connects her with the sun as the horseman of the heavens. It also connects her with the rituals of kingship, for – as we shall see – these rituals often involved equine symbolism. Thus she and Eochaidh illustrate the use of the solar mythology in connection with the Tara kingship. By serving drink to the king, she directly acts out the part of the goddess of sovereignty in Irish tradition.[19]

Midhir was also a deity, and was described as the brother of the Daghdha. His name is cognate with that of the Continental god Medros and – deriving it from Celtic *med- ('to measure') – it has been interpreted to mean 'judge'.[20] It may, however, be connected also with another Celtic word *med- meaning 'ale' (Irish midh),[21] which is found in the name Meadhbh. This name (Old Irish Medb, Celtic Meduva) originally meant 'she who is mead' or 'she who intoxicates'.[22] This was the name more usually given to the goddess of sovereignty at Tara (Medb Temrach), and the literature claims in fact that one fortress there was known as hers, Ráth Mheadhbha.[23] With her was associated the ban-fheis, or feast of inauguration to the kingship, but which literally meant 'sleeping with a woman'.[24] The cultus of Meadhbh as a personification of sovereignty has a long and venerable background in the culture of the Celts and further afield. For instance, Aristotle describes how the original Greek colonists of Marseilles arrived at that place just as the daughter of a Gaulish king was about to offer a drink to a man in token of choosing him as her husband. She changed her mind, and instead chose the Greek leader.[25] That such a rite was known also in ancient India is apparent from accounts of the princess Madhavi, whose name is cognate with that of Meadhbh, and who is described as having been the consort of several kings.[26] In the Tara cultus, however, we find the role of the lady magnified from a personification of sovereignty into that of a veritable goddess, who is in many ways more powerful than the kings with whom she associates.

In this context, and returning to the story of Étaín, it is notable that the *feis* of Tara is there made synonymous with the marriage of Eochaidh to Étaín. Meadhbh is in several texts described as the daughter of Eochaidh Feidhleach,[27] and when dislocation is taken into account it seems likely that Étaín herself and Meadhbh were once one and the same. The peculiar twist given to the motif of identical women in the Étaín story, indeed, by which king Eochaidh ends up with a daughter identical with his wife, may well echo such a dislocation. The interpretation of the name Étaín to mean one who evokes jealousy gives further support to her identification with Meadhbh, whom the literature describes as a continual focus of contention. She was known as Meadhbh Leathdhearg, which epithet means 'half-red' and suggests that the sacral kingship alternated between periods of war and peace.[28] The literature states that Meadhbh could be 'fierce and merciless', and underlines her role as a symbol of the sovereignty thus:

> Great indeed was the strength and power of that Meadhbh over the men of Ireland, for it was she who would not allow a king in Tara unless he had her as wife.[29]

Given his role in the story as the figure to whom Étaín properly belongs, and who eventually retakes her from the king, there is a strong case for regarding Midhir as the male-patron of the kingship. He resides at Brí Léith ('the mound of Liath'), which though located by the literature in present-day Co. Longford, may originally have been a synonym of Tara. A poetic name for Tara was, indeed, Liathdruim ('the *Liath*-ridge'),[30] and one source explains this as deriving from a personage called Liath mac Laighne who constructed the ridge (*druim*) there.[31] From this, one can suppose that Liath was another name, or a descriptive, of Midhir and that he had a special connection with Tara. The word *liath*, meaning 'grey' or 'the grey-haired one' is used for some otherworld characters in the literature[32] and may have been an appellative for the father-deity in opposition to his young son. If so, Midhir as a grey-haired personage would have represented the father-aspect of the patron deity as he bequeathed the kingship for a while to the incumbent.

It is clear that the story of Étaín incorporates several of the focal points of ancient Irish mythology, and there is one intriguing hint as to its antiquity. This relates to the task imposed on Midhir of building a causeway over a bog, for an enormous roadway, laid across a marsh, has been discovered at Corlea (*Cor Léith*) in Co. Longford. The roadway, made from oak planks and up to 2 km in length, is within a few miles of Midhir's reputed dwelling of Brí Léith. The roadway was constructed in the middle of the 2nd century BC, but it was never completed and fell into disuse soon afterwards.[33] This situation is in fact paralleled in the text, where we read of how Eochaidh sent his steward to survey the work being done, and of how this so displeased Midhir and his men that they did not complete the causeway properly. The text states that 'there would be no better causeway in the world if they had not been watched, and defects were left in it on account of that'.[34]

Corlea has not been definitely identified with the bog (*móin*) of Lámhraighe, but the townland of Lehery or Leheries at the northern end of the Corlea bog may preserve the original name. The locations of the other tasks – lower Meath, Tethbha, and Breifne, are all – like Corlea – in the area of the north midlands.[35] The strong likelihood, therefore, is that the tellers of the Étaín story in antiquity knew of this roadway, and included its building among the impossible tasks assigned to Midhir. It has been suggested that it may have originally been a corvée imposed on a population group in the area, and that memory of it had survived for some time.[36] With regard to the actual narrative itself, the role of difficult tasks, as well other elements in the story such as the transformation into swans and the choice from identical women, were based on an international folktale (known to modern scholars as 'The Girl as Helper in the Hero's Flight').[37] The combination of the road-building with the folktale plot may have taken place at a very early period, however, for that folktale is considered to be one of the oldest stories known to man.[38]

New deities

There are many indications that population movements took place from Britain to Ireland in the first two centuries AD, probably in the main due to the suppression of Celtic groups in the sister isle by the Roman legions,[39] and reflections of this are to be expected in the Irish mythological sources: for instance, the case of Nuadhu, a leading personage among the divine community, who was also known as Nechtan and Nuadhu Necht. He is described as husband of the lady Bóinn – in early poetic rhetoric the river Boyne is referred to as 'the forearm of the wife of Nuadhu' and its source as being within 'the *sídh* of the wife of Nechtan'.[40] Although the two names do not correspond exactly, there is clearly some connection between this Nuadhu and a Celtic deity in Britain called Nodons.

The principal known shrine to Nodons is by the river Severn at Lydney in Gloucestershire. He is represented there as elsewhere as a god of healing, and some coins from the site depict a figure hooking a fine salmon.[41] Because of its vigour, the salmon is a natural symbol of health, and a likely interpretation of the name Nodons is 'catcher',[42] so it seems that this British deity had a quite elaborate and developed cult associated with him. Such a cult could easily transfer to the Boyne in Ireland, given the lore of a divine salmon symbolising wisdom and welfare in that river (see Chapter 4), and thus the Irish Nuadhu can be viewed as a borrowing of the British Nodons. It may be relevant that a small bronze arm was found also at the Lydney site, for the Irish Nuadhu is said to have lost an arm and to have had a silver replacement made for it.[43] In Welsh tradition, the character-name Lludd is considered to be a corruption of Nudd; and significantly this Ludd is given the epithet Llaw-Ereint ('Silver-Handed').[44]

Nuadhu himself shows signs of being an interloper on the Irish scene. Although Bóinn's husband was appropriately called Elcmhar ('the envious one') in the story of the conception of Aonghus,[45] Nuadhu is the name by which that husband came to be known. Also Nuadhu is represented as an ancestor figure,[46] in which role he tends to edge out the Daghdha. His additional name of Nechtan may provide a clue to his actual importation into Ireland, for the Romans in Britain identified Nodons with their own Neptunus.[47] Nechtan would have been a tolerable Irish borrowing of the Latin Neptunus, and the Irish would easily deduce an adjective 'necht' from the proper noun Nechtan, thus calling the god Nuadhu Necht.

At Lydney, Nodons is depicted as a full Neptunus figure, riding in a chariot through the sea and brandishing a trident – but this belongs to a fully Romanised stratum on the site, which stratum dates to the 3rd century AD. The Irish Nuadhu does not have Romanised imagery, so the borrowing to Ireland would have taken place at a time when Nodons had as yet been assimilated to Neptunus in name only. This would presumably have been sometime in the 2nd or early 3rd century AD. The earliest references to Nuadhu in Irish literature are in Leinster genealogies, in which he is presented as a royal ancestor of such worthies as Find mac Cumhaill and Find File.[48] It would therefore appear that his cult was first adopted by the Leinstermen at a time when they controlled the Boyne valley and the Tara kingship, and this would also accord with the above dating.

It is interesting to note that Nuadhu was put in the role of husband to Bóinn, and accordingly in the role of father of Aonghus. This Aonghus is described in Old Irish literature as *Mac and Ócc*, which is ungrammatical and is considered a corruption of *in Macán Ócc* ('the young son').[49] The name Macán is in fact a direct Irish parallel to that of a young Celtic deity in Gaul and Britain, Maponos. Like Nodons, Maponos was a patron of health at British shrines,[50] and it might therefore be that his name was borrowed along with that of Nodons into Ireland. The contention here would be that, when Nuadhu was made the husband of Bóinn, the celebrated son of that lady was given an additional designation. In this way, the long-established character Aonghus came to be known also as the 'Macán'.

The young defeats the old
The imagery of the sun-deity found further expression in the figure of Balar, whose name is derived from Celtic *Boleros* and can be connected with a very ancient root *bhel*, meaning 'flash'.[51] His name seems also to have been known in Britain, for a promontory in the southwest of that island was called

Bolerion.[52] Interestingly, there was an Irish tradition which associated Balar with Mizen Head, the furthest southwest point of Ireland.[53] The most dramatic trait of Balar shows him clearly to have been a symbol of the sun – he had a blazing eye which destroyed all on which it looked.

The only full narrative concerning Balar has him opposed and destroyed by the son of his daughter. This was the champion Lugh, a major figure in Irish myth whose name in Celtic was Lugus. We know from toponymics and from inscriptions that Lugus was a very important deity among the Continental and British Celts.[54] Furthermore, when Latin writers mentioned a multi-skilled Celtic god who presided over oaths and bargains, they were almost certainly referring to this Lugus.[55] We know that the original name of Lyons in France was Lugudunum or Lugudunon ('fortress of Lugus'), and a great August festival was held there in Roman times.[56] In Ireland, the harvest-festival and consequently the month of August was called Lughnasa after the Irish version of the same deity. It is very likely, therefore, that the accounts of his slaying of Balar are residue of an early harvest-myth.

The story involves a prophecy made to Balar that if his daughter has a child, that child will kill him. Unfortunately, this detail is not specifically mentioned in literary accounts of the rivals, but it occurs clearly in some other early sources which can be shown to be based on the story of Balar and Lugh. Moreover, the full plot is evidenced from folklore of Balar and Lugh over a wide area, and we can therefore take it for granted that the prophecy was part of the original narrative. Because of the prophecy, we are told, Balar tried to keep his daughter away from men, but he failed in this and she became pregnant. Balar ordered that the child be slain as soon as it was born, but his soldiers took pity on the baby boy and put it out to sea in a basket. Little Lugh was rescued, and when he grew up he confronted his tyrant grandfather and slew him.[57]

This plot is of a type quite uncommon in Europe, but several examples of it are known from the ancient cultures of the eastern Mediterranean. It is reflected in the Sargon inscription at Babylon and in the Exodus account of Moses, and the Greeks heard it told of the Persian king Cyrus and told it of their own hero Perseus.[58]

From a comparison of these two latter versions, it would appear that the plot was borrowed by the Greeks from the Middle East in the 5th century BC, but was not applied to Perseus until some time later.[59] The ancient Greek tradition of slaying a Cyclops-figure had long been attached to Perseus[60] and this – when the new plot from the Middle East was added – meant that the opponent of Perseus could be imagined as either his grandfather or the Gorgon Medusa. It is interesting to note that the portrayals of Perseus in the Classical literature keep these two opponents as different characters, and from this we can gather that the story of Lugh and Balar does not derive from these literary versions. The Celts, therefore, must have picked it up from Greek popular tradition. They may perhaps have heard it from Greeks in eastern or central Europe, but it seems more likely that it was the Celts of Gaul who heard it from a Greek colony such as that at Marseille. At any rate, they soon connected it to two dramatic figures in their own culture, Lugus and Bolerus.[61] It is notable that the destructive eye is much more pronounced in the case of Balar, who moreover is the one great opponent of Lugh. It would thus appear that the Celtic, and particularly the Irish versions, assimilated the Balar-figure to an earlier image of a Bronze Age sun-god. The combination of the Cyclops image, as well as the Middle Eastern plot, ensured that, while obviously representing the sun, Balar does so in a negative and destructive way.

The destructive nature of his eye indicates that Balar represented a specific effect of the sun as distinct from the general function of that body. In such circumstances, he may have been taken to symbolise an excess of sun such as would destroy crops and wreck the harvest. It has been suggested that the cult of Lugus did not in fact reach Ireland until the 1st century BC,[62] and an even later date could be proposed.[63] The literature portrays him as a strange newcomer to Tara and, though this may be nothing more than creative design on the part of the writers, it might also be taken to reflect a feeling that his pre-eminence there was secondary in time. On these lines of interpretation, the myth of Lugh and Balar would have first gained currency in Ireland, and that in connection with the harvest festival, sometime in the 1st or 2nd century AD.

Concerning Lugh, we read that there was 'an assembly held by him at the beginning of harvest each year', and this assembly is identified with the great fair of Tailtiu (Teltown, Co. Meath).[64] Lugh is claimed to have introduced ball-games, horse-racing, and chess to Ireland, and this accords well with his patronage of such an assembly.[65] Tailtiu was an ancient burial-place,[66] and the holding of assemblies at such locations evinces once again the close connection in Irish religion between the realm of the dead and the society of the living. The placename itself, however, is of an unusual type, and it has been interpreted as a borrowing of a British-Celtic word such as appears in Welsh as *telediw*, meaning 'well-formed'.[67] It is possible that there was a settlement of British Celts in this area and that it was they who brought the cult of Lugus with them to Ireland.

Since it is within a dozen miles of Tara, the assembly of Tailtiu would easily have been brought into the ambience of the great ritual site. A connection between the two sites is clear from records of the early historical period,[68] and no doubt it had existed in the late centuries of prehistory also. Lugh, with his imagery of harvest, commerce, and social life, would have been a very appropriate adjunct to the Tara cult of kingship. But it is likely that earlier Celtic tradition portrayed this deity as being particularly suited to a leader's role, for in Irish he is known as Lugh Lámhfhada – the epithet meaning 'long-armed', a suitable image for a good king.[69] The mediaeval literature, in its own fanciful way, echoes something of this by describing how Conn, king of Tara, once had a vision while in the company of his druids and poets. In the vision he found himself in a wonderful house in the company of a very handsome man and a beautiful woman. The stranger explained that he was Lugh and that the woman was Sovereignty. She gave a drink to Conn, to indicate that he was the king, and Lugh foretold a long list of kings who would succeed him.[70]

The primordial battle

The residual outline of the Celtic solar cult on regal tradition is instanced by another account found in the mediaeval literature. According to this, a young woman of the Tuatha Dé Danann,

Ériu daughter of Delbáeth, was on the shore once when she saw a boat of silver come in from the sea. A man with gold-yellow hair and garments embellished with gold stepped from the boat, and asked her to lie with him. She agreed, and before he left he gave her a gold ring as a token which she should only give to a person whose finger it fitted. He then revealed that he was Elatha son of Delbáeth, king of the Fomhoire. He further told her that she would bear his son, who would be called Eochu Bres. This child, more commonly referred to simply as Bres (which meant 'the beautiful'), grew up and became king of the Tuatha Dé.[71]

It is curious that both man and woman in this text are said to have had a father named Delbáeth, and indeed this name is given to several figures in genealogies of the Tuatha Dé. We read, for instance, that Delbáeth was the father of Danu herself, and that he begot 'the three gods of Danu' on her.[72] The name seems to be a corruption of *Delbáedh* ('fire-shaped'), and if so would refer directly to the sun. As a character in the hero-lore, Delbáeth is given the alternative name Tuirill, which may be a compound of the word *tuir* ('a pillar' – see below). Such confusion has developed within the literature due to the multiple characterisation of these figures that it is difficult to discover the original ideas. It is notable, though, that the name Eochu is used in the story. This was a variant of the name Eochaidh[73] for the Daghdha, and was closely associated with the solar imagery of that father-god. Although in this text the name is given to a child rather than to a father-figure, this can be considered a dislocation within the tradition. Perhaps most significantly of all, the woman who is fertilised in the story by a male sun-like figure is called Ériu (literally 'Ireland') and thus provides a clear example of the figure of the land-godess. The parental coupling of sun and soil was obviously the mythic idea from which this account grew.

Viewed from a wider perspective, the dislocation of character-names may not be so great. We have seen in Chapter 4 that the figure of the child-deity in some ways reciprocated that of the father-deity. Moreover, some characters from the Find-complex – for example Fintan and the Findbhennach – are reborn with different shapes and personalities,[74] and it is therefore likely that the story of the birth of Bres is a late development based on the wisdom-lore of Find. We can even date that development, for an account of the birth of another character derived from Find, Mongán, also has the mother impregnated by a deity who comes from the sea.[75] The source of these plots must be the pseudo-Fredegarius chronicle, from the 7th century AD, which tells of how Merovech, founder of the Frankish Merovingian dynasty, had a sea-spirit for a father.[76] This plot, however, has merely been superimposed onto earlier Irish tradition – which made use of solar symbolism, probably rationalised within the druidic teaching. As we have seen in Chapter 1, rebirth was considered basic to the nature of divinity itself, and it has been suggested that this was one of the reasons for the prominence of incest in tales of ancient Irish heroes.[77]

Incest would in itself be a symbol of continuity, a link between the generations in social life which was otherwise expressed by the druidic tradition of seeking inspiration from the dead in the tumuli. The aspects of the story which tend to conceal this can easily be distinguished as later layers of tradition. The ring by which the offspring will be identified, for instance, is a motif from a quite ancient international hero-tale.[78] The plot of this hero-tale was known in early mediaeval Ireland,[79] and versions may have been current here at an even earlier period. In the context of the story of the conception of Bres, however, it is clearly a secondary development.

The other layer of tradition which tends to conceal the basic idea of the story is more difficult to define. This is the complex of lore concerning the rival communities of Tuatha Dé Danann and Fomhoire, who are temporarily reconciled by the birth of Bres. The names of these two communities are very significant. That of the more benevolent of them, literally 'Tribes of the Goddess Danu', relates them directly to the lore of the land-goddess. We cannot say exactly how old this actual designation is, but since the literature does not expressly describe Danu as presiding over them, it would appear to reflect a very ancient tradition which had become clouded by fictional stories. The first element in the designation, tuath, is the usual word in early Irish for a sept, but there is some warranty for considering it to have also had a special mythical application.

The Tuatha Dé are referred to in a leading text as *fir Trí nDéa* ('men of the three gods' or 'men of the three goddesses'),[80] and we have alluded in Chapter 2 to the tradition of *trí dée Danann* ('three gods of Danu'). Elsewhere a triad called Mac Cuill, Mac Cécht, and Mac Gréine are described as three kings of the Tuatha Dé Danann – their names indicate that they were 'son' of hazel, ploughshare, and sun respectively – and they were grandchildren of the Daghdha. Their royal and exalted status is indicated by their marriage to ladies called Ériu, Banba, and Fódla (all names for Ireland).[81] It is clear from this that the early Irish, like other European peoples, sometimes triplicated their divinities. Interestingly, Lucan refers to a triad of deities worshipped by the Gauls and calls them by the names Teutates, Esus, and Taranis.[82] Teutates is known also from inscriptions in Gaul and in Britain. Based on the Celtic word *teutá*, the name would have meant something like 'tribal god'. From inscriptions such as 'Mars Teutates', the designation would seem more properly to have been a descriptive title rather than a name.[83] This is borne out by Irish sources, for Celtic *teutá* is the same word as Irish *tuath*, and an Irish warrior's oath was taken to 'the god to whom my tribe (*tuath*) swear'.[84] There is, in fact, a mention in mediaeval Irish literature to the three gods of Danu as *trí dée Tuath*.[85] The Tuatha Dé of Irish literature, then, may have derived from a ritual reference to the tribal gods who were presided over by the goddess of fertility Danu.

Similarly, the rival community of Fomhoire must have been mythical in origin, their name meaning 'under-spirits'[86] and referring to the less benign aspect of the divine realm. One source calls them 'the strong men of the *sídh*',[87] and their imagery may therefore have grown out of the dark and dreary world of the tumulus which – as we have seen in Chapter 4 – was viewed as being in opposition to, and yet complimentary to, the brighter otherworld. It is clear from this why the Tuatha Dé and the Fomhoire were not completely separate from each other, and why several mythical or fictional characters could be variously named as belonging to either community.[88]

At some stage, the contrast between the Tuatha Dé and the Fomhoire came to be dramatically expressed in terms of a great contest between them. It has been suggested that this was the invention of mediaeval writers,[89] but the origin is far more likely to be of ancient vintage – paralleling primordial contests between sets of deities in other cultures.[90] The early setting for this Irish contest would appear to have been at sea, and concerning a maritime *tuir* ('pillar'). Garbled versions of such a narrative are found in the mediaeval literature, which has such a pillar in the possession of the Fomhoire and being attacked by the followers of a character called Neimheadh (literally 'sacred person') or by the Tuatha Dé themselves.[91] The pillar may be described as a great golden, silver, or crystal tower, which was typical Irish symbolism for the sun.[92]

This calls to mind the many 'Jupiter'-columns erected by the Gauls, which are topped by a horseman overcoming a humanoid monster.[93] In this Gaulish iconography, the column may represent a cosmic pillar which at once divides and unites sky and earth, whereas the horseman parallels the Irish name Eochaidh for the Daghdha, and the defeated monster is a tolerable equivalent of the Fomhoire. We have suggested in Chapter 4 that a basic teaching of the druids dealt with the contrast, yet complement, of darkness and light, of earth and sky, and that this reflected in a mystical way the basic dualism between the dead and the living. The cosmic pillar would therefore represent the joining together of the high sky and the underground depths. Due to the idea that the sun sinks down into a mystical western island of the living dead, the pillar would be situated in the sea.[94]

The story of the great primordial contest, as we know it from the mediaeval writers, however, is much coloured by literary speculation. Among the changes, the setting has been brought to land and, probably from a confusion due to the word *tuir*, the action is situated at Magh Tuireadh (Moytirra in Co. Sligo). The following is a synopsis:

The Tuatha Dé brought with them to Ireland four wonderful things – the stone of Fál, the spear of Lugh, the sword of Nuadhu, and the cauldron of the Daghdha. They made an alliance with the Fomhoire, and to seal it Cian of the Tuatha Dé married Eithne, daughter of Balar of the Fomhoire. From this union was born Lugh, 'the wonder child'. They fought the incumbent race of Fir Bolg, conquered them and gained possession of the country. The hand of king Nuadhu was cut off in that battle and since the loss of it rendered him ineligible for the kingship, the Tuatha Dé appointed Bres to rule over them in his stead. Bres was the son of a Tuatha Dé mother and a Fomhoire father. When he had assumed the kingship he was oppressive towards the Tuatha Dé, and even imposed heavy servitude on the Daghdha and on Oghma.

Moreover, the new king was extremely niggardly, never providing feasts or entertainment. When the poet Cairbre mac Étaíne was given a miserable reception by Bres, he satirised the king, and as a result the land was blighted. The Tuatha Dé, growing increasingly uneasy, began to pressurise Bres to resign, but he prevailed on them to allow him to continue in office for seven more years. He used this respite to go to the northern areas of the world and to seek help from his Fomhoire relatives to secure the kingship of Ireland for him. He got particular support from Balar, who had a fiery eye which destroyed all on which it looked, and under Balar's leadership a mighty force of the Fomhoire landed in Ireland.

Meanwhile, the physician Dian Cécht had fashioned a hand of silver for Nuadhu, which was as mobile as a natural hand, and in this way Nuadhu was restored to the kingship by the Tuatha Dé. He held a great feast at Tara, and during the feast a stranger arrived who was master of all skills and arts. The stranger was Lugh, grandson of Balar. Nuadhu held a council, at which it was decided to refuse to pay tribute to the Fomhoire and to give the leadership to Lugh in the impending crisis. Lugh was therefore allowed to preside in the king's chair for thirteen days, and he immediately set about preparations for battle with the huge Fomhoire army.

The Daghdha and Oghma played a leading role in these preparations. Goibhniu, the great smith, fashioned weapons for the Tuatha Dé; while Dian Cécht, the great physician, prepared a magical well which could heal all wounds. When the preparations had been made, the Daghdha went to a tryst with the Mór-Ríoghain, and she promised to use destructive magic against the Fomhoire. As the two armies faced each other at Magh Tuireadh, the Tuatha Dé appointed nine warriors to keep Lugh away from the fighting, for they feared that on account of his great ability he would be a prime target for the foe.

As soon as battle was joined Lugh escaped from his guard and encircled the enemy, going on one foot and with one eye closed and chanting a spell against them. The slaughter was terrible, Nuadhu being among those slain. Then Lugh came face to face with Balar. The cover was being removed from Balar's eye so that he would gaze upon the Tuatha Dé and thereby destroy them, but Lugh cast a sling-stone at him and drove the eye to the back of his head so that it was turned against the Fomhoire. Balar fell dead, and much of his army was destroyed by the baleful effect of his eye. The Tuatha Dé redoubled their efforts and the Fomhoire were completely overthrown.

Bres was seized, and in return for his life he promised that the cows of Ireland would always be in milk and that there would be a fine harvest each year. The Daghdha then recovered the whole herd of the cattle of Ireland which had been taken by the Fomhoire, and the Mór-Ríoghain announced the great victory with a rhetoric.[95]

This version is found in a text dating from the 11th century, but based on earlier materials. We know that the story of the great battle of Magh Tuireadh was already in existence by the 9th century AD,[96] and there is every reason to believe that – prior to that – its elements had been in the process of development for quite some time. The earliest stratum would appear to have involved the Daghdha as a figure bringing light into darkness and thereby resolving the conflict between sun and earth. This would have attracted the Indo-European myth of a conflict between two sets of deities, expressed in Ireland in terms of the Tuatha Dé and the Fomhoire. The plot concerning how Lugh overcame Balar would easily become domiciled within such a setting. These basic elements were probably all in the story before the spread of Christianity throughout Ireland in the 5th and 6th centuries, but miscellaneous incidents concerning other deities and personages may have been added by the writers after that.[97]

Other figures with divine attributes
From the association of his cult with so many sites, and from the

frequency of his name in the mythological literature, it is clear that Lugh was a favourite deity among the late pagan Irish. This is further underlined by the popularity in the same period of names, such as Lughaidh, which were derivatives of his. There are, however, other figures who loom large in the accounts given by mediaeval writers of the mythical and semi-mythical past, and whom we must regard as deities or quasi-deities of Celtic Ireland. Those with names easily identifiable with Celtic deities abroad have already been discussed, but there are also some with what appear to be distinctly Irish names. The names of these may well be developments on Irish soil, but their general attributes were paralleled abroad. Though their names are all Gaelic they, like the Irish versions of the more widespread Celtic deities, probably also had elements in their make-up which survived from cultures of pre-Celtic Ireland.

The divine leech Dian Cécht fulfilled a function which was, of course, indigenous to any human society. His name seems to have meant 'he who swiftly travels',[98] and he is described in one text as 'going roads of great healing'.[99] This could have referred equally to the speed with which he could be invoked and to how quickly his cure worked on the patient. Dian Cécht was referred to as a 'god of power' and a 'god of health',[100] and this function is strongly indicated by one early reference to a salve given by him and which heals various ailments.[101] Like most divine figures, however, he is generally portrayed in the literature as a celebrated character of ancient history. Thus we find him referred to as 'the healing sage of Ireland'[102] and the following words are put into his mouth before the battle of Magh Tuireadh: 'Any man who is wounded will be fully healed by me, unless his head be cut off, or the membrane of his brain or his spinal cord be severed.'[103]

The exalted status of Dian Cécht is underlined by the attribution to him in early law tracts of wise judgements which lay down precedents on a variety of issues.[104] That he belonged to the leading rank of the Tuatha Dé is confirmed by the account of the Magh Tuireadh battle, for in that text Nuadhu is described as holding a conference which lasted for a whole year. Present at that conference were the Daghdha and Oghma, and Nuadhu saw to it that 'his two kinsmen Goibhniu and Dian Cécht' were also summoned.[105] This Goibhniu has already been referred to in Chapter 4 as presiding over an imagined feast of the gods. Like Dian Cécht, he is appealed to for protection in an early Irish charm, viz. 'very sharp is Goibhniu's science, let Goibhniu's goad go out before Goibhniu's goad!'[106] and both his name and his cult must be very old.[107]

His name is a simple derivative of *gabha* ('smith') and his profession of smithcraft has often been invested with special supernatural importance in early cultures. It is not surprising, therefore, to find him listed among the leading artisans of the Tuatha Dé, for whom he fashions their wondrous spears. His manufacturing skill was so marvellous that he could boast as follows: 'No spearpoint which my hand forges will make a missing cast, no skin which it pierces will taste life after that.'[108] So strong was this ancient cult of Goibhniu, indeed, that various echoes of him have survived in Irish folklore to the present time. Most dramatic of these is the Gobán Saor, a peripatetic figure who is described as the greatest craftsman who ever lived and to whom many adventures are attributed.[109]

The figure of Flidais in the mediaeval literature has also been alluded to in Chapter 4. Her special connection with milk shows that she was an emanation from the mother-goddess, but her herding of the deer suggests that she represented the wilder aspect of that divinity. In this, she belongs to a very ancient tradition – that of deities presiding over wild animals – which long predates the Celtic culture in Europe.[110] It is very likely that beliefs of this sort existed also in pre-Celtic Ireland, and ideas concerning a patroness of animals both wild and tame may well have been subsumed into the goddess cult at an early date.[111]

Traces may also be distinguished in the lore concerning the Cailleach Bhéarra ('hag of Beare'), who is described in the early literature as having the personal name Boí (a derivative of *bó*, 'a cow'). We read that she lived on the island off the Beare peninsula, in the southwest of Ireland. Her great age was proverbial, and perhaps indicative of the archaism of her cult.[112] Stories of her survive in folklore throughout the Gaelic world, and in these she is often described as possessing very keen eyesight by which she can distinguish her cattle at a great distance. She has taken over other roles in some areas, such as that of harvest-spirit in Connacht and the north midlands, where she is described as reaping the corn at a phenomenal speed. Perhaps of greatest interest is the general portrayal of her in Gaelic Scotland as a fearsome protectress of wild animals. This seems to be a late development in the context of her specific name, but in itself is no doubt a continuation of such beliefs from earlier epochs.[113]

That early Irish hunting lore had a strong supernatural content is suggested by a story which is told in an 8th-century text concerning the sage and hero Fionn mac Cumhaill. According to this, Fionn had a servant called Dearg Corra, who had the habit of leaping to and fro over the hearth as food was being cooked. After a woman had made false allegations against this Dearg Corra, he was banished by Fionn. He went to live in the forest, and he was wont to go about there 'on shanks of deer, if that is true, he was so light'. Then one day, while in the forest: 'Fionn saw a man on the top of a tree with a blackbird on his right shoulder, and a bright bronze vessel in his left hand, with water in it, in which was a leaping trout; and a stag was at the foot of the tree.' This stranger was sharing nuts with the blackbird, sharing apples with the stag, and sharing the water from the bronze vessel with the trout. He could not be recognised, because he was surrounded by a cloak of concealment (*féth fiadha*). Fionn, however, put his thumb of wisdom into his mouth, and then sang an incantation. 'It is Dearg Corra, son of Daighre's descendant,' he said, 'who is in the tree!'[114]

The supernatural attributes of Dearg Corra in that account can hardly be explained except as survivals of a cult of some divinity. The name Dearg, meaning 'red' was – as we have seen in Chapter 2 – a usual one for a god in early Ireland. Furthermore, the name given to the character's ancestor, Daighre, meant a flame,[115] and his leaping over the hearth is symbolic of the flames which cook the food. Since he thus symbolises the provision of sustenance, his reign among the wild animals makes sense to the hunter, for he protects the quarry so as to ensure a sufficient amount. Furthermore, he is concealed from ordinary eyes, and the vision of him is vouchsafed only to a seer like Fionn who has the power of magical incantation. It may even be that Dearg Corra represents the Irish version of the horned animal-god of the Continental Celts called Cernunnos.[116] At any rate, this story again demonstrates the belief that natural and supernatural agents inhabit the environment side by side with each other and that these two worlds can interface at points of social importance.

The reason why Fionn himself was not included in the pantheon of the Tuatha Dé is of interest. As we have seen in Chapter 4, his cult was used by the Leinstermen in their efforts to regain the Boyne valley in the 5th to 6th centuries AD, and this caused him to be regarded very much as an historical figure. In Chapter 7, we will discuss a further incentive for such historicisation, in that his status as a seer was used by Christian missionaries to have him foretell the coming of the new faith. Another celebrity, well-known to Irish tradition but also not included in that company – at least not until the later mediaeval literature – was Manannán.

In this case the reason was that the personage had a particular connection with the sea rather than with tumuli in the landscape. Manannán was, in fact, given the patronymic *mac Lir* (meaning 'son of the sea'). His name appears in Welsh in the form Manawydan,[117] which is based on the toponymic Manaw, the Welsh term for the Isle of Man. The origin of this toponymic is not entirely clear, but Pliny calls the Isle of Man 'Monapia',[118] and this suggests a population name. Such a name, 'Manapii' or the like, was the same as that of the Menapii, a section of the Belgae people in northern Gaul.[119] Many of the Belgae had been crossing from the Continent into southern Britain, probably from as early as the 2nd century BC,[120] and it has been suggested that groups of them may have pushed further and established colonies in the west.[121] It is more likely, however, that the designation Menapii or Manapii was applied in general by the Celts to groups who lived beside the sea, for the root of the word would appear to have meant 'water'.[122] We know from Ptolemy that some 'Manapii' were settled in the southeast of Ireland, and these came to be known in Irish as Fir Monach, just as the Belgae were known as Fir Bolg.[123]

It would appear likely that the Menapii – like other Celtic groups – took their name from a special designation which their tribe had for the ancestor-deity. This would have been *Mena-pios, with a meaning like 'the water-controller'. That the Irish had heard of such a god-name, and pronounced it as *Mon-akwos, is strongly suggested by the name Monach given to some characters in the early literature.[124] The names Manannán and Manawydan, however, differ so much from such a divine designation that their connection with it would be unrecognisable. These character-names must come from a period – probably as late as the 4th century AD – when the designation Manapii had become quite corrupted and when the tribal deity survived only as a memory of some obscure personage who inhabited the Isle of Man. Such a lingering memory could easily become fused with the well-known Celtic notion of an otherworld island off the western coast where the god of the dead dwelt (see Chapter 2), and it was from such a fusion that the Welsh imagined a sea-dwelling deity who periodically mingled in human affairs.

Manu was the Old Irish name for the Isle of Man; and it could only have developed after the term Manapii, or more specifically a variant 'Manavii', had in British Celtic become Manaw.[125] The Irish 'Mannanán' is a diminutive (affectionate in function) of a genitive form of Manu, whereas the Welsh 'Manawydan' comes from the nominative Welsh form Manaw; and accordingly these names of the personage were two separate developments from the same lore. It would appear that it was the Irish who first gave the title 'mac Lir' to him, and that this was in turn borrowed by the Welsh as 'map Llyr'. In line with this, the Irish preserved in fuller form the original lore of the personage, describing Man-annán as a wonderful mariner who rode the maned horses of the waves, and to whom the sea – 'the plain of Mon' – was full of flowers. He was believed to control the weather, and stories told of how he came periodically to intervene in the affairs of the men and women of this world.[126]

His residence being in Manu, Irish storytellers made much of the ancient lore concerning the otherworldly nature of that place, and from this came a new legendary name for the Isle of Man. The designation of the mound venerated by the prehistoric

Ulstermen, which had a special otherworld significance, was
Eumania (see Chapter 6). Probably from a play on the name of
that mound – which could easily be confused with the different
word *emuin* ('twin')[127] – otherworld islands came to be regarded
as doubles of that mound,[128] and so in Irish stories the Isle of
Man became known as Eumania (later Eamhain). This legendary
name seems to have been attached to Manu some time before the
Christianisation of Ireland, for in a 7th-century biography of St
Patrick that island is referred to as 'Eumonia' as if that were its
ordinary name.[129]

Perhaps some indication of the origin of the placename in that
of the ritual mound of the Ulstermen survived, however, in the
earliest of our texts dealing with Manannán. This text, *Immram
Brain*, was written in the 7th or 8th century in east Ulster[130] and,
curiously, it claims that there was a unique tree on the island of
Eamhain, and that 'four legs of white silver' were under the
island, holding it up.[131] This may be a confused echo of the great
tree-trunk and the timber stakes in the structure of the Eamhain
of the Ulstermen (see Chapter 6). With regard to the great tree
on the otherworld island, it was imagined that wonderful apples
grew on it. This must have been in origin a separate tradition[132]
– similar to that of the Hesperides in Greek lore – and it may
have been part of the original ancestor-cult of the Manapii or
Manavii on the Isle of Man. So Manannán was said to reside in
Eamhain *Abhlach* ('of the Apples') where all of life came to its
full fruition,[133] and we can see how he himself developed –
charmingly if somewhat fortuitously – from lore of an ancient
Celtic population-group.

− 6 −

The Rites of Sovereignty

T HE IRISH WORD for a king is *rí* (earlier *rígh*), which is cognate
with the Gaulish *ríx*, the Latin *rex*, and the Indic *raj*; and this, as
one might expect, was regarded as an especially sacred office.[1]
For instance, the idea of nature being in equilibrium with the
beneficent rule of a proper king was a very archaic aspect of culture which the Celts held in common with many other peoples.[2]
There are several allusions to this belief in mediaeval Irish literature, and we can take these to be surviving echoes from
rhetorics which accompanied the actual inaugurations of kings.
Details given in some texts are quite mystical and impressive, as
one would expect in such rhetorics. One poem, for instance, says
that 'truth in a ruler is as bright as the foam cast up by a mighty
wave of the sea, as the sheen of a swan's covering in the sun, as
the colour of snow on a mountain . . . A ruler's truth is an effort
which overpowers armies, it brings milk into the world, it brings
corn and mast.'[3]

In illustrating the benign and dignified bearing desirable in a
king, the same text states that the three best things for him are
'truth, mercy, and silence'.[4] It was appropriate for a king to be
sparing in his speech, for the office of kingship was a sacred one,
and the words uttered by him were not only formal but also had
effect on the environment. The good fortune connected to a reign

was conceptualised as *firinne flatha* ('truth of a sovereign'), and the opposite of this – illustrated by accounts of natural and social disasters – was *gó flatha* ('falsehood of a sovereign'). We read that 'by a ruler's truth fair weather comes in each fitting season, winter fine and frosty, spring dry and windy, summer warm with showers of rain, autumn with heavy dews and fruitful. And it is the ruler's falsehood that brings perverse weather upon wicked peoples and dries up the fruit of the earth.'[5]

There is evidence that the Celts of Gaul had by the late centuries BC evolved a form of government in which the power of kings had been greatly curtailed by the nobles, and that the central role of sacred kings in Ireland was a survival of an older Celtic system.[6] The only apparent derogation from the power of kings in Ireland was due to the influence of the druids, who tended to take the right of making pronouncements and passing judgement to themselves.[7] Whereas the king was the intermediary between the society and destiny, the druids claimed to be the only true interpreters of this situation. Their claim – as we have seen in Chapter 4 – was that their understanding of mysterious things made their words as necessary to the people as physical food, and this claim was institutionalised in the process of kingmaking. There are many indications, for instance, that at the inauguration of a king the druids recited rhetorics with allusions to mythical, genealogical and other lore which qualified the new man for his office and promoted the welfare of his people.[8]

The ideal king

Iron Age Ireland was divided geographically into five general regions. From these come the surviving names of the four provinces – Ulaidh, Laighin, Mumhain, and Connachta (earlier Ol nÉcmacht). The fifth province was Midhe (meaning 'middle'), the region which included the rich and prestigious Boyne valley, with its ancient cemeteries and the ritual centre of Tara. There were many local kings, each ruling a *tuath* (population-group) of a few thousand people. Collections of local kings owed fealty to superior kings, each of whom was known as a *rí ruirech*.[9] The usual method of choosing a king was in the hands of the male members of the *derbfine*, a group comprising four generations of relatives.[10] We may presume that the greater the power of a king, the more sacred his office, but rituals and beliefs of some kind must have attached to them all.

A text which may be as early as the 7th century AD has the mythical jurist Morfhind – one of the wise *Find*-figures of Irish tradition discussed in Chapter 4 – giving instructions to a prince on how to govern. He states that truth in a ruler keeps plagues and misfortunes away from the people, maintains peace, and causes an abundance of fruit, milk, corn, fish, and children.[11] One recension of that text places the king and his proper quality at the very centre of the social universe: 'So long as he preserves truth, good will not be lacking to him, and his reign will not fail, for it is by the truth of a sovereign that great kingdoms are ruled.'[12] By 'truth' was meant conformation to the mythically ordained role of a king – the upholding of social structures and rituals, the making of wise decisions and the avoidance of any act which was thought to tempt fate.

On the issue of fate, this was rationalised in the literature in a rather esoteric manner by the concept of *geis* (plural *gessa*, later *geasa*), which can best be described as 'prohibition by destiny'. We read of several kings being surrounded by such prohibitions, but the basis and purpose of many of them is unexplained. By mediaeval times, of course, the writers had become quite speculative in their accounts of such things.[13] For example, a long poem from the 11th century describes seven purported *geasa* on the king of Tara, and five each on the provincial kings.[14] After allowing for imaginative additions and for over-neat enumeration, the actual things mentioned can be reduced to two types – which we may term 'mythical' and 'historical'.

To the 'mythical' type belong such things as where a king should be at sunrise or sunset, or the way in which he should position himself at certain places – these could well be residue of sun-myths and of sacred rituals, which lingered on as superstitions for a long time. They were probably always viewed selectively, only being referred to in order to bolster political or personal preferences. To the 'historical' type of *geasa*, on the other hand, belong prohibitions of a very specific and unique type. These may reflect some disaster which happened to either king or people on an earlier occasion, and there would naturally be a superstitious dread of a similar event happening again. Or they may reflect prophecies which had been made for some king or other. Examples of such 'historical' *geasa* are many and varied – for instance, that on the Leinster king to 'ride on a dirty black-heeled horse across the plain of Maistiu', that on the Munster king 'to hold a border-meeting at Gabhrán', that on the Connacht king 'to go to an assembly of women at Seaghais', and that on the Ulster king 'to attend the horse-fair of Ráth Line in the company of the youths of Dál nAraidhe'.

It should be remarked that this belief was not confined to the affairs of kings. Warriors also had their *geasa*, if the literature is to be credited, and it appears that what was basically intended was that a special destiny was allotted to each individual person in life.[15] The ending of an individual's life, being ultimately unavoidable, could be rationalised in this way, and it is noticeable that the occurrence of *geasa* in Irish literature is perennially linked to the breaking of them and therefore to death. A similar rationale was behind another strong belief in early Ireland – that a person might have a *fód bháis* ('sod of death') allotted to him by destiny, although unknown to himself, and that the person would inevitably die at that spot.[16] The importance of what was destined for a ruler, of course, would be greatly magnified to include not only his personal fate but also the fate of his followers. The *geasa* of a king would therefore involve social as well as personal issues, and would have been dramatised through imagery related to these issues.

The kingship of Tara

Tara was a sacred centre from time immemorial, and it was situated in the richest part of Ireland. Accordingly, great prestige attached to the gaining of the kingship there. In reality, the ancient kings would have come to power through a combination of factors – such as wealth, diplomacy, and fighting – but no doubt they felt the necessity to legitimise their position. In this way, a compromise had to be reached between personal ambition and social convention. On the conventional side of the equation, the rituals of installation were of great importance, enacting as they did the right of the king to his throne and the right of his people to benefit from him. To guarantee all of this, the involvement of otherworld forces – even if contrived – was necessary, and what the mediaeval literature tells of ritual echoes this. For example:

> This is how they did the bull-feast (*tarbhfheis*) – a white bull was killed and one man consumed his fill of its meat and of its soup, and he slept after that meal, and a charm of truth was sung by four druids over him, and it would be revealed to him then in a vision the identity of the man to be made king, as to his form and his appearance and the nature of the actions he would do.[17]

We note here the parallel between the white bull and the bulls of the same colour sacrificed by the ancient Gaulish druids and the early lore of white cattle in Ireland. We have seen in Chapters 3 and 4 that such animals and their colour reflected both prosperity and benign otherworld forces. The king, having been selected at the direction of spiritual forces, was no longer an ordinary man and must exercise the wisdom and caution appropriate to his office. His reign itself was something of a ritual, and his behaviour and actions were invested with supernatural import. One text describes sacred prohibitions which were on the king of Tara:

> The sun must not rise upon him in his bed in the plain of Tara. He must not traverse the plain of Cuilleann after sunset. He must not launch his ship on the next Monday after Bealtaine (May-feast). He must not leave the track of his army on the plain of Maighean on the Tuesday after Samhain (November-feast).[18]

Some of the details here may be mediaeval fancy, but it is significant that emphasis is on the sun and also on the ancient two-part division of the year. The strong suggestion is that the reign of a king was brought into a causal relationship with the sun and the year-cycle, thus reflecting a religious myth which concerned agricultural welfare. Another text stresses that rituals of kingship symbolised natural productivity. This is a literal translation:

> There was a king's chariot at Tara. Two steeds of one colour, who were never before harnessed, were yoked to the chariot. He to whom the sovereignty of Tara was not due, the chariot would tilt up before him so that he could not control it and the steeds would rear up at him. And there was a king's mantle in the chariot – he to whom the sovereignty was not due, the mantle was too big for him. And there were two flag-stones in Tara – *Blocc* and *Bluigne*. He whom they accepted, they would open before him so that the chariot would go between them. And *Fál* was there, the stone penis, at the head of the course – he to whom the sovereignty of Tara was due, the *Fál* used to call against the axle of the chariot so that all heard it.[19]

The imagery here is very much based on sexual intercourse, and it may be viewed as a reflection of the primordial mating of sun and soil. This would mean that the kingship was synony-mous with the life-giving forces, and the importance attributed to the *Lia Fáil* as a wondrous gift of the Tuatha Dé (Chapter 5) can therefore be explained as a rationalisation of ancient ritual.[20] This explanation dovetails with the general tendency by which early ritual practices of ancient times are reflected as epical motifs in the literary period. The patronising role of the sun itself appears in a very distinctive way in mediaeval epic, its imagery being connected with the obscure but magnificent figure of Cú Roí. This personage, partly shapeshifter and partly warrior, is described as son of Dáire, which seems to have been an alterna-tive designation for the Daghdha. All three of these characters share some characteristics, including the possession by each of a mighty cauldron, and so – in function at least – they can be regarded as identical.[21] One text claims that thirty oxen would fit in the cauldron of Cú Roí, and he is also said to have had a huge vat and a dish wrought from silver and gold.[22] The solar imagery of this epical Cú Roí is striking, He is described as being a great traveller over sea and land, and 'he chanted over his fortress every night, so that it revolved as quickly as a millstone, and the entrance was never to be found after sunset'.[23]

In the mediaeval literature Cú Roí was associated with the area of Co. Kerry, where his name was given to a very conspicuous and near inaccessible hill-fort of the late Bronze Age viz. *Cathair Chon Roí*.[24] This south-western location may in itself have been an affirmation of his solar connections, but it is also due to the predominance in that part of the country of the Érainn septs,[25] with whom both he and Dáire were closely associated. Originally – according to both mediaeval and modern scholars – the Érainn had been at Tara,[26] and it is therefore likely that the figure of Cú Roí preserves vestiges of lore from that most prestigious cultic centre. The early literature repeatedly claims that a celebrated leader of the Érainn, Lughaidh mac Con, had once ruled at Tara.[27] He is variously referred to as a son of Cú Roí and a son of Dáire, and this underlines again the identity of these two mythical personages. It is thought that the name Lughaidh was a later addition to his designation, and that originally he was known simply as *mac Con* ('son of hound', with the figurative meaning 'son of a warrior').[28] This would be an apt ritual title for a great leader, and it may reflect an idea that the Érainn kings were in relation to the solar deity as a son was to his father.

The Érainn at Tara

The story in which the sacred rituals of Tara are described was committed to writing in the 8th century AD, and is principally concerned with the accession to that kingship of a hero called Conaire. His name probably signified 'warrior-lord', and thus it seems to be an echo of the same ancient title as found in *mac Con*. As in the case of the bearer of the latter name, Conaire is connected to ancestral beings with shapeshifting and solar traits.

The literature deliberately grafts him on to the tradition of Eochaidh and Étaín (for which see Chapter 5). He is claimed to have been a direct descendant of that union,[29] and this could well be an echo of how the Érainn combined the god-goddess myth with the antiquarian prestige of Tara so as to forge a ritual of kingship there. There is also a strong social dimension to the legend of

Conaire – we read of how he gained the throne through the aid of
druids and satirists and hornblowers, and an army which came
from a tumulus.[30] Thus the role of priestly caste and of ceremony,
as well as of the otherworld community, is expressed as crucial to
the kingship. The ritual practices associated with the reign of a
king are clarified by a version of the story which uses the whole
life-span of Conaire to symbolise his sacred office.

According to this, the princess Mes Buachalla was abandoned
as a child and was raised by a herdsman. When she grew up, she
was betrothed to the Tara king Eterscéle. On the night before her
wedding, a stranger came to her in the form of a bird and, lay-
ing aside his feathers, made love to her. He told her that she
would have a son and that this son should not kill birds. After
she was married to the king, she gave birth to the child Conaire,
and he was taken to be the son of Eterscéle. He was put into fos-
terage away from home, along with three sons of a champion
called Donn Désa. The boy Conaire possessed three great skills
– he had great hearing, seeing, and wisdom in giving judgements.
In time, king Eterscéle died and his followers assembled for the
'bull-feast' to select a new king. The man performing the ritual
saw in a vision 'a stark-naked man, as night ended, on the road
to Tara with his stone in his sling'.

Meanwhile, Conaire had been travelling towards Áth Cliath
(Dublin) in his chariot, when he saw huge white-speckled birds.
He followed them as far as the sea, with the intention of shoot-
ing at them from his sling, and they suddenly turned and faced
him with spears and swords. One of them protected him, telling
him that it was his father, and reminding him that he was for-
bidden to cast at birds. The bird further instructed him to go to
Tara. He did so, naked and at daybreak, and was met by men
who put a garment on him and brought him to the citadel to be
installed as king. Then Conaire revealed the prohibitions which
the bird-man had put on him, as follows:

> You must not go right-handwise around Tara or left-
> handwise around Breagha; you must not hunt the wild
> animals of Cernae; you must not venture each ninth night
> out of Tara; and you must not stay in a house from which

firelight can be seen to emerge after sunset or can be seen
from outside; and three reds must not precede you to the
house of Dearg; and no plunder must be taken in your
reign; and a company of one woman or one man must
not come to you in your house after sunset; and you must
not intervene in a quarrel between two of your servants.

During the reign of Conaire there was an abundance of wealth
and peace, and the weather was wonderfully calm. His three
foster-brothers, however, took to plunder and murder, and he
had no choice but to banish them from the country. They made
an alliance with a British king called Ingcel the One-Eyed and
prepared to invade Ireland. Meanwhile, when trouble broke out
between two local rulers in Munster, Conaire intervened to make
peace between them, thereby breaking one of his prohibitions.
Returning home, he found the countryside devastated, and in his
desperation he forgot the other prohibitions also. He passed with
Tara to his left and Breagha to his right, and then hunted in Cer-
nae. When he wondered where to spend the night, his leading
warrior Mac Cécht advised him to go to the hostel of Da Dearga.
On his way there he noticed three red horsemen riding ahead of
him, and at the hostel he found himself besieged by the invading
army. The hostel was set on fire, and druids who were with the
foe caused a great thirst to come on Conaire. He was thus weakened, and was slain in the fighting. Mac Cécht gave a drink of
water to the decapitated head of Conaire, and it spoke a quat-
rain in thanks.[31]

This text preserves several elements of pre-Christian belief in
Ireland, though these elements are couched in narrative form.
The role of the birds in the story might be interpreted as a survival of some form of totemism, but there may have been a more
basic belief that birds in certain contexts carried messages from
the heavens to the earth. The author of this text seems to have
regarded them as the form which the otherworld beings take in
their relationship with Conaire. It is they who impose the prohibitions on him which limit his activities as king. Significantly, the
text states, after he had broken some of the prohibitions, that 'he
was on this account the king whom the spectres banished'.[32] The

word used for spectres here, *siabrai*, is used in another text on his accession, viz. 'that was the Conaire then whom spectres brought to the kingship'.[33] The parallelism between the two phrases is striking, and expresses the notion that just as a king was appointed by the spiritual powers he was also deposed by them. It is noticeable also that the birds make the announcement of his future power to Conaire when he is on the plain of Dublin, and that his destruction takes place in the same region (the hostel in question was near Bohernabreena in the Dublin mountains).

The coming of Conaire to Tara is told as the adventure of an ancient hero, but the story-line is based on rituals concerning the installation of a king. It is likely that the basic idea was that the sun – symbolised as the bird-father – appointed the king to rule as its ritual son. Accordingly, the prohibitions, which are placed on Conaire and which he dramatically breaks, are echoes of ideas centring on the sacred rules which kept the community in equilibrium with the natural and cosmic realms. The fire within the king's household would therefore be a symbol of the king's own reign, and it should not be seen to contend with the heat of the sun just as the reigning king should accept the ultimate mastery of the heavenly body. Finally, the hostel in which he meets his death belongs to Da Dearga, which name can be translated as 'the Red God' – this, as we saw in Chapter 2 – was a designation of the sun as god of the underworld. The 'son' of the sun was destined to be favoured only for a while.

The story of Conaire, as we have it, cannot be dated much earlier than the 8th century text – that much is clear from the supposition that the king of Tara was the overlord of Munster and perhaps also from the name Ingcel ('Angle'?) for a British king. The actual writer of this text seems not to have understood very clearly that the old narrative was derived from a mythic rationale of kingship, and so he presented the story as the epical life and death of a famous king of yore. The idea that the sun appoints a king to his office must, however, be of far greater antiquity than any pseudo-historical account, and we have argued that this was a basic element in the ancient Érainn concept of kingship. Other, and only slightly less antique elements, can also be distinguished. For instance, the hostel of death is clearly a variant of the house of Donn, but the name Donn Désa occurs also in early Leinster genealogies, and so it would seem that the story encompasses a Leinster development of ancient death-lore. From this, it has been deduced that in the prehistoric background was a memory of how the Leinstermen first took Tara from the Érainn.[34]

The Leinstermen at Tara

All indications are that the Laighin ('Leinstermen') had possession of Tara some centuries before the Christian period. Their legends told of the mythical king Labhraidh,[35] whose name literally meant 'he speaks' and may reflect the duty of a sacred king to make solemn pronouncements.[36] He is often referred to as Labhraidh *Loingseach* ('the mariner'), and is also given sobriquets like *Lonn* ('fierce') and *Lorc* ('savage'). The actual establishment of their kingship, which by implication in the Conaire story is connected with the taking of Tara, seems to have been a matter of great ritual importance to the Leinstermen. As we have seen, Conaire was slain in a hostel by besiegers who had Leinster associations.

Another regnal story, which survives in a verse fragment from the 6th century AD, tells of a parallel victory gained by the Leinstermen in a siege. The location of this action is at Dind Ríg (the moat of Burgage, south of Leighlinbridge in Co. Carlow) and the Leinster leader was Labhraidh himself. The early fragment can be translated thus: 'Red is Dind Ríg, a kindled fire the hill-face, thirty chieftains have died sorrowfully. He crushed them, laid them low, fierce Labhraidh the boar-warrior, the champion of Ireland, grandson of Loeghaire Lorc. A bull-calf was Lughaidh, fierce and grasping was Sétne, famous was Cobhthach Coel, a wise leader was Muireadhach Mál. He trod down the weapons, the father of Ollamh's father; the dumb one killed the sons of glorious Aughaine.'[37]

The later literature amplifies the description. We read that Loeghaire Lorc was king of Tara, but that he was assassinated by his jealous brother Cobhthach Coel. The latter also poisoned Loeghaire's son Ailill, and then usurped the kingship. Ailill had a young son who never spoke and was therefore known as Moen ('the dumb'). While playing hurling one day he was struck on the shin and cried out in pain. The other players remarked in astonishment that 'the dumb speaks' (*labhraidh Moen*), and this as a result became the name of the youth. Later, Cobhthach asked his poets who was the most generous man in Ireland, expecting that they would give the honour to him, but they replied 'Labhraidh Moen'. Overcome with jealousy, the usurper then banished Labhraidh from the country. The young man was very successful abroad, however, and brought an army back to Ireland with him and laid siege to Cobhthach at the strong fortress of Dind Ríg. The fortress was set on fire, and all within perished. Thus was the kingship gained by Labhraidh.[38]

Some elements of this story may be of antique vintage. The contrast between dumbness and speaking – as we have suggested – may be a remnant of royal ceremonial, whereas scholars have speculated that the fierceness of Labhraidh and his coming from abroad might reflect the original seizure of territory by the Leinstermen.[39] The burning of the fortress is a notable detail, and is developed by the literature into a claim that Labhraidh first took it by storm, and then invited Cobhthach to a feast there. A great banqueting-hall was constructed for this feast, all of iron, and it took a year to complete. None of the builders spoke a word of their work, and we read that from this a proverb grew up to the effect that 'every Leinsterman has his own secret'. When all was ready, Cobhthach arrived with his retinue. It was, of course, a trap, and when the visitors were within, Labhraidh had the door fastened and the building set on fire by blowing bellows which had been secretly installed in the structure.

This burning is likely to be an echo from some ritual. In the mediaeval literature, the mythical warrior Fionn mac Cumhaill saves Tara from the fire-breathing spirit Aillén.[40] Fionn was very much a product of Leinster tradition, and his alter-ego Find File was represented as an ancient Leinster king.[41] It would be logical to consider brightness and wisdom – as indicated by the name Find[42] – to be traits proper to a king, and the Leinstermen may therefore have dramatised the gaining and loss of kingship by a fire ritual. Fire, like Labhraidh, was both startling and fierce. Apart from this portrayal of a basic or original king-type, the

Leinstermen laid particular stress on another king of theirs, called Cathaoir Mór, whose reign the historians put down variously to the 2nd, 3rd, and 4th centuries AD.[43] The name Cathaoir Mór meant 'great battle-lord' and may in fact have been a title borne by Leinster kings at Tara for, as we have seen, the sovereignty there was a matter of acute contention.

The Connachta kingship

Around the year 400 AD, the whole plain of Meath was taken from the Leinstermen by an ascendant sept called Connachta. In taking possession of Tara, these new rulers also took over the cult of the place. Their great king in the early 5th century was Niall Naoi-Ghiallach ('Niall of the Nine Hostages'), whose epithet referred to the sureties taken by him from other groups for his overlordship.[44]

Niall is described as the son of Eochu Muighmheadhon (the soubriquet here meaning 'lord of slaves') and a captive girl from Britain called Caireann. This may reflect historical fact. We read that Caireann was resented by Eochu's legal wife, who gave her servile tasks to perform, and that Niall was therefore born in the open air. Birds attacked the baby, but the poet Torna took up the child, named it 'Niall' and prophesied its future greatness. Niall was reared by the poet, and when he was of age Torna brought him to Tara. A druid-smith was appointed to compare Niall with Eochu's four legal sons, and he did this by setting fire to a forge where the young men were working. Each of them saved an implement from the fire, but the anvil was saved by Niall who thereby showed his superiority. Then follows a most striking vignette of the goddess of sovereignty. The five young men went hunting, and in the wilderness one of them went to fetch water. Coming to a well, he found an extremely ugly hag there guarding it. She asked him for a kiss, but he refused. His three brothers similarly refused, and as a result they got no water. Finally, Niall came to the well:

> 'Water to me, woman!' said Niall. 'I will give it,' she said, 'and give me a kiss!' 'I will lie with you as well as giving a kiss!' He threw himself on her then and gave her a kiss.

Then, when he looked on her after that, there was not in
the world a maiden with a more pleasant deportment or
mien than her . . . 'You are multishaped, woman,' said
the youth. 'That is true,' said the woman. 'Who are you?'
said the youth. 'I am sovereignty,' she said, and spoke
thus: 'O king of Tara, I am the sovereignty; I will tell you
its great value!'

She then explained to him that 'just as you saw me loathsome,
beastly, and horrible at first and beautiful at last, so is the sovereignty, for seldom is it gained without battles and conflicts, but
at last a person finds it beautiful and comely'.[45] This account
makes use of a common folktale plot concerning a magical trans-
forming kiss,[46] but the plot is used to illustrate the dual nature
of kingship, which must have been a very old concept. We have
already discussed (in Chapter 5) the 'half-red' nature of the Tara
goddess Meadhbh, and how the very name of this goddess
(Celtic *Meduva*) refers to the ritual drink proffered to the new
king. The word used for such an inauguration was *feis* (literally
'spending of the night'),[47] with the import that the new king had
sexual intercourse with the goddess. All of the main themes of
the Tara inauguration rituals are therefore featured in this
account of Niall.[48]

The Connachta developed a variety of special myths which
dramatised the seizure by them of Tara, and in the Christian
period they began to claim the high-kingship of all Ireland. Some
of these myths had vestiges of antiquity within them. Their septal name, Connachta, for instance, meant 'the people of Conn'.
This Conn derives from Celtic *Condos*, which is attested from
Gaul as a personal name.[49] It had the meaning of 'head' in the
sense of 'wise leader', and it is easy to see how an ascendant sept
in ancient Ireland would have thought it appropriate for them.
They called their great eponymous leader *Conn Céadchathach*,
the epithet meaning 'of the hundred battles'. In describing the life
of this Conn, the literature again evidences some ancient mystical lore which was associated with kingship, and clearly shows
how the propaganda of the Connachta sought to encompass the
landmarks of the Boyne valley.

We read that a seer named Fínghein was visited on the night of Samhain (Halloween) each year by a woman called Rothni-amh from a tumulus, and how she once told him that on that night Conn would be born. The child would be a great king over Ireland. Other wonders would occur on the same night – including the bursting forth of the river Boyne, the finding of treasures in various tumuli, the discovery of the five great roads of Ireland, and the coming of thrice nine white birds who would sing on the ramparts of Tara. Significantly also, Rothniamh states that an ancient tree called Mughain would be discovered at the birth of Conn.[50]

Here the birth of a dynasty is represented as a primaeval event which determined the nature of the environment. This is, of course, dynastic propaganda, but it is also a mythic portrayal which utilises an ancient sacred rationale. We have referred in previous chapters to the persistent and recurrent theme of rebirth in the balancing of natural and social forces, and have noticed that this was particularly developed in the long and ethnically-varying tradition of power in the Boyne valley. That origin legends of cosmic character were known to the early Irish is beyond dispute. We have met with an original ordaining of cattle and food in the text concerning the primordial Battle of Magh Tuireadh (Chapter 5), and several other aspects of natural and social formation are referred to in a less direct manner in that same text.

In the Conaire story, we have noticed that the druids sacrificed a white bull as a preliminary to forecasting the new king. Given that the selection of a king had ramifications concerning the good fortune and prosperity of society, this reference must be an echo of an ancient rite. Such a rite is recorded of the Gaulish druids;[51] and the early Romans, too, sacrificed a white bull and then dismembered it and distributed the parts to the various groups which constituted their nation.[52] Similar sacrifices are attested for other ancient peoples, and it was usual for the parts of the victim to be scattered or buried at different locations.[53] This can be viewed as a repetition of the original creation of the world, a cosmogonic act which socialises the environment according to the desired cultural forms. We read in the great epic of the Ulster Cycle of how the two bulls meet when the battle is ended, and how the dark one kills the white one and scatters its remains. The different parts of the white bull's body, dropped from the other's horns at different places, give rise to a series of placenames.[54]

A further echo of the same notion may be found in folk versions of the youth of the hero Fionn. As he races away from his pursuers, with his nurse on his shoulders, she is torn asunder by the projecting branches of trees. Several toponymics, we are told, arise from the parts of her body thus dropped.[55] A 9th-century glossarian states that Fionn's nurse was called Búanand, which he then explains as *búan-Anand* ('good Anu') a compound of the name of 'the mother of the gods'.[56] Anu was an alternative for Danu, and we have seen in Chapter 2 that the land was metaphorised as her body. A better interpretation of Búanand would be 'she who is constant',[57] but this merely underlines the reason for the glossarian's statement. This, therefore, is a complex of imagery which brings together a dismemberment and the origin of culture. It may be that the detritus of both strands – the cosmogonic sacrifice and the land-goddess – had come together in early Irish metaphor, but it might also be that both strands were linked from the beginning in ritual. If so, the white bull may have originally symbolised the sun-deity, who along with his earth-wife gave of his body in order to vitalise the world.

Of equal interest is the use made in the birth-story of Conn of the cult of great individual trees. The famous yew-tree of Mughain was near Ballaghmoon in Co. Kildare, while others of equal celebrity were the yew of Ros at Old Leighlin in Co. Carlow, and two great ashes in Co. Westmeath called the Craebh Dháithí (at Farbill) and the Craebh Uisnigh (at Ushnagh). Most notable of all was a gigantic ash, the Bile Tartain at Ardbraccan in Co. Meath.[58] The word used in Irish for such a great tree was *bile*, and this was also a common metaphor for a champion or a protector. The great tree would therefore have symbolised the reigning king as an intermediary, who stood between heaven and earth and thus kept both in equilibrium for the welfare of his subjects. It is no coincidence that the inauguration of a local king often took place at a special tree in the territory of his sept.[59]

We can accordingly see why the tree of Mughain is brought into association with the reign of Conn. One mediaeval text associates a similar image with the Leinster symbol of Tara kingship, Cathaoir Mór. We read that Cathaoir once dreamed of a fragrant tree full of fruit and emitting music, and his druid explained to him that the tree was himself. Its music was his eloquence in public gatherings, and its fruit was his great generosity – both attributes which were considered proper to a king.[60] The image of a king as a protecting tree may be as old as Celtic kingship itself, for the Indo-European *reg-s* has been interpreted to have meant 'one who stretches forth'.[61] The Irish language, indeed, preserved – alongside *rí* ('king') – the verb *rigid* ('to rule'), and the word *righe* for the forearm continues in use to this day.

The text on Fínghein and Rothniamh goes on to describe the reign of Conn as a wonderful time without wars or strife, disease or bad weather. There was plenty of fruit and of dew and of corn, the cattle thrived and the rivers were full of fish. Regarding the trees, 'a hundred clusters grew on each stem, a hundred nuts in each cluster'. Finally, at his death – according to another text – wars began to recur, rivers broke their banks, and the salmon screamed out in the river Boyne, trees fell, and the four great waves of Ireland lamented his passing.[62] Two of these four waves were in the southwest, in Tralee Bay and Kenmare Bay; and the other two were in the northeast, in Dundrum Bay and at Ballintoy.[63] The idea that waves cried out at the death of a great king accords, not only with the equilibrium between the environment and the king's reign, but also with the ancient druidic lore which regarded water as a source of spiritual wisdom (Chapter 3). That sea-waves at specific places should formally cry out, however, seems ultimately to derive from the idea that subterranean dwellings of the dead lie underneath some great breakers in the sea. Thus a lady of the Tuatha Dé, Clíodhna, is said to have been drowned at the location of the great lamenting wave in Kenmare Bay, while another mythical lady is said to have been drowned under the wave at Ballintoy.[64] The crying wave of Tóim in Tralee Bay, indeed, seems to have got its name from the word *túaim*, which meant 'bank' but was often used as a term for a tumulus.[65]

Another obscure figure whom the Connachta used in their propaganda was Cormac. From the frequent occurrences of variants of this name in early Leinster genealogies, it would appear that the lore of Cormac was borrowed by the Connachta from their predecessors at Tara. By the 6th or 7th century AD a special legend had been developed by the Connachta concerning this character, whom they called Cormac mac Airt. His patronymic comes from the Celtic word *artos* ('bear'), found in the names of Gaulish divinities Artaios and Artio,[66] and attests to the proximity of such Irish lore to that of the Celtic culture abroad, for bears had been extinct in Ireland for the previous thousand years at least.[67] Most of the motifs in the legend of Cormac have the marks of borrowing from Christian and Latin sources, but there are a few aspects which reflect earlier native ideology. Principal among those are the imagery of the 'true' king who gives wise judgements.[68] This is graphically expressed in one recension of the legend, which has a wall of the palace at Tara begin to collapse when the usurper Lughaidh mac Con gives a false judgement, but when Cormac rectifies this the wall steadies itself of its own accord.[69]

The sacred nature of kingship is illustrated in another story of Cormac. According to this, he was accidentally struck in the eye and blinded by a link from the chain of a huge spear which was being wielded by a raider at Tara. Due to this physical blemish, Cormac had to vacate the kingship and went to live at the rath of Cleiteach (near Slane in Co. Meath).[70] This idea of a blemished king being unsuitable to reign is an old one, expressed in a few striking prototypes in Irish saga. The most celebrated instance is that of Nuadhu, who had to vacate the kingship of the Tuatha Dé when his arm was cut off (Chapter 5). Another instance concerns an early Ulster king called Fearghus mac Léide, whose mouth is twisted with horror when he sees a monster in Loch Rudhraighe (Dundrum Bay, Co. Down). He remains in the kingship only by concealing the blemish, but when taunted concerning it by a slave-woman he returns to the bay and dies fighting the monster.[71] The motif of a blemished king features also in the account (discussed in Chapter 3) of how Caier vacates the kingship of Connacht when his face blisters due to the satire of a poet.[72]

Since the proper king kept nature and society in equilibrium, it is clear that any defect in his sacred person could be thought to affect his reign. This kind of homeopathic magic was given credence to varying degrees in certain ancient societies.[73] There is a distinct lack of evidence for the actual displacement of kings or leaders in early Ireland due to such blemishes, however, and it would appear that – like *geis* – it was just another device which could be used as propaganda in unstable political circumstances. It is significant that the mentions of it in the Irish literature tend to be in the context of a king being satirised, and indeed the usual words for such a blemish (*oil* and *ainimh*) were standard words for the effect of poetic satire. The likelihood, then, is that the idea of a blemished king bringing misfortune on his people would only have force when some failure in the king's rule was evident to all.[74] The nature of such failures is clear from a text on the results of a king's 'falsehood' – they include defeat in battle, famine during his reign, and lack of milk, fruit, and corn.[75]

The idea of the natural surroundings, and especially of water, being in equilibrium with the personality of a good king, is expressed in a curious way in a mediaeval fiction that Cormac mac Airt had been a convert to Christianity through his own wisdom before the coming of the new religion. Here we read that, on his death, Cormac left instructions that he be buried not in Brugh na Bóinne (Newgrange) – where the text claims that the pagan kings of Tara were buried – but on the other side of the river Boyne. After his death these instructions were ignored, and his body was being carried across the river to Newgrange for burial, but 'the Boyne rose up three times' so that they could not cross. 'They then realised that it was a transgression of a sovereign's judgement to go against the will of the king' and they buried him at Ros na Rí where he had desired.[76]

The Ulster kingship

Apart from Tara, the most celebrated site in the old literature was Eamhain Mhacha (the hill-fort of Navan, a few miles west of Armagh city). There are several references to the *óenach* or assembly of Eamhain, and no doubt its importance stretches well back into prehistory.[77] The archaeology of the site is of great interest. It was inhabited since the neolithic era,[78] but traces of earlier structures were erased by ploughing before the major settlement there, which began in the 7th century BC.[79] These Bronze Age inhabitants erected a palisaded enclosure on the top of the hill, with wooden huts inside it. At the beginning of the 1st century BC a whole new and larger enclosure was raised, within which were four concentric rings of oak posts and a circle of timber uprights towards the centre. In this circle again was a large timber post sunk into a hole. It is thought that the whole inner structure may have been roofed. There are no traces of human habitation, and there is therefore scarcely any doubt but that the function of the site was ceremonial.

Curiously, at some stage the inner structure was filled with limestone blocks and its walling burned, and finally it was sealed by covering it over with sods.[80] Although it has been suggested that this destruction was a ceremonial act carried out by the devotees themselves, the destruction may rather have been a hostile act, and if so it may have marked the overthrow of a Bronze Age people at the site by an incoming Celtic group.[81] At any rate, the striking circular plans, the use of great oak posts, and the sealing off of the whole building, leave little doubt but that those responsible for both construction and destruction were in awe of the site and regarded it as sacred. The largest timber post might have been intended as a sort of 'world-tree', at the sacred centre of the community's territory with a ceremonial function of linking the earth with the skies. As such it would have been a symbol of the prosperity of the tribe or sept, and important ceremonies would have centred on it.[82]

That the site had such a mystical importance emerges also from the literature, which – in addition to celebrating the place as the headquarters of the ancient Ulstermen – uses the term 'Eamhain' in general as a designation for otherworld places.[83] In fact, scholars are generally of the opinion that a reference which long predates any writing in Irish is the first mention of the actual site – this was the reference to *Isamnion* in his description of the country by the Graeco-Egyptian geographer Ptolemaeus in the 2nd century AD.[84] If so, the original form of Eamhain would probably have been Celtic 'Isomnis',[85] with a meaning such as 'sturdy posts'.[86] The development of this within archaic Irish would have been of the following order: *isomnis > ihomniah >*

eumania. This latter form is in fact attested in early Irish literature as the designation of the Ulster capital, and from it the standard form Eamhain derives.[87]

The importance of this ancient site is reflected by the high prestige which continued to attach to it, for a great heroic saga was woven around its name, and some of the elements of that saga preserve old ritual ideas. The literature always has Eamhain Mhacha as the royal seat of the Ulaidh, whose leading sept was the Rudhraighe. It is not known when they founded their kingdom, but it may have followed on that enigmatic destruction in the 1st century BC. In keeping with time-honoured tradition, these Rudhraighe would have expropriated to themselves the sacred significance of the place, while synchronising it with sacred lore of their own. It was such an amalgam which, many centuries later, was shaped into an heroic saga for the descendants of the Rudhraighe.

The narratives as we have them are no older than the 6th or 7th century AD, from which time they underwent rapid development in a romantic mould. Traces of the original mythology, however, peep through, as in the rather strange political arrangement which is basic to the cycle. According to this, Fearghus, who has been king, has handed the kingship over to the younger Conchobhar, and he remains as a kind of seneschal within the kingdom. We may suspect the occurrence here again of the ancient concept of the elder succumbing to the youngster. In the specific context of kingship, we have already noted this outline in the Étaín story, where the elder Midhir can be viewed as the presiding deity who hands the kingship over to the reigning monarch.

Indeed, the story of how Aonghus gets possession of Newgrange through the help of Midhir (see Chapter 5) is also a parallel, and the close resemblance between the names Aonghus ('real vigour') and Fearghus ('male vigour') calls for comment. The full name of the latter is *Fearghus mac Ró-eich* ('male vigour, son of great stallion'), and it is possible that – in the original Ulster formulation of the outline – Fearghus was the name of the younger character, and the elder had divine equine imagery. The name Conchobhar literally meant 'beloved of warriors', and this may have at first been a secondary title given to the incumbent king, who ritually represented the fecundity of male vigour. The complex, at any rate, is clearly related to the installation of the kings of the Ulstermen in the late prehistoric period.

The equine connections of the patron-deity parallel the designation Eochaidh Ollathair ('horsemen all-father') for the Daghdha, and it is therefore probable that the conceptual framework of the ancient Ulster kingship was derived from the Boyne valley. A strong indication that this was the case is provided by a mediaeval story concerning the origin of Lough Neagh (*Loch nEachach* – 'the lake of Eochaidh') in the territory of the ancient Ulaidh. That lake, we read, was formed from the urine of a great horse, on which a warrior called Eochaidh had abducted the wife of his father. Eochaidh had been assisted in this escapade by Aonghus of Newgrange and opposed by Midhir.[88] The occurrence of these divinities in the story is hardly coincidental, and it is best to regard it as débris from the form in which the cultus was borrowed by the Ulaidh. As we have seen, the Tara cultus of kingship was a development of the idea of intercourse between sun and earth.[89] The special stressing of equine imagery in the context of Eamhain seems to represent a very ancient aspect of Indo-European culture, for Sanskrit and Norse sources connect the sacrifice of a horse with the rites of kingship.[90] The land-goddess, to whom the king was being symbolically wedded, could be envisaged in the form of a mare. The energy and fertility of this animal was desirable to the tribe just as the milk of a cow was, and the goddess could take either form.[91]

It is clear that, on the eve of the introduction of Christianity, the term Eamhain had come to denote a sacred tumulus in general. In order to specify this particular tumulus the element 'Macha' was added, thus giving the full name by which the site is known to tradition, Eamhain Mhacha.[92] The word *macha* meant a designated portion of land, and was the name by which the surrounding plain had come to be known.[93] The title 'king of Macha', as applied to the legendary Conchobhar,[94] originally referred merely to the status of a ruler over that plain, and was no doubt a designation used for the leader of the Ulaidh in the area. In ordinary usage, however, the word *macha* acquired the secondary sense of 'enclosure',[95] and this would have caused a developing tendency to interpret 'Eamhain Mhacha' as 'the tumulus within the enclosure'. Yet further development in the interpretation led to the conjecture that the toponymic meant 'the tumulus of Macha', and accordingly Macha came to be imagined as a mythical personage in the lore of the site.

We have seen that the functions of male personifications in the embryonic Ulster Cycle, such as Fearghus and Conchobhar, paralleled those of similar males within the Boyne valley cultus of kingship. The third important character in such a cultus would have been a land-goddess, such as Danu or one of her several emanations. Several literary sources list Macha and the Mór-Ríoghain as two in a triad of sisters, and some sources actually claim that the two were one and the same.[96] There can, in fact, be little doubt but that the designation originally used by the Ulaidh for their cult-goddess was in fact Mor-Ríoghain. This was superseded by the new name Macha, which gave the Ulaidh a special goddess of their own and helped to distinguish the sacred nature of their kingship from rival groups to the south of them. Thus the title 'king of Macha' took on a new and much more prestigous meaning, the ruler of the Ulaidh being portrayed as an appointee of a goddess who presided exclusively over the famous otherworld mound of Eamhain.

The Ulster Cycle always represents Macha as a wonderful lady after whom the prestigous site was named. One account describes how she offered her favours in turn to three kings, but physically overcame each of them and tied them up. She then forced them to build the fort of Eamhain for her.[97] In this case she emerges clearly as a goddess of the land and of sovereignty who desired the sacred enclosure to be a symbolic dwelling. A lingering memory of this idea is indicated in a fanciful interpretation (viz. 'neck-pin') of the word Eamhain given in an early glossary. Here we read that she sat on the hill and planned the perimeter of the mound with the pin from her mantle. 'Her pin stretched further eastwards in front of her than behind her to the west – thus the mound is uneven.'[98]

More significant in terms of actual ritual is another story, according to which Macha came from the otherworld and became the wife of an Ulster farmer. She was a great runner, but

she warned her husband not to tell of that. At the assembly of
Eamhain, he boasts that his wife could outrun the king's horses
and, although heavily pregnant, she is brought and made to run
against these. She wins the race, but dies on the finishing line
after giving birth to twins there. As she dies, she lays a curse on
the Ulstermen for their ill-treatment of her.[99] The twins (*emon*)
are an incidental addition to the narrative, no doubt based on a
misinterpretation of the name of the mound (*Eumania,* etc.).
Otherwise, however, this account is very significant, for it brings
into focus the equine imagery in the Ulster cultus of kingship.
This imagery, deriving from the sun-lore of Eochaidh as patron
of the kingship, would naturally spread into the context of that
god's partner, the divine patroness of the land.

We have seen that the ancient Ulaidh referred to their patron-
deity as a great 'stallion', the word in use being *each* < **ekwos*.
The cognate of this word in Continental Celtic was **epos*, and
the Gauls did indeed have a very influential goddess of horses
called Epona, who was adopted as their patroness by the Roman
imperial cavalry.[100] There would be no great difficulty, then, for
the Mor-Ríoghain to be portrayed in the context of horses, and
it may even be that influence was at work from the Epona-cult
among the Romans in Celtic Britain. Certainly, the British Celts
knew of an association of the same land-goddess with horses, for
the title Mor-Ríoghain derives from a Celtic **Rigantona*, and the
Welsh avatar of this personage, Rhiannon, was said to have been
an otherworld woman riding on a large white horse which out-
stripped all her pursuers.[101]

Stories of otherworld ladies who leave their husbands after the
breaking of a prohibition are found widely in folklore,[102] and no
doubt the theme of Macha leaving her husband has been deliberately borrowed from floating lore. The reason would be that it
was considered suitable to the Macha-personage, for the lady of
the folklore plot belonged to the otherworld, just as the Irish
goddess (Mor-Ríoghain > Macha) did. We may speculate that
the actual situation entailed in the folklore plot was also suitable.
This left her human husband dependent on her and able to gain
the continuation of her goodwill only by taking extreme care in
his handling of a supernatural condition. The borrowing would

accordingly have taken place in the context of a belief in the importance of placating the goddess Macha and maintaining her protective function. It may even be possible to suggest a date for the addition of this narrative plot to the cult of Macha, for the idea that she cursed her people seems to have arisen as an explanation of the overthrow of the Rudhraighe kingship by the Connachta of Tara in the 5th century AD.[103]

The actual horse-racing, however, must belong to the original Celtic material. This is also indicated by the name of a famous chariot-horse in the Ulster Cycle, the *Liath* ('grey') of Macha,[104] which according to one source was owned by the goddess.[105] We have already encountered this imagery of greyness in the case of the patron-deity Midhir, and it may be that the *Liath Macha* was originally another name for the *Ró-each* or 'great stallion', the divine patron of Ulster kingship. That the deity in the guise of a stallion should bequeath the sovereignty – envisaged in the form of a mare – is a direct and reasonably logical concept. It may be that rhetorics or even rituals developed this further. The ordeal by which a hero defeats in a race a fleet-footed woman is found as a very ancient motif in international stories,[106] and it was utilised in order to flesh out the equine symbolism.

The race of the goddess would have been considered a suitably mystical way to refer to the course of a king's reign. We recall the description above of the rites accompanying the ancient Tara inauguration, which has a new king coursing a chariot with unbroken horses between sacred stones. This way of symbolising and ritualising a reign ordained and limited by destiny must have been central to the early Irish concept of kingship. We can take it to derive from the imagery of the sun itself coursing the heavens, which – as we have seen – was intimately connected with the *geasa* on kings. While functioning under the patronage of the solar ancestor-deity, a king and his career would naturally have to conform to the cosmic system. This was the system from which his power got its license, and on which the well-being of the people ultimately depended. The orientation of the entrance to the timber-structure at Eamhain is to the west;[107] and it is possible that the image of the enclosure (*macha*), and a ritual custom of circumambulating it sun-wise, may have contributed to

the adaptation of the running-motif.[108] This may have happened
quite early, for there is also a reference to Meadhbh, the Tara
goddess of sovereignty, racing against horses.[109] The combination of her (whose name refers to ale) and horses would have
been especially apt to the age-old cultus of kingship, for the
meaning 'horse-mead' is found in a Gaulish royal title *Epome-
duos* as well as in the title of the Hindu inauguration ritual
asvamedha.[110]

Kingship in the west

Mention of Meadhbh brings us to the issue of the kingship of the
western province. Whether or not the powerful Connachta originated within that area, it is at any rate clear that by the time that
they gained possession of Tara in the 5th century AD they were
already in the process of forming another strong kingdom in the
west, centring on Cruachu (later, Cruachain – near Tulsk in Co.
Roscommon). No doubt they chose this site because of its
impressive appearance, for a large number of earthworks and
cairns are spread over a wide area. The largest and most celebrated of them is Ráth Chruachna (Rathcroghan), a large flat-
topped tumulus. There are several parallel pairs of linear
earthworks in the area, and the longest of these is orientated
directly towards Ráth Chruachna itself. Although no major excavations have yet been carried out at Cruachu, it is thought that
megalithic tombs were situated there, as well as cairns of the
Bronze Age.[111]

After the 5th century AD, Cruachu acquired a new mythic
dimension. As the leading branch of the sept at Tara took on the
new name of Uí Néill ('descendants of Niall'), the designation
Connachta was increasingly understood to apply to the branch
at Cruachu, and indeed the western province in general came to
be known as 'Connachta'. Moreover, due to the comprehensive
expropriation by the sept of the Meadhbh lore at Tara, that goddess had become known as Meadhbh of Connachta, and with
the shift in meaning of the septal designation her name came to
be associated with Cruachu. Thus it happened that the mediaeval heroic tales of the Ulster Cycle – which had their basis in the
defeat of the Ulaidh by the Connachta of Tara – described

'Meadhbh of Cruachu' as a Tara princess who became queen of
the western province. An ogham-inscription, on the roof of the
cave at Cruachu is dedicated to one 'Vracos son of Meduva'.[112]
This was probably written in the 6th century, and the Vracos in
question is likely to have been a noble of the Connachta, hence
his title 'son of Meduva'. The inscription would therefore bear
witness to the translation of the Meadhbh cultus to Cruachu at
that time.[113]

The mediaeval literature refers to a great – probably annual –
assembly at Cruachu, and it is clear that the place's prestige was
high in the early Christian period.[114] It was claimed that the celebrated king Nath Í, brother of Niall Naoighiallach, was buried
at Cruachu and that a red sandstone pillar marked his grave
there.[115] This may instance a continuity in sepulchral tradition
associated with the site. In the early historic period, indeed, the
vicinity of Cruachu was regarded as one of the great cemeteries
of Ireland.[116] There was also a tradition in the Middle Ages that
the declivity at Cruachu, known as *Uaimh na gCat* ('the Cave of
the Cats'), was an entrance to the otherworld.[117]

Kingship in the southern half
One of the largest hill-forts in Ireland was situated on Aillind
(Knockaulin in Co. Kildare). Here also indications of neolithic
habitation have been found, and the same process of Celtic culture taking over from pre-existing ones can be deciphered.[118]
There is Iron Age evidence at Aillind for circular trenches, on
which timber palisades were erected, and there was a circle of
large timber posts at the centre of the enclosure. Again, no traces
have been found of contemporaneous habitation at the site, but
there was much evidence of burning taking place near the stand-
ing-posts. As at Eamhain Mhacha, the most compelling suggestion is that the whole purpose of Aillinn was a ritual one.[119]
Situated in the heart of the territory of the Leinstermen, it must
have been an important site for them during their occupation of
Tara, which seems to have lasted until the 4th century AD. In the
century or two after this, its cultic significance would have
increased, as the shrinking Leinster kingdom transferred some of
the lore of the Boyne valley southwards with it. Thus, in the 6th

and 7th centuries, we find Leinster genealogies claiming that a great king of theirs called Find File ruled at 'round Aillinn'.[120] As we have seen in Chapter 4, this Find File was a personage based on a mythical Vindos. He is described as a descendant of Nuadhu, another aspect of the Boyne cult to which the Leinster-men clung.

Another emanation from Vindos was the celebrated Fionn mac Cumhaill, who was also mentioned in these genealogies and described as a descendant of Nuadhu. This latter seer-warrior was said to have had his headquarters at Almhu (the Hill of Allen in Co. Kildare) – there was formerly a burial cairn on this hill and the association of the great mythical figure with it would indicate that it had a sacred status in Leinster prehistory. It is interesting to note the attempts at locating the Vindos tradition in two different areas of Leinster. Aillinn and Almhu are at opposite ends of the plain of Kildare – about seven miles apart – and they may have been the foci of two rival subsepts of Leinster, the Uí Garrchon and the Uí Fáilghe respectively. A new subsept, the Uí Dúnlainge, took the Leinster kingship in the late 5th century AD, and they upheld the ritual status of Aillinn. They claimed that the hill-fort (called Dún Aillinne) had been constructed by an ancient king called Mes Delmonn, who was a mighty warrior against his foes in this world and against the Fomhoire in the afterlife.[121] The Uí Dúnlainge also seem to have kept up the practice of public assembly at the site for some centuries, for traces of large-scale feasting have been found there.[122]

The literature has little to tell us of culture in Munster during the Iron Age. At the beginning of the historical period, it was ruled over by the Eoghanacht.[123] They claimed descent from an eponymous Eoghan Mór,[124] and the saga which they told of him shows clear Leinster influence. According to it, a Leinster king called Dáire Barrach wished to fortify Dún Aillinne, and employed Nuadhu – described as a great builder – for the task. Eoghan was standing by with a group of other youths observing the work, and when he saw a huge stone in the trench he removed it without effort. A druid remarked: 'You have a noble servant today, o Nuadhu!' Thus Eoghan became known as Mugh Nuadhat ('servant of Nuadhu').[125] The stone can still be seen at

Knockaulin, at the side of the hill-fort there. As king of Munster, Eoghan is described as fighting continuously against Conn Céadchathach, and the two are claimed to have divided the country equally between them – the northern half (*leath*) being Leath Choinn and the southern half Leath Mhogha.[126] All of this is mediaeval elaboration of earlier propaganda data, and the ultimate origin can hardly be earlier than the 4th century AD, given the presuppositions regarding characters and lore on which it is based.

The Eoghanacht were not predominant in Munster until the 5th century AD or thereabouts, and there are several hints in the literature that a branch of the Érainn had previously been dominant there as at Tara. How the Eoghanacht displaced the Érainn in the south is symbolised in stories of a contest between the Érainn hero Lughaidh mac Con and the ideal king of Eoghanacht tradition, Ailill Ólom. One such story preserves a sympathy for Lughaidh, by having both men embrace each other in friendship, but Ailill has a poisoned tooth with which he nips the cheek of Lughaidh. As a result, Lughaidh's face began to melt away.[127] Such a 'loss of face' (usually termed *meath n-oineach*) was a symbolical way of describing loss of honour in ancient Ireland,[128] and its occurrence here is no doubt to illustrate how Lughaidh's power was at an end. We further read that, in order to be sure of his triumph, Ailill engaged the seer Ferchess to assassinate his rival. Finding Lughaidh amongst his own relatives and supporters, Ferchess chanted a spell over his spear: 'Point of spear past a follower directed towards a blemished king between two namesakes!' He then threw the spear at Lughaidh, and it went straight to him and killed him.[129] Conspicuously, the words of the spell are a play on the idea of kingly status – Lughaidh has lost his honour, and is therefore blemished as a king and will be replaced.

The name Ailill itself is worthy of note. In its earlier form it was 'Eilill',[130] and it has been explained as cognate with Welsh *ellyll* which meant 'a phantom' or 'a spirit'.[131] What appears to be a diminutive of the name, Ellén, is given to a triple-headed destructive being which emerges from the cave of Cruachu;[132] and also to the fire-breathing phantom who threatens Tara but is overcome by the seer-hero Fionn mac Cumhaill, who thereby becomes the 'king' of the Fianna warriors.[133] The designation Ellén therefore would appear to have attached to the detritus of the sun-god, the divine patron who relinquishes his role as controller of the community to human leaders. We can presume that Ailill was originally another term for the figure of the father-deity presiding over the institution of kingship. The role assigned to Ailill Ólom as ancestor of the royal Eoghanacht sept accords well with this. We seem to be dealing with an adaptation to the Munster context of the same allegorical language, rooted in inauguration rituals, which is expressed more clearly in the lore of the kingships of Tara and Eamhain.

The soubriquet Ólom (earlier Aulom) meant 'bare-eared', and the actual name is paralleled by that of Ailill Molt ('Ailill the Wether'), a Connachta king of Tara in the 5th century AD. In the case of the latter personage, this must have been a case of attaching to a real king a mythical name entailing kingship and wealth.[134] Its roots must go back very far, for the Gauls had a wether-god whom the Classical writers referred to as 'Deus Moltinus'.[135] An ancestral figure of early Leinster tradition, indeed, had the name Augaine, which may have meant 'wether-conceived'.[136] This latter name is of interest, for it is close to *Éugan*, the earliest attested form of the patronymic of the Eoghanacht sept.[137] Thus Ailill 'the bare-eared' would have symbolised the wealth of a king in terms of sheep-herds. Such imagery was, of course, very appropriate to a dynasty which controlled the grasslands of Munster.

Although the septal name may have derived ultimately from a sheep divinity, it came to be interpreted as based on *eó*, meaning 'stem' and later 'yew-tree'. This element is found in the early literature also in the names of the personages Eoghabhal and Fer Í (literally 'son of yew'), otherworld beings associated with the Eoghanacht dynasty.[138] There was much confusion with regard to mythical data in this literature, as can be noticed also in the similarity which these names have with that of Eoghan Mór, who is furthermore described as a son of Ailill Ólom.[139] It is best to unravel this by postulating that both the divinity name Ailill and the septal name Eoghanacht derive from the one complex of ritual, which involved a phantom patron of the sept's welfare. The identity of this patron is underlined by his further designation of Ailill Áine. The soubriquet here meant 'fieriness' or 'brightness' and would refer to the sun. When used on its own, the soubriquet was considered to refer to a masculine divinity[140] but, due to the theme of sovereignty in the form of a goddess, the Eoghanacht tradition developed the notion of Áine as a female personage of the otherworld.[141] For the sept she came to supplant the role of the ancient Munster land-goddess Anu or Danu.[142]

Early mediaeval literature describes an adventure of Ailill Ólom with this otherworld lady, who resided in the heart of the Eoghanacht territory – in a cairn on top of Cnoc Áine (the hill of Knockainey, Co. Limerick). The account comes from a somewhat hostile source, but the outline of an indigenous ritual can be deciphered in it. We read that the grass used to mysteriously disappear overnight from the hillside at Knockainey. On the advice of the seer Ferchess, Ailill went to the hill on the night of Samhain (the November feast) to investigate. He fell asleep there 'while listening to the grazing of the cattle', and awoke during the night to see the beautiful maiden emerge from the cairn, accompanied by her father Eoghabhal. He forced his attentions on her, and in the struggle she bit his ear off – hence the nickname ó-lom ('bare-eared').[143]

Other sources make it clear that Áine was the patron-goddess of the Eoghanacht,[144] and the union of king with the land-goddess must lie behind the above account. The role of Ailill's seer-druid as instigator, and the midnight awakening from sleep in order to encounter the goddess, suggest that the story is débris from an actual rite of inauguration. Here again one notices the antiquity of the cultural landscape, for Knockainey lies within a short distance of Lough Gur, at which there is continuous and copious archaeological evidence since the neolithic period.[145] The Eoghanacht kings of Munster were at one with their counterparts in other parts of the country in seeking the prestige of pre-Celtic sites for their dynasty.

−7−

The Triumph of Christianity

THERE WERE CHRISTIANS in Ireland before the coming of St Patrick. That is clear from the fact that Pope Celestine appointed Palladius as the first bishop to the Irish in or about the year AD 429.[1] Their numbers must have been very limited, however, and Christianity was still at this time unknown and irrelevant to the vast majority of people on the island. The new religion was known only to those who, through trade or otherwise, had met with people from Britain or the Continent, or to those who had come from abroad. It is indeed likely that the majority of Christians living in Ireland, at this stage, were slaves who had been brought here from the Irish raids on the west of Britain.[2] Most of them would have been in the south of Munster, but there probably were small communities of Christians also in parts of Leinster and of east Ulster.[3] These people tried to preserve their Christian faith as best they could in the alien and difficult environment.

Life may not have been so difficult for all of those in bondage, and some of them indeed may have had access to important strata within Irish society. For example, the literature states clearly that the very powerful 5th-century Tara king, Niall, was himself the son of a girl who had been captured in Britain. She had the Latin name Carina, but was called by the Irish 'Cairenn', and had been taken by Niall's father Eochu, who had the soubriquet Muighmheadhon meaning 'lord of slaves'.[4] When Niall grew up, we are told, he brought his mother with him to Tara and clothed her in the purple robe of a noble lady. His claim to kingship was underlined by the story (Chapter 6) of how he gained it in accordance with the imagery of the pagan inauguration rites.[5]

Leader of the predominant Connachta sept, his name seems originally to have been Nél ('cloud'), a mythical one given to him for prestige. Known to posterity as Niall Naoi-Ghiallach, the literary accounts of him, though several centuries later than his floruit, can be taken to contain some reliable tradition. His soubriquet (originally 'Noígiallach') meant 'having nine hostages' and refers to the custom of an over-king taking hostages from lesser rulers. During his reign, he and his sons extended their power far beyond their power-base in Breágha (the plain of Meath), conquering large areas of Connacht and Ulster. He was famous for his raids abroad, which – it was claimed – carried him as far as the Continent itself. In reality, these raids were probably confined to the coast of Britain. He was slain on one such campaign – variously described as in the Channel Islands and in Scotland – in or about the year 452 AD. The tradition that his slayer was a Leinster nobleman, who had earlier been exiled by him, is probably true. One account has his followers, after his death, raising aloft his body so as to ensure victory in battle. He was brought home to Ireland and buried at Faughan Hill, near Navan in Co. Meath.[6]

The celebrated mission
In his raiding abroad, Niall took after his father, and – although there is no direct evidence for this – it may be on one of his raids that the sixteen-year-old boy Patrick was captured somewhere in the west of Britain. Certainly the raid on which Patrick was taken was a large and co-ordinated one, of a type which only a powerful leader could organise – in his autobiography, the *Confessio*,[7] the saint himself states that 'a great number of people' were taken. He spent six years as a slave in Ireland, pasturing flocks in wooded and mountainous terrain probably in the area

of present-day Co. Mayo. Then one night, in his sleep, he heard a voice telling him to escape. He travelled two hundred miles to a ship, but was refused passage by the sailors because he refused 'to suck their nipples'.[8] This was apparently a pagan practice of swearing loyalty. There are other references to it in Irish literature, as – for instance – the boast attributed to the early seer-poet, Néidhe mac Adhna, that in the process of acquiring his wisdom he 'drank' from the breast of the chief-poet of Ireland.[9]

Eventually the sailors agreed to take Patrick on board their ship, and so he got away from Ireland. Some years later, when he had become a priest and had returned to his relatives in Britain, he had a vision in which a man came to him bringing a letter with the heading 'the Voice of the Irish'. He then heard 'as with one voice' those same people whom he had been among 'beside the western sea', appealing to him to 'come and walk among us'. Thus St Patrick explains his resolution to return to Ireland as a Christian missionary. In the *Confessio*, Patrick is pre-occupied in general with the spiritual rather than the temporal dimension of his mission, and accordingly he gives little precise information about the actual circumstances of his work in Ireland. It is clear from the text that his mission lasted up to thirty years, but scholars are divided as to the precise dates. The date of his death is usually given as AD 461, but there is also some evidence indicating that it may have been as late as AD 493.[10] Although there were definitely other Christian clergymen in the country at that time, and some even involved in missionary work, there is scarcely any doubt that the work of Patrick was the most significant and that it proved to be the crucial turning-point in Irish religious history.

Patrick was a very courageous and determined man, but he appears also to have been very shrewd in his dealings with the Irish, and to have made himself acutely sensitive to the structures of power which existed in the country. Concerning the difficulties which he encountered, and the strategies adopted by him, the following remarks of his are the nearest hints which he gives to the actual situation: 'And all that time I used to give presents to the kings, in addition to paying wages to their sons who travel with me; and nonetheless they seized me with my companions, and on that day they were keen to kill me, but my time had not yet come; and everything they found with us they seized, and myself they bound in irons; and on the fourteenth day the Lord freed me from their power; and all our belongings were also restored to us, for the sake of God and the close friends with whom we had provided ourselves beforehand.'[11]

Although Patrick, in his text, gives few indications of the actual beliefs which he encountered among the pre-Christian Irish, some ideas can be gained concerning these beliefs through a study of the way in which his teaching was represented in subsequent Christian sources. For instance, the biography of him written in the 7th century by the monk Muirchú shows how his teaching contradicted pagan tenets and, in some very interesting ways, coalesced with them. In his *Confessio*, Patrick was very scrupulous about attributing the success of his mission, not to any qualities of his own, but to the grace bestowed on him by God. For instance, he states that he must 'exclaim aloud to make some return to the Lord for such great favours of his here and in eternity, favours which it is beyond the mind of man to measure',[12] and again he refers to Christianity as 'that gift so great, so salutory'.[13] A favourite phrase of his was *gratiam ago Deo meo* ('I render thanks to my God'), and he insists that he would do thus 'not only when circumstances favour me, but also when I am afflicted – so that whatever happens to me, good or bad, I must accept with an open mind and thank God always'.[14] In that passage, he is deliberately echoing the sentiments of Job in the Old Testament, who faced adversity with the motto 'the Lord gives and the Lord takes away – blessed be the name of the Lord'.[15]

From these references made by Patrick in his *Confessio*, we can see that he stressed a great and generous gift given by God to him, and that he accepted that God had every right to withdraw comforts as He pleased. The phrase of Patrick which encapsulated that attitude was 'gratiam ago'. It is noteworthy that a variant of this phrase *grátes agam* ('let me render thanks')[16] is found in a corrupted form, *grazacham*, in a story related by Muirchú concerning Patrick's attitude to a gift given to him by a pagan potentate in Ireland. The story goes as follows:

Dáire went out to honour holy Patrick, bringing with him a marvellous bronze cauldron from overseas which held three measures. And Dáire said to the holy man: 'Look, this cauldron shall be yours!' And Patrick said: 'Grazacham!' When Dáire came home he said: 'This man is a fool, if he has nothing better to say for a marvellous bronze cauldron of three measures but only "grazacham".' And then Dáire said to his servants: 'Go, and bring us our bronze vessel back!' They went out and told Patrick: 'We are to take the bronze vessel back.' Nonetheless on that occasion also holy Patrick said 'grazacham, take it', and they took it away. And Dáire asked his companions and said: 'What did the Christian say when you took the bronze vessel back?' And they replied: 'He said "grazacham".' And Dáire answered and said: 'Grazacham for the gift, grazacham for its withdrawal; his saying is such a good one, with these grazachams his bronze vessel shall be brought to him again!' And Dáire this time came in person and brought Patrick the bronze vessel and said to him: 'This vessel shall be yours, for you are a steadfast man whom nothing can change. Besides, I give you now that piece of land for which you once asked, so far as it is mine – dwell there.' This is the city which is now called Armagh.[17]

It should be noted that the biographer Muirchú was a monk of the Armagh church,[18] and that he tells us that he had picked up traditions of Patrick from 'knowledgeable men' in that area.[19] He describes Dáire, the bestower of the gift and of the site for a church at Armagh, as 'a wealthy and honoured man' in the area who had initially refused the saint's request for a site and had quarrelled with him. When Dáire gave orders to have Patrick killed, he himself was miraculously struck down. He was revived by the saint, and it was in gratitude for this that he had brought the valuable cauldron as a gift. It is clear from this that the Dáire in question was very much a pagan, but that after some hesitation he succumbed to the saint's preaching and became a Christian. There must have been many such individuals among those who encountered Patrick, and indeed the gaining by the saint of a site at Armagh can be accepted as historical fact, for that place became the headquarters of his mission. The name Dáire may perhaps have been borne by the man who presented the site to Patrick, but there are some aspects of the Dáire described by Muirchú which appear to be symbolical rather than historical, and from studying these it will be clear that the oral legend which Muirchú picked up from the local lore of Armagh was much influenced by mythical material.

First of all, the name Dáire occurs as that of a mythical ancestor of several septs in early Irish genealogy.[20] Of likely relevance is the fact that one of these septs, called the Dáirine, inhabited an area in east Ulster,[21] and accordingly the name in this case may spring from their tradition. 'Dáire' meant literally 'the fertile one',[22] and from this we may consider that he is an echo of the Irish ancestral deity, more usually known as the Daghdha.[23] Such an identification is much strengthened by Dáire's role in the story as a bestower of land, which accords well with the agricultural function of the Daghdha. Most of all, however, Dáire parallels the Daghdha by possessing a marvellous cauldron, which in both cases is described as brought from overseas. The cauldron of the Daghdha signified plenty and generosity,[24] and indeed the very name of this ancient deity meant, and was understood to mean, 'the good god' in this sense of bounteousness.[25]

Attributes of goodness and bounty would easily cause the traditional lore of the Daghdha to become confused with the references which Patrick had made to the gracious and generous Christian God. The confusion would have arisen as the result of contemplation and discussion among those to whom portions of Patrick's *Confessio* were cited. This audience we can easily imagine as a mixed one of newly-converted monks and half-converted laymen in the Armagh area. The teacher would have stressed Patrick's indebtedness to God, the phrase of thanks which the saint was wont to use in that context, and the example of Job which the saint had followed. The teacher, or someone of his audience, would speak of the generosity of God, which extended to both spiritual and temporal matters. This would have given rise to comparison with the bounty of the Daghdha, whose

'goodness' would have been described as far less impressive than
that of the Christian God. Such a demotion of the Daghdha is
reflected in the naive and subservient role which Dáire plays vis-
à-vis Patrick in the legend.[26]

It is significant, however, that Dáire plays the role of a good
Christian by granting the site to Patrick. This would be felt to be
especially relevant to a people like the Dáirine, who claimed
descent from an ancestor figure with that name. It may well be,
therefore, that the legend emanated from a newly-Christianised
group of this sept, for the motif of posthumous baptism for an
ancient worthy was very popular in the lore concerning St
Patrick. This motif was part of Christian lore for quite some time
– a version was told in the 7th century, for instance, of how the
dead Roman Emperor Trajan was revived by Pope Gregory the
Great in order to be baptised.[27] In the preamble to the story of
Dáire, indeed, Muirchú describes that pagan worthy as having
died and been revived by Patrick;[28] and this circumstance would
indicate that the legend, in its original oral form, accommodated
the idea that the ancestor-figure of the Dáirine had been granted
salvation through the donation by his people of the site for
Patrick's church.

The motif of a dead pagan resuscitated, so that he can be baptised by Patrick, occurs more directly in the other biography of
the saint written in the 7th century. In this work, Tíreachán
describes how Patrick came upon a very large grave in Ulster, and
his followers remarked that they did not believe that there could
have been a man so tall. The saint struck the grave-stone with his
staff and made the Sign of the Cross, whereupon the dead man
arose and revealed that he was a swineherd who had been killed
by a band of warriors. He was baptised, and then was laid again
in his grave.[29] In succeeding centuries, this motif of the baptism
of a dead pagan by Patrick was applied to many worthies of Irish
legend, including Cormac mac Airt, Cú Chulainn, and Fionn mac
Cumhaill.[30]

The assault on sun-worship
Resuscitation and baptism are featured in another legend
recorded by Muirchú, and in this case the worthy in question has

even more dramatic echoes of pre-Christian Ireland. Muirchú writes of how a certain pagan of Ulster, whom he calls Macuil moccu Greccae, was 'an impious and savage tyrant, so much so that he was named cyclops'. Macuil was a robber who infested the mountains and slaughtered travellers. On seeing the saint approach one day, he ordered one of his own followers to feign illness so as to test the saint's miraculous ability. On meeting the 'patient', Patrick remarked that he was not surprised that the man was ill, whereupon the pagan's followers noticed that he was indeed dead. Macuil then repented, confessed that he had intended to slay the saint, and accepted baptism. Patrick revived the dead man, and imposed penance on Macuil. The penance was that he be tied with chains and set adrift in a boat on the sea. This was done, and Macuil was blown southwards to Evonia (the Isle of Man). He there met with two clerics, and remained with them on the island, where he eventually became a bishop.[31]

It is clear that Muirchú pictured Macuil as an ordinary human, though fierce and 'wearing emblems of the most wicked cruelty'. The story which he had heard had been influenced by social factors of the time – such as clerical opposition to the *díbhfheirg*, groups who lived by reaving in early Ireland;[32] and the practice of setting adrift as punishment.[33] The genesis of the story, however, appears to be of greater antiquity. The name, in its more standard Irish form of Mac Cuill, occurs in the mediaeval literature as that of one of a trio of Tuatha Dé Danann personages.

The trio are Mac Cuill, Mac Cécht, and Mac Gréine (literally 'son of hazel', 'son of healing' and 'son of sun'). They are the otherworld husbands of Banba, Fódla, and Ériu – three mythical ladies whose names all signify the land of Ireland.

These husbands have solar associations. The name Mac Gréine embodies this explicitly, while Mac Cécht is described significantly in one early text as travelling Ireland before morning with a golden goblet in his possession.[34] There can be little doubt but that Mac Cuill himself belongs to the selfsame context. Muirchú equates the name Macuil with 'cyclops', thus indicating that the true form would be Mac Guill – 'son of Goll' – for the word 'goll' meant one-eyed. We have already related the name Eochaidh Aonsúla ('Horseman One-Eyed') to the Daghdha in his image as sun-deity, and Goll is cited as an alternative name for him.[35] No doubt this imagery was very old, for the Irish word for an eye (*súil*) is a cognate of *sauél*, the Indo-European word for the sun.[36] The name Mac Guill, therefore, in its devoiced form Mac Cuill, is fully redolent of the ancient Irish format of the male sun as mate of the female earth. His trip as described by Muirchú to the Isle of Man, moreover, may be a transformed version of the old theme of the sun's journey to the mystical island in the west. Admittedly the journey in this case is eastwards, but as mentioned in Chapter 5 the Isle of Man had the reputation of being an otherwordly place from antiquity.

Patrick certainly disapproved of sun-worship, as is clear from the following discourse in his *Confessio*:

> For that sun, which we see, rises daily at God's command for our sake; but it will never reign, nor will its splendour abide; but all who adore it will come, as unhappy men, unfortunately into punishment. We, on the other hand, who believe in the true Sun and adore Him, Christ, will never perish. And neither will he who does His will; but he will abide for ever, as Christ abides for ever.[37]

He obviously regarded solar religion as a particularly powerful pagan phenomenon. This attitude was general in his time, for the Christian church had just succeeded in overcoming such an official cult within the Roman Empire itself. In the latter half of the 3rd century AD the Emperor Aurelian had established the 'Sol Invictus' or 'unconquered sun' as the supreme deity of the state,[38] but within one generation the Empire had been Christianised. The first Christian Emperor, Constantine, had been brought up in this solar cult, but had converted on seeing his celebrated vision of the Cross elevated higher in the sky than the sun.[39] In this case, however, Patrick must have been referring to the particular challenge which sun-worship presented to his own mission in Ireland. That such a challenge was a major one is clear from the frequent use of sun-symbolism in pre-Christian Irish tradition concerning gods and goddesses. The strength of solar worship is indicated by the fact that, even in the Christianised Ireland three centuries after Patrick's mission, prehistoric spiral engravings on rock were explained as 'the figuration of the sun' which was adored long ago.[40] One Irish text – which may be as early as the 6th century – describes how the pre-Christian poets 'extolled the sacred sun of the sky', thus echoing the old tradition.[41]

Patrick's contemporaries noted his insistence on the contrast between ordinary physical light and the light of heaven. So much so, indeed, that traditions developed which used such imagery to show his triumph over Irish paganism. The most celebrated instance of this is how the light of a Paschal fire lit by him on the hill of Slane was seen nearby by Laoghaire, the king of Tara. Laoghaire was angry because Patrick had lit the fire in violation of a rule that on that night nobody should kindle a fire before the king himself did so, and his druids warned him that if Patrick's light were not extinguished on that night 'it will never be extinguished at all'.[42] This led to a tête-à-tête between the saint and Laoghaire, and Patrick is described as proving his point to all and sundry through a dramatic contest with a druid.

Two versions of this contest are featured in the biographies compiled in the 7th century, and the fact that these versions differ considerably from each other suggests that the story was then in existence for quite some time. It concerns a fire-ordeal, and it should be noted that one of the designations of the sun-god in Irish tradition was *Aedh*, which literally meant 'fire'.[43] The account given by the biographer Tíreachán is brief and to the point – it tells of a druid of the high-king Laoghaire, called Cruth, engaging in the ordeal with Benignus, a Christian servant of Patrick:

The chasuble of the druid was burnt about the body of Benignus and reduced to ashes. The holy boy was saved by his firm faith in God in the presence of the king, the people, and the druids. But the chasuble of Benignus, Patrick's (spiritual) son, was worn by the druid, and the druid was burnt to death in it. And Patrick said: 'In this hour all paganism in Ireland has been destroyed!'[44]

The other version, told by the biographer Muirchú, has the same initial situation but is much more elaborate. According to this, Laoghaire and his druids confronted Patrick at Slane, but they were completely confounded by the miracles performed by the saint. Patrick then came to Tara on Easter Day, which he entered through locked doors. He accepted an invitation to eat with the pagans, and survived an attempt to poison him. Challenged to a contest in magic by the druid Lucat Máel, he again triumphed by his miracles, and then king Laoghaire suggested that they undergo an ordeal by fire. The druid was afraid to contend with Patrick himself in such an ordeal, but agreed to a contest with one of the saint's servant-boys. Patrick directed that the two contestants exchange garments and enter a divided and closed house, which was to be set on fire. Accordingly, a house was built, half of green wood and half of dry wood:

> The druid was placed in the green part of the house and one of holy Patrick's boys, Benineus by name, wearing the druid's garb, in its dry part. Then the house was closed from outside and, in the presence of the whole crowd, was set on fire. And in that hour it so happened through the prayer of Patrick that the flame of the fire consumed the druid together with the green half of the house, and nothing was left intact except the chasuble of holy Patrick, which the fire did not touch. On the other hand, happy Benineus, and the dry half of the house ... the fire did not even touch him, and brought him neither pain nor discomfort. Only the garb of the druid, which he had donned, was burnt in accordance with God's will.[45]

This whole account is lavishly ornamented with detail from the Bible. The high-king and his cohorts are expressly compared by Muirchú with the Babylonian king Nebuchadnezzar and his satraps,[46] and he further admits that his description of the fire-ordeal has been influenced by the *Book of Daniel*.[47] Also in the author's mind was the contest of Moses with the magi of the Egyptian Pharaoh in *Exodus*, as well as that of Elias with the priests of Baal in the *Book of Kings*. The reference to green and dry wood echoes a passage in Luke's Gospel.[48]

It is therefore obvious that the account given by Tíreachán is truer to the original oral form of the story. We can perhaps come closer still to the genesis of this fanciful anecdote by considering the fact that both biographers admit that they took material from a description of Patrick written by Ultán, bishop of Arbraccan in Co. Meath.[49] This description is lost, but scholars are of the opinion that it included the anecdote. Ultán himself seems to have spent some time as abbot of the monastery of Louth,[50] in the vicinity of Tara and Slane, which had been founded by a disciple of Patrick called Mochta[51] and in which the writings of the saint were especially venerated.[52] It would appear likely, therefore, that the anecdote actually developed within that monastery, due to contemplation and discussion of what Patrick had written in his *Confessio* concerning sun-worship.

The druids confounded

The overcoming of druids is a favourite theme in the Irish hagiographical literature, and there must be an historical basis for this. Indications of the nature of the original conflict may be gained from the names given to some of these druids. The Lucat Máel referred to above is a good example. 'Lucat' can best be explained as a corruption of 'Lugaid', a diminutive form of the divine name 'Lugh'; while 'Máel' meant 'shaved' and by extension 'servile'. Perhaps, if there really was such a druid, he was a special devotee of the Lugh cult, but it is much more likely that he was an invention of the hagiographers as a disparagement of Lugh himself. Other druids cited by the biographers as being in conflict with Patrick, such as Lochru and Lochlethanu, may well be intended as further caricatures of the Lugh-cult. To a Christian of the time, the name Lugh would have suggested the Latin *lux* ('light') and Lugh's involvement with the sun-imagery of Balar (see Chapter 5) would have strengthened such an interpretation. The story cited above concerning Macuil has Patrick overcoming a cyclopic figure, and this may have been suggested by Lugh's mythical triumph over Balar. A tendency can certainly be observed in Irish tradition to have Patrick usurp the position

of Lugh, and from the early mediaeval period onwards the saint
has been portrayed in folk culture as triumphing over a great
pagan potentate at the harvest festival of Lughnasa, which originally belonged to Lugh.[53]

The impersonal and ideological portrayal of druids is further
suggested by other names given to them in the Christian literature, such as the 'Cruth' cited above. This word meant 'form' or
'shape', and a variant of it in the form of *creth*, was used to
denote seer-poetry and magical craft.[54] The actual portrayal of
the druids in Irish hagiographical literature is, however, usually
quite unhistorical – most of it being borrowed from the accounts
of magicians described in the Bible and other Christian literature.
Tíreachán, for instance, had been shown a stone at Tara onto
which Lochlethanu was dashed after being miraculously lifted
into the air by Patrick's prayer.[55] Muirchú tells this of Lochru,
and cannot hide his suspicion that the episode was borrowed
from the *Acts of Peter*, an apocryphal text which has St Peter
overcoming the magician Simon Magus.[56] As is clear from
Tíreachán's version of this episode, it had already become part of
ordinary lore prior to the labours of both writers, and we can
thus assume that it was current in or about the time of Patrick
himself. Perhaps the saint, or someone of his company, referred
to the druids as equivalents of Simon Magus, and such a reference was the embryo of the story.

That there was some argument between the early Christian
missionaries and the native druids is to be expected. One early
echo of this is provided by a prophecy which appears in both
Irish and Latin texts, and which may be as early as the 6th century. Muirchú claims that, before Patrick's mission began,
Lochru and Lucat Máel 'by their magical art prophesied frequently that a foreign way of life was about to come to them'
and that they 'described the man who was to bring this way of
life'. The prophecy was to the effect that the new faith would be
'honoured by all' and would 'reign for ever'. It was couched in
the form of a poem 'which these men often recited, and especially
during the two or three years immediately before the coming of
Patrick'. Muirchú then quotes a Latin translation of the poem,
which he says is 'not very intelligible'.[57] Although the surviving

Irish text comes from a manuscript later than Muirchú, there are reasons to believe it closer to the original poem.[58] The original can be reconstructed as follows:

> *Ticfa Tálcend*
> *tar muir mercend,*
> *a thí thollcend,*
> *a chrand crombcend;*
> *[canfaid cáidi]*
> *a mías i n-airthiur a thige;*
> *fris-gérat a muinter uile*
> *'Amen, amen!'*[59]

Muirchú commented on the obscurity of this poem, but failed to notice the deliberate ambiguity of it. The meaning to a pagan Irish listener would be as follows: 'Adze-head will come, across the sea, crazed in the head – his cloak with a hole in the head, his stick bent in the head; he will chant an imprecation from his table in front of his house, all his people will answer "be it thus, be it thus!"' The *tálcend* ('adze-head') is a reference to Patrick's tonsure, the holed cloak is his cowl, and the stick is his crozier. The ceremony referred to is the celebration of the Mass, with the Hebrew word *amen* misunderstood to be the Old Irish *amin* ('let it be like that').[60] Moreover, the words *tálcend* and *cáidi* are ambiguous, while *mercend* could be taken to refer to the sea. So, to a Christian listener the phraseology could be interpreted in the following way: 'The head which bestows (wisdom) will come over the tempestuous sea . . . he will chant holiness . . . all his people will answer "amen, amen!"'

Not only such a content, but also the form of the language in the poem, can hardly predate the 6th century.[61] We can therefore be sure that this poem was not composed by pre-Christian druids, but rather by a Christian in or around the 6th century, as part of the argument between Christians and pagans which was still taking place at that time. The unknown composer wanted the audience to believe that it was a genuine druidic prophecy, and may have borrowed some uncomplimentary descriptions which he had heard from pagans in order to make it more convincing. Yet the point of the poem is to prove the inevitable triumph of Patrick, as is clear from the remarks of Muirchú. It must have worked as a strong argument against paganism – albeit not quite an honest one – for how could a pagan counter such a prophecy if he were convinced that it was made by his own druids?

That such a method of arguing the supremacy of the Christian faith continued in use for some time is indicated by other sources. For instance, a stone-cross at Drumhallagh in Co. Donegal has a carving, which dates to the 8th century, of two duplicated figures. One of the figures is of a bishop holding a crozier, and underneath him is the figure of a man in sitting posture and with his thumb in his mouth.[62] The lower figure calls to mind the lore concerning Fionn, the great warrior and prophet to whom all was revealed through the sucking or biting of his thumb. We have cited aspects of the Fionn-lore which indicate that he was of symbolic importance to the druids (Chapter 4), and the carvings on the Drumhallagh stone can therefore be interpreted as the great seer Fionn foretelling the coming and the triumph of St Patrick. As if to underline the continuity of this Christian propaganda, a mediaeval text imagines Fionn's friend, Caoilte, as saying the following to Patrick when the saint visited the Rock of Cashel: 'We never had knowledge of heaven until Fionn sat on this rock and put his thumb a hundred times under his tooth of knowledge, so that heaven and earth were illumined for him, as well as the faith of the gilded true God, and your coming to Ireland, o Adze-Head!'[63]

Cultus old and new

Although the coming of Patrick represented a sea-change in ritual practice, it is clear that the promulgators of the new religion in Ireland were anxious to maintain a certain degree of continuity in non-theological matters. This is reflected in the adaptation of Christianity to the existing social order, and its purpose was undoubtedly to guarantee a smooth and, in so far as possible, an unchallenged transition. Such a policy can be deciphered behind the narratives concerning Patrick's triumph at Tara, which in pre-Christian culture was the most sacred place in Ireland. In referring to the contest between the saint and Lochlethanu, which culminated in the death of the latter at the druid's stone,

Tíreachán reports that the stone was 'in the southeastern parts of Tara, and I have seen it with my own eyes'. To judge from this, there was already by the 7th century an established tradition that Patrick had visited Tara. It is quite conceivable that he did indeed do so, but how he fared there in reality is a fact lost to history.

Patrick, in his *Confessio*, alludes to 'the twelve perils in which my life was at stake, in addition to many plots against me', and furthermore to how he 'endured insults from unbelievers' and was 'taunted for being a foreigner'. He also says that his followers were persecuted and reproached by their families, that the slave-girls who followed him suffered most, and that he himself was held for a while against his will.[64] Nevertheless, he managed to convert 'many thousands of people' and travelled on his mission 'even to the remotest parts'.[65] In order to facilitate his work, he made payments 'to those who wielded authority throughout the districts I more frequently visited'.[66] That he met with increasing success is suggested by his reference to 'sons of the Irish and daughters of their kings' who adopted the clerical life.[67]

As his mission progressed, therefore, opposition seems to have waned, but we have no means of ascertaining exactly what areas had been the focus of his work at different times. The indications are that he was initially more involved with the Ulaidh kingship in the Armagh area.[68] This kingship was overthrown around the middle of the 5th century AD, which also seems to have been the period of the death of the great Tara king Niall. That king was succeeded by his son Laoghaire, and in his time the sphere of influence of Tara extended, not just throughout the north midlands, but into much of Ulster as well. Laoghaire's obit is given as 461 AD and, if Patrick did really make a missionary visit to Tara, it would very likely be towards the end of his reign. He may have gained some influence there, for there was an early tradition that Laoghaire's brother Conall Gulban adopted the new faith[69] and, whether this be true or not, Tíreachán felt confident enough of Christian influence on Tara to reckon two of Laoghaire's own daughters among Patrick's 'daughters of their kings'.[70]

Muirchú's claim that Laoghaire himself was converted after being overwhelmed by Patrick's miraculous power[71] is hardly tenable. Tíreachán is doubtless more accurate in stating that he remained a pagan till death, though he qualifies this by suggesting that he persisted in his paganism only because his father Niall had enjoined it on him.[72] It could well be that Christianity was beginning to have an influence on the policy of Tara during Laoghaire's reign, for within a few decades his successors would be, nominally at least, Christians. Within this period, closely following on the deaths of both Laoghaire and Patrick, a corpus of lore would have been forming which projected glory onto the memory of the indomitable saint within the context of Ireland's most celebrated place. Although describing Patrick as overcoming the druids in a test of supernatural power at Tara, Tíreachán is otherwise quite restrained in his account, and may be near to giving a picture of the actual historical situation when he states that Patrick made a pact with Laoghaire 'that he should not be killed within his realm'.[73]

Muirchú greatly dramatises the situation, claiming that Patrick, through his prayer, worked stupendous miracles on both the king's company and the environment, causing great terror and consternation to the pagans. Leaving the Biblical and other miraculous borrowings aside, the special detail of this situation is striking. Tíreachán – as we have mentioned – heard traditions that the saint had been at Tara and in its vicinity, and he refers to the fire lit at Easter by him at the ancient burial-place at Slane, and to candles given by him to Bishop Kannanus 'so as to kindle the incense into the eyes and nostrils of king Laoghaire and his druids'.[74] Muirchú, probably quite unhistorically, claims that this was Patrick's first Easter in Ireland, but the description given of the pagan ritual is of interest. 'A feast of pagan worship was being held, which the pagans used to celebrate with many incantations and magic rites', and the chieftains, druids, and representatives of all the arts and skills were assembled with the king. On seeing Patrick's fire, Laoghaire with his followers rushes forth for the first of his great confrontations with the saint. Significantly, Laoghaire brings with him his two leading druids and 'thrice nine chariots . . . according to the tradition which they had received from their gods'. On arrival, however, the king is advised by the druids not to enter the perimeter of the place illumined by the fire, but to order Patrick to come out to meet him 'lest perhaps you afterwards adore him who lit it'.

The terms of reference are clear here – the author is using the rites and tabus of Tara as his theme, and showing how Patrick is the triumphant one in that context. A stranger has come to Tara on a solemn occasion and is to become the true ruler there. In other words, Patrick is the new champion, the new Lugh or Conaire or Cormac, except that he is infinitely more authentic than they, for he represents the triumph of the true God of heaven and earth. As well as from the Christian culture, therefore, some imagery has been borrowed from the pre-Christian culture. The sequel in Muirchú's account brings this out clearly for, having confounded the pagans, Patrick and his nine companions disappear in the form of deer.[75] This is an example of the druid-trick called *féth fiadha*, which we have discussed in Chapter 4, but which is here represented as performed by the Christian saint.

The use of tradition
As one would expect, the Christian missionaries strongly opposed the practice of rituals which they understood to be incompatible with their own ideology. We have seen how Patrick himself alluded to one such ritual which he found demeaning and to which, at his own peril, he refused to submit. In time, the Christians extended their objections to substantial parts of the social order. Within a few generations, church ordinances were forbidding clerics to appeal to secular judges and, significantly, condemning the Christian who 'swears before a seer like the pagans'.[76] Any recognition of spiritual power or spiritual authority outside of the Christian domain was thus being contested, but this did not rule out a *modus vivendi* with non-spiritual aspects of culture. So long as such aspects did not contradict Christian beliefs and morals, they were accepted.

This situation is exemplified by the early biographers of Patrick who state that, on the arrival of the saint at Tara, a leading poet called Dubhthach maccu Lughair was the only one to extend a welcome to him there.[77] We read that this Dubhthach accepted Christianity, and a later account states that the saint blessed his mouth and that as a result the blessings of the Holy

Ghost were in his words.[78] This encounter of Patrick and Dub-hthach can hardly be taken as historical, but it illustrates a tendency in early Irish Christianity to reject the magical side of druidry and to accept those elements of it which were confined to rhetoric and poetry. This critical process is exemplified in an Old Irish glossary which – in discussing the rites by which seer-poets were inspired (see Chapter 3) – claims that Patrick forbade the practice of *imbas forosnaí* and *teinm laída* because these were rites involving the convocation of idol deities, but allowed the practice of *díchetal do chennaibh* because it entailed natural and genuine knowledge (*soas*).[79]

Such a policy had repercussions on a wide level, including the cult of the saints themselves. Popular practice and belief was allowed to persist, and even was lauded, so long as it was not seen to transgress Christian theology. The most interesting example of this tolerance is the tradition concerning the celebrated St Brighid (in Old Irish *Brigit*) who died in or about the year 524 AD. We know little about the actual woman herself, except that she belonged to a branch of the Fotharta, a sept subject to the Leinstermen, and was the abbess of a convent in Kildare. The most likely theory is that – in those times when the new religion was still a minority one – she Christianised a pagan sanctuary located near an oak tree, thus giving rising to the placename *Cill Dara* ('the oak-cell').

It is difficult to say whether or not her own personal name was Brighid, but the fact that she shared the name with an ancient goddess (see Chapter 4) was to prove very important in the development of her cult. If she did indeed Christianise a pagan sanctuary, it may be that *Brigit* (literally 'the exalted one') was in fact a title given to the leading lady there. That her cult from an early date took on the nurturing aspect of a mother-goddess is clear from the tribute paid to her in the very earliest reference which we have. In that reference, from about the year 600, 'the truly pious Brigeoit' is described as 'another Mary'.[80] This is the nearest that a Christian writer could go to assigning divine status to her, and indeed *Muire na nGael* ('the Mary of the Irish') has always been a popular title for her in Irish tradition.

The biography of Brighid, in Latin, entitled *Vita Brigitae*, dates
from in or about the year 650. It was assembled by a monk at Kildare who called himself 'Cogitosus', and whose real name is
thought to have been Toimtenach.[81] It is very much a Christian
document, and for the miracles attributed to the saint it makes
use of several motifs which occur in Continental hagiography.
Traces of the cult of the Celtic goddess can be deciphered in parts
of the text, however, especially when the author describes her ability to multiply such things as butter, bacon, and milk, to bestow
sheep and cattle miraculously, and to control the weather. It is no
accident that the first day of Spring came to be assigned to St
Brighid as her feast-day. This day was originally known as *oimelg*,
which in primitive Irish meant 'lactation'. It is thus apparent that
this Christian saint took on the functions of the mother-goddess
who guaranteed agricultural prosperity, functions which remain
hers in the traditional culture of all Ireland to the present day.[82]

The earliest biography of St Brighid states that she spent her
youth engaged in agricultural labour, such as shepherding flocks,
churning butter, and tending to the harvest. Other biographical
accounts of her in both Latin and Irish from the 7th to the 9th
centuries contain several extra details of interest. In these we read
that her mother Broicseach was a slave who was made pregnant
by her master, who then sold her to a druid. The child Brighid
was thus born and reared within the druid's household.[83] There
may well be an historical basis to this, for an acquaintance with
druidry would have been important to a person who later undertook to Christianise a pagan sanctuary.

One account has the druid recognising from the noise of a
chariot in which Broicseach was being conveyed that she was
carrying a marvellous child in her womb. It further states that
Brighid was born as her mother was bringing milk into the
druid's house at sunrise – Broicseach had one foot 'neither within
nor without the house' when she gave birth.[84] These motifs recall
the tradition of sacral kingship (see Chapter 6) and seem to be
vestiges of druidic lore. Since it suited the druids to concern
themselves with good fortune emanating from the symbolic marriage of kings with the goddess of prosperity, it is understandable
that such vestiges would be found in this context. It should also

be stated that there is continuity between the 'the dew of a goddess' (*druchtu déa*)[85] as a symbol of agricultural wealth in the
early literature and the surviving folk custom of leaving a piece
of cloth outdoors on St Brighid's Night in order to gather the
moisture which brought good fortune to a household.[86]

The third great saint of early Irish Christianity, Columba
(known in Irish as Colm Cille), represented in his very person the
final union of formal native tradition with the new religion. Born
around the year 521 in north Donegal, he was a member of the
leading Irish sept of his time and was in fact a great-grandson of
Conall Gulban, brother of Laoghaire and son of Niall. Columba
founded many monasteries, including those at Derry, Durrow,
and Kells, before he went to the island of Iona off the west coast
of Scotland, from where he undertook his very influential mission to the Picts and the Irish settlers in Scotland. He died at his
monastery in Iona in 597. Between the years 688 and 692 one of
his successors as abbot there – who was in fact a kinsman of his
– Adhamhnán, collected the memories of him into the biography
in Latin entitled *Vita Columbae*.[87]

Notwithstanding his natural tendency to support the political,
and sometimes even military, interests of his aristocratic relatives,
Columba was a Christian monk through and through, and had
little tolerance of paganism. And indeed his biography shows
that paganism was becoming completely redundant in his time.
The many instances of clairvoyance, prophecy, and miracles
attributed to him show that whatever supernatural functions
were required from druids could now be exercised in a fully
Christian context by the leading holy men. Columba was reputed
to be able to produce food miraculously, to control the weather
at sea, and to emulate and exceed the wisdom of the druids by
seeing 'many secrets hidden since the beginning of the world'.[88]
To him, as to many other early missionaries, paganism was a disease which blighted the environment and made it dangerous. In
what is believed to be a genuine composition of his, the long
Latin poem *Altus Prosator*, he borrowed imagery from the Apoc-
alypse of John to warn against paganism as a 'great horrible
frightening dragon' which dwells in the depths of land and sea.[89]
By the time that Adhamhnán wrote his biography, this reference

had developed into a story of how Columba banished a great water-monster into Lough Ness,[90] thus giving rise to one of the most enduring local legends in the world.[91]

Although not directly engaging in maledictive rhetorics like the druids, Columba is stated in the biography to have made several prophecies of disaster concerning people of whose actions he disapproved. Perhaps the most striking instance of this is the case of Aodh Dubh, a noble of the Dál nAraidhe sept of the Antrim and Down area. This Aodh had been 'a slayer of many men', but had come to Iona and, unknown to Columba, was ordained a priest there. Among those whom Aodh had killed was the high-king of Ireland, Diarmaid mac Ceirrbheoil, a kinsman of Columba. When the saint heard of the ordination he was very angry, and prophesied that Aodh would return to his former life as a murderer and 'at last, pierced by a spear, will fall from wood into water, and die by drowning'. This prophecy proved to be true. Aodh Dubh afterwards returned to his warrior-life, and was treacherously speared while on the prow of a ship, causing him to fall into the water and be drowned.[92]

The annal entries show that king Diarmaid was slain by Aodh Dubh in the year 565, and that Aodh himself was slain in 588.[93] Both events, therefore, took place while Columba was abbot of Iona, and it is quite credible that he would be displeased at the acceptance into his monastery of his kinsman's assassin. It is therefore understandable that the dramatic circumstances of Aodh's death would suggest the notion that Columba had prophesied it, and we can distinguish the general lines along which that notion developed. The motif of a duplicated or triplicated death was current in folklore, the purpose of it being to illustrate a destiny which could not be avoided.[94] It thus was a suitable motif for a prophecy, and would have become embedded in the lore concerning Columba's reactions to these events. It is apparent that this account was an addition made by Adhamhnán to his text in the year 695[95] and, if so, he is likely to have first heard of the supposed prophecy at that time.

Tradition in this case provides a good illustration of how dramatised lore can gain a currency of its own, for in time these same circumstances came to be applied to the death of king

Diarmaid mac Ceirrbheoil himself. The mediaeval literature claims that Diarmaid was cursed by St Ciarán of Clonmacnoise, and that this curse was fulfilled when he made a tryst with a woman at a rath in Co. Antrim. Diarmaid was run through by the spear of Aodh Dubh, the rath was simultaneously set on fire, and the king died after scrambling into a vat of ale to avoid the flames. Diarmaid was a benefactor of St Ciarán, and indeed the misdeed which reputedly caused him to be cursed by that saint was an ill-judged attempt to procure an ecclesiastical site. By slaying the previous occupier of the land at Clonmacnoise, the king had created a particularly embarrassing situation for St Ciarán.[96] This tradition illustrates the rather ambiguous position of Diarmaid himself. Although nominally a Christian and a close acquaintance of several saints, he is nevertheless portrayed by the literature as keeping druids and soothsayers in his entourage.[97] Fifteen years into his reign, he felt secure enough to celebrate the inauguration rite called the *feis* of Tara in the year 560 – for the last time in history.[98]

This sense of an ending cast its shadow forwards onto subsequent tradition. With Diarmaid the official pagan lore of Tara finally died, and so it was natural that he would in time be regarded as having been deposed by a Christian saint. Such indeed is the focus of a very dramatic tradition concerning St Ruadhán (of Lorrha in Co. Tipperary), according to which that saint was responsible for the desertion of the great stronghold. Ruadhán died in or around the year 584, but Tara was not abandoned as a royal dwelling until several generations after his time. The story that he had caused this is therefore unhistorical, but it may be based on some actual dispute over a hostage between the saint and his famous contemporary.[99] According to the story, Ruadhán gave sanctuary to a man who had slain an overbearing tax-collector in the king's employ, but Diarmaid seized the man in violation of the sanctuary. Ruadhán thereupon went to Tara and fasted against the king there. Diarmaid was slow to relent, and Ruadhán placed a curse on both him and Tara. The two men were reconciled, but the curse – having been put – could not be avoided. Thus further was explained the misfortune of Diarmaid, as well as the desertion of the prestigious centre.[100]

The practice of fasting would have been no stranger to a Christian saint like Ruadhán, but he would have undertaken it for penitential reasons. In this story, however, the purpose is quite different – it is to compel a powerful man to submit to the will of a faster, and this perspective comes from a much older source in Ireland. This is the ritual fast against a person in order to obtain satisfaction from him. Such a fast must be justified, in which regard it is on a par with other rituals of constraint, such as the use of satire (see Chapter 3). The early mediaeval laws mention fasting against nobles, clerics, and poets and make it clear that 'one who does not give a pledge in response to fasting is an evader of all things'. The major stress is on a creditor fasting against a debtor, and this must be very ancient, as it is referred to also in Sanskrit literature. It is most likely that the practice of fasting as a ritual way of demanding one's rights was Indo-European in origin.[101] It is significant that – in the story of the desertion of Tara – such an archaic means of constraint has coalesced with a devout Christian practice, and that when the Christian personality triumphs, he does so only by means of such a long-established pre-Christian rite.[102]

The connection between native ideas and Christian culture is, however, often more difficult to decipher. A case in point also concerns fasting, but in a different context – that of funereal custom. In a heroic text from the 9th century, after the tragic death of a fictional young warrior 'his cry of lament and his grave and his headstone were completed, and for three days after that no calves were let to their cows by the Ulstermen'.[103] Such a rite, which entailed the sounds of lamentation being heard throughout the countryside as the hungry calves bawled out, is mentioned in a later source also,[104] but it parallels an account in the Book of Jonah so closely that it appears to have been a literary borrowing from the Bible.[105]

The druidic image dissected

There is every reason to consider that Diarmaid mac Ceirrbheoil was the last semi-pagan king of any real importance in Ireland. The most celebrated of his soothsayers was one Beag mac Deadha, who is recorded as having died in the year 553. In line with the general tendency to have pagan prophets foretell the triumph of Christian saints, this Beag is reputed in the literature to have prophesied the successes of Sts Ciarán, Brendan, and Columba. His name Beag means 'small', by which we may consider that he was diminutive in size – perhaps he was a dwarf, and if so his unusual physical appearance would have added to the mystique which accompanied his sayings. His patronymic connects him with some branch of the far-flung Deadh sept, but in time the literature tended to misinterpret this as Dé, the genitive of Dia ('God'). Such a propitious designation of Beag as a 'son of God' would naturally bring him into the ambit of Christian imagery. Writers many centuries after his time, in fact, even claimed that Beag himself was a Christian saint.[106]

The rapprochement reached between Irish Christianity and the less druidic aspects of seer-poetry is historically manifest in the very existence of the literature itself. Writing was introduced into Ireland by the Christian clergy, and much of the ancient mythological tradition was committed to the parchment within the monasteries. This rapprochement had begun as early as the 6th century, and the earliest clear example of it is furnished by the long poem composed in Irish in praise of St Columba by the poet Dallán Forgaill. The poem was entitled the *Amhra* ('marvel'), and tradition has it that Dallán had begun the composition of it before the death of the saint, but had been asked by the humble Columba to postpone it until after his death.[107] Columba himself has long been regarded as especially partial to the poets, and it is not surprising to find that Adhamhnán ascribes powers of clairvoyance to him of a similar nature to those attributed to druids. Indeed, one early mediaeval text has Columba, just like the seer-poets discussed in Chapter 3, interpreting the voice of the sea. His colleague St Cainneach asks him 'what does the wave chant?', and Columba answers 'your community was in danger out at sea, and one of them perished!'[108]

All improvisations, whether positive or negative, in the portrayal of druidic traditions were intended solely for the promotion of Christianity. The clearest illustration of how the druidic image was transformed by the writers with a negative intent is furnished by the lore concerning a druid called Mogh Ruith. It is probable that the name of this personage was a survival of that of an ancestor figure of the Rothraighe, a sept in east Munster.[109] At some stage his name came to be associated with solar symbolism. This must have been due to antiquarian speculation, which took the name to mean 'servant of the wheel'. It was accordingly claimed that Mogh Ruith had a wondrous instrument known as a *roth rámhach* ('oared wheel').[110]

The idea of such an instrument would be suggested by the survival of prehistoric solar symbols engraved on stone. One such stone, at Cleghile near Tipperary town, was even said to be a remnant of the great wheel of Mogh Ruith. It was known as the Roth Fáil ('wheel of enclosure', i.e., circular or sacred wheel),[111] which designation calls to mind the sacred stone known as the Lia Fáil at Tara (Chapter 6). We read of this stone at Cleghile that 'everyone who saw it was blinded, everyone who heard it was deafened, and everyone who struck it was dead'.[112] It is not, therefore, surprising that other débris from ancient solar beliefs became attached to him. It was claimed, for instance, that he had lost one eye,[113] which circumstance aligns him with the several other mythical characters who have solar associations. One mediaeval pen-portrait has him travelling in a lustrous chariot which made the night seem as bright as the day.[114] In general, the Mogh Ruith tradition came to bear witness to the genesis in sun-worship of so much Irish lore, and to the lingering notions that supernatural power was secluded in stone.

How Mogh Ruith was transformed from a quasi-mythical ancestor figure into a druid is an intriguing question. Lore of his wheel at Cleghile stretches back to a very early period, but the earliest literature has no mention of him as an actual druid. The probable reason for the latter function being attributed to him was speculation by scholars schooled in Latin. From the 8th or 9th century his name was being misinterpreted as the Latin *magus rotarum*, literally 'magician of the wheels', with the claim that 'it is by wheels that he used to make his druidic divinations'.[115] The false identification here of *mugh* (from Celtic **magus*, meaning 'servant' or 'slave') with the Latin word *magus* ('magician') had a further result – by way of name-attraction – in the extraordinary fiction that Mogh Ruith had learned his magic from the charlatan of Christian tradition Simon Magus. Mogh Ruith was then further denigrated by the claim that he had entered the service of King Herod and had been the executioner of John the Baptist.[116]

The fact that Mogh Ruith is listed in the genealogy of several septs indicates an attempt to disparage these septs by including such a disreputable character among them.[117] A case in point is Fir Mhaighe Féine, who inhabited an area of central Munster, with Eoghanacht septs belonging to the royal Munster dynasty on either side of them. One genealogical entry states that the ancestors of these two royal septs, Maine Muinchaoin and Dáire Cearba, were brothers, but that their mother had a vision before their birth to the effect that in her womb there was 'a beetle between them, Mugh Ruith the druid, so that neither of them could help the other'.[118]

Continuity in practice

Although the general situation in Irish Christian literature is to have the saints perform standard Christian miracles and to triumph easily over the druids,[119] some motifs of saintly prowess can be interpreted ambiguously. The Venerable Bede, for instance, commented in the 7th century on the vindictiveness of Irish clerics[120] and, if the biographies are to be credited, the holy men of Ireland had indeed a predilection for cursing their foes.[121] This must be influenced by the very strong native idea that seer-poets could use their satires to great physical effect.[122] Things so basic to social structures as the definition of values do not die easily, and the idea that the poet has magical powers has survived in Ireland almost down to our own time.[123]

Some motifs in the biographies of Irish saints can also be connected to druidic imagery. Several accounts in the hagiography echo the old druidic art of magical concealment, the *féth fiadha*. We read, for instance, that a person who invoked the name of St Kevin could become invisible, that the tunic of St Fintan Munnu could equally render its wearer invisible, and that the cowl of Columba guaranteed protection from weapons to its wearer.[124] We further read that St Maodhóg of Ferns protected the local cattle-herd from invaders by making the Sign of the Cross with his crozier or by drawing a line with it on the ground around them.[125] This is strongly redolent of the power anciently attributed to druids to stop armies in their tracks or to erect a protective barrier of magic.

The issue of designating a particular space as sacred is, of course, in religious terms an all-pervading one.[126] It springs from psychological factors within the human person, and as such can be applied in any imaginative context. We have noted the megalithic alignments of stones, the Bronze Age stone-circles and henges, and the circular enclosures of the Iron Age; and there can be no doubt but that all these served sacred functions of their own. Similarly, the circumambulation of areas would have been intended at all stages to set such areas apart, whether for secular or religious purposes – or, as is most likely, for both purposes at once.[127]

The importance attributed to moving in the same direction as the sun, and the concomitant belief that the right hand is propitious, have been alluded to in previous Chapters. This must arise from the position of facing the rising sun, in which stance the right hand is towards the south, where the sun shines. Contrariwise, the left hand and the northerly direction were regarded as suspect. A similar way of dividing good and bad fortune is, indeed, evidenced by many Indo-European languages,[128] and in Irish the word *deas* and its derivatives are used in the senses of both 'south' and 'fortunate', whereas the word *tuath-* and its derivatives are used to mean both 'north' and 'dangerous'.[129] Such a distinction is clear from many Irish sources, including the heroic literature, where the turning of a war-chariot in a circle to the right is done to bring good fortune to a campaign, whereas a turning to its left side is a threat of imminent danger to opponents.[130] In an allegorical story concerning the 6th-century poet and antiquarian Seanchán Toirpéist, the spirit of poetry assists Seanchán and his students in composition and then turns right-handwise around them before disappearing.[131] Elsewhere the literature refers to passing to the right around a rock for good fortune, and turning to the right in order to find a lost valuable.[132] This was regarded as constructive magic, but the word for 'left' was used to denote sorcery and more destructive magical acts,[133] and there are several references in the old literature to the dangerous power of an individual with a blind left eye.[134]

The Christian culture in Ireland concurred with such imagery, principally due to the fact that one faced east also towards the Holy Land and, more coincidentally, due to Biblical references such 'the right hand of God'[135] and 'the sheep on His right hand and the goats on His left'.[136] It is not surprising, then, to find an 8th-century Irish source referring in the following way to the Crucifixion and to the soldier Longinus piercing Christ with a lance: 'Westwards was Christ's face on the Cross, and eastwards was the face of Longinus – what to him was the left to Christ was the right.'[137] That such ideas were strong in Irish religious lore – at least at the popular level – is clear from several references in the mediaeval literature. Some of these express the age-old folk view of magic, that the ritual itself is neither bad nor good, but that the morality depends on the purpose of its use. Thus, we find a mediaeval text (admittedly late in date), stating that St Maodhóg of Ferns was angered against two men and that as a method of cursing them 'he turned his sandals and enduring relics around them three times left-handwise'.[138]

This view of the saints was general. An account of St Findchua of Brí Ghobhann (Mitchelstown in Co. Cork), has him assisting a Munster army in the following way against the forces of an Ulster king: 'Findchua goes in the van of that battle-force, with the *Ceannchathach* – that is, his crozier – in his hand; and he strengthens the counsel and heartens the force, and comes three times right-handwise around the host, with his crozier in his hand.'[139] The name of the saint's crozier in that reference means literally 'the head-battler', and it is interesting to note that – at the other end of the country – a relic of St Columba with a similar name was used in battle by the Cineál Chonaill (O'Donnells of Donegal). This was the *Cathach* ('battler'), a manuscript copy of the psalms, which may have originally been written by the saint himself. One account says that, before a battle, the Cineál Chonaill used to have this relic carried three times in a right-handed direction around their army.[140]

The most enduring folk belief concerning such practices is that a person can be cursed by turning a stone in the left-hand direction 'against them'. This belief has remained strong until recently in the north and west of Ireland, and is also mentioned in the later lives of the saints.[141] It may have been influenced by popular interpretations of Biblical lore, such as the accounts of Elijah erecting an altar of stones and calling down fire to destroy an enemy,[142] but in all likelihood the basic ritual action was in existence from antiquity. 'Every left-hand turn is bad' states an old glossary,[143] but another glossary exhibits a Christian development of the idea when it refers to the need for protection from 'the pagans who turn left-hand, the *sidhaighi*.'[144] This latter term originally meant 'mound-dwellers' but had come to signify the fairies, and the literary tradition identified the fairies with the Celtic deities, the Tuatha Dé, who it was said had gone to live 'in the hills and tumuli' of Ireland.[145] These Tuatha Dé were usually portrayed by the mediaeval Christian writers as an ancient race who once inhabited Ireland, but some strands of Christian thought remained uneasy with the lore and chose to look upon the ancient spirit-people in a negative way.

Ambiguity towards the Tuatha Dé is shown by a mediaeval writer, who on the one hand calls them 'demons', but on the other hand cannot refrain from describing the genuine tradition. He states that they 'used to fight with men in bodily form, and used to show delights and mysteries to them, and people believed that they were immortal'.[146] As we have seen, the left-hand and the north were united in archaic symbolism, and it is therefore not surprising that the sunless and mysterious northern regions of the world were associated with magic. The mediaeval writers picked up on this, describing how the Tuatha Dé, before coming to Ireland 'in dark clouds', sojourned in northern islands 'learning druidry and wisdom and prophecy and sorcery, so that they became skilled in the pagan arts of wizardry'.[147] This was another attempt to demonise the old gods, who – as we have seen – in ancient Irish belief were often associated with water and with otherworld regions far out in the sea. Perhaps such a negative way of portraying the pre-Christian deities was the origin also of the curious Irish belief that hell is cold and wet,[148] although this notion may owe something to climatic considerations!

One mediaeval text portrays walking right-handed around a
cemetery as a salutary gesture,[149] and it is interesting to note the
survival of this into modern times in popular Irish religion, for it
is still customary in some places to parade right-handed around
a cemetery before interring a corpse. More widespread is the custom of making rounds in a right-handed direction while reciting
prayers at a holy well.[150] This tradition of holy wells is yet
another case in point when one tries to distinguish between pre-
Christian and Christian traditions. All holy wells in post-
mediaeval Ireland have a Christian significance, and most have
actual named patrons, so that resort to a well is primarily done
on the feast-day of the particular saint.[151] The significance of a
convenient water-supply for baptism was very real to the early
missionaries, and thus the holy well tradition has a specifically
Christian orientation.

Nevertheless, there is evidence from early Celtic culture for
sacred springs and for the healing cults of gods and goddesses in
association with them. An instance is actually cited in Tíreachán's
7th-century biography of St Patrick, where the well of Slán, in the
west of Ireland, is described. 'The druids honoured the well and
offered gifts to it as to a god' and it was referred to as 'the king
of the waters'. Tíreachán explains that this well was covered with
a square stone and that it was believed that 'some wise man had
made a shrine in the water under the stone to bleach his bones per-
petually'. Patrick denied that such a man was under the stone,
claiming instead that nothing was there except 'some gold and
silver from your wicked sacrifices'.[152] This is a clear reference to
the veneration among the pre-Christian Irish of a god within water,
and to the deposition of valuables in order to propitiate him.

There are other, but more obscure, references in the literature
to burials at wells,[153] and the motif – common in traditional Irish
storytelling – of a *gruagach* or wizard who resides in a well is no
doubt another survival of such beliefs. The idea that a deity or
divine hero was living on in the world of the dead underneath the
well is evidenced in an onomastic poem of the 10th or 11th century, which alludes to a natural well which 'is above the bed of
the warrior Lughaidh'. 'Virtues and strong taboos' attached to
this well, and these are explained as freedom from disease for a

person who walks around it to the right but failing health and
death before long for one who does so to the left.[154]

This well is in the area of Sliabh Riabhach, in southeast Co.
Limerick, and the hero in question was Lughaidh Loíghde, a
mythical ancestor of the sept which inhabited that area.[155] It is
interesting to note that the well has traditionally been dedicated
to St Molua, and all its qualities are attributed to that saint.[156]
We read that the original name of this Molua was in fact
Lughaidh,[157] and it is obvious that we are here dealing with the
transference of the well from a pre-Christian to a Christian context. The ancestor deity and original patron, Lughaidh Loíghde,
was an alter-ego of the celebrated Lughaidh mac Con;[158] and the
ultimate origin in the god Lugh of the whole local cultus is further underlined by the actual date of St Molua's pattern, August
3, which brings it neatly into line with the festival of Lughnasa
itself. There may well have been an historical St Molua, but the
culture surrounding him is surely a survival of Iron Age pre-
Christian religion.

Both literature and folklore attest to the importance of wells
and springs in the lore of Irish saints.[159] One belief, which survives strongly in folklore to the present day, is that a supplicant
at a holy well can be assured of his request if he sees a little mystical fish in the water.[160] This belief in the sacred fish in wells can
be traced backwards through the hagiographical literature, and
it may well be a survival of the pre-Christian lore of the salmon
of wisdom in the river Boyne. It is significant that this Boyne
salmon can be connected with the salmon of health, as icono-
graphically represented at the ancient British Celtic temple in
Gloucestershire dedicated to the god Nodons.[161] Similarly, the
presence of trees at holy wells, and the custom of attaching offerings to them,[162] recalls the very archaic and pre-Christian veneration of individual great trees in Ireland.[163] In this context, a link
between the ancient and modern traditions is furnished by the
mediaeval accounts of the wondrous tree of St Ruadhán at Lorrha, the sap of which gave full sustenance to all the monks of the
monastery and to their guests.[164]

More than anything else, the early religious ideas of Ireland
survive in the context of festival lore, and especially in the cases

of the ancient seasonal junctures.[165] Much custom and belief is attached in folk tradition to the 'eve', or night before, such a festival. The tendency to regard such an eve as a sacred time, somehow outside of ordinary time, has not yet quite died out in Ireland; and traditions of ghosts appearing at these times persist, as well as attempts to ensure good luck during the ensuing season.

All four seasonal festivals have to an extent been Christianised. The ancient spring festival of *oímelg* has long been dedicated to St Brighid, but this appears to be a continuation of the cult of her pagan namesake. The *Bealtaine* (May) festival has more recently been connected with the Virgin Mary, though this has not transformed either its celebration of the coming of summer with flowers and greenery, or the symbolic practices to promote agricultural prosperity. Since mediaeval times, the harvest festival of *Lughnasa* has been portrayed as the occasion of Patrick's victory over paganism, but the hill-climbing, games, and other celebrations associated with it are in direct continuity with ancient rites. The festival of the dead, *Samhain*, at the beginning of winter, retains much of its old sombre but imaginative atmosphere, although the Feast of All Souls two days later has in recent centuries tended to submerge it. Yet the outstanding fact remains that in Irish popular tradition these four festivals have a corpus of custom and lore attached to them which is rivalled only by the two leading church festivals of Christmas and Easter.

Notes

Chapter 1

1 Herity/Eogan (1977), 16–24; Harbison (1988), 16–26; O'Kelly (1989), 13–38; P C Woodman in Ryan (1991), 38–41.
2 Herity/Eogan (1977), 24–56; Harbison (1988), 27–41; A Sheridan in Ryan (1991), 47–52.
3 Cooney/Grogan (1994), 17, 19, 37.
4 *ibid.*, 12–24.
5 See, for instance, James (1962) for an analysis of religions in the ancient Near East and Eastern Mediterranean areas.
6 See the many examples and sources cited by Campbell (1983).
7 See Maringer (1960).
8 A discussion of the various interpretations is in Bahn/Vertut (1988).
9 For a critique of Emile Durkheim's theory of social projection, see Evans-Pritchard (1981), 153–69.
10 For anthropological approaches to symbolism, see Firth (1973), 15–53.
11 Harbison (1988), 21.
12 Maringer (1960), 51, 130; James (1961), 277 and in Bleeker/Widengren (1960), 24–5; Brandon (1962), 10–12; Smart (1971), 62–3; Dyer (1990), 19, 28; Briard (1979), 23, 47.
13 For a critique of Frazer's theory of 'sympathetic magic', see Evans-Pritchard (1981), 132–52.
14 See Ó Súilleabháin (1942), 426; Opie/Tatem (1992), 181–2.
15 On the issues of magic, science, and religion in human culture, see Malinowski (1974), 17–92.
16 Instances of such primitive beliefs cited in Tylor (1930), 2, 92–104; Collins (1978), 190–227. For Irish environmental folklore, see Ó hÓgáin (1995), 29–49.
17 Frankfort/Frankfort (1949), 12–14
18 See E O James in Bleeker/Widengren (1969), 34.
19 For the moon as interpreted by ancient cultures, see Kristensen (1960), 77–87, 523; J R Bram in Eliade (1987), *10*, 83–91. For later Irish folklore concerning the moon, see Ó hÓgáin (1995), 32–6.
20 See Cooney/Grogan (1994), 28–33.
21 For such a tendency in human thought, see Eliade (1957), 42–7.
22 See Cooney/Grogan (1994), 18– 22, 50–2.
23 Herity/Eogan (1977), 24–7; Harbison (1988), 27–32; O'Kelly (1989), 35–7.
24 Herity/Eogan (1977), 27–36; O'Kelly (1989), 85–92.
25 Maringer (1960), 159–88; Mohen (1990); Hutton (1991), 21–2.
26 Childe (1940), 46–80 and (1958), 124–34.
27 Herity/Eogan (1977), 85–90; Harbison (1958), 52–6; O'Kelly (1989), 92–7.

28   For distribution maps of court-cairns, portal chambers, and passage-graves respectively, see O'Kelly (1989), 86, 93, 98.
29   O'Kelly (1982) and (1989), 97–115; Eogan (1986); Herity/Eogan (1977), 57–79.
30   O'Kelly (1982), 140; Eogan (1986), 134.
31   Herity (1974), 132; Eogan (1986), 136–40.
32   See Bergh (1995), 151–162.
33   Mohen (1990), 216–19.
34   Eogan (1986), 114–15, 216–224; O'Kelly (1989), 122–4. For an analysis of how different cultural and social groupings tend to regard and relate to each other, see Bromley (1984); Renfrew (1987).
35   McMann (1993), 43.
36   O'Sullivan (1993), 33.
37   *ibid.*, 10–12, 33; Mohen (1990), 244–53, 269.
38   Eogan (1986), 178.
39   This phenomenon seems to have been noted in the folklore of the area before archaeologists began to investigate it – see O'Kelly (1971), 92–5.
40   O'Kelly (1982), 137–40. See also Hutton (1991), 59–60.
41   See Herity/Eogan (1977), 178–9.
42   See O'Kelly (1971), 68; T Condit in *Archaeology Ireland* 4/1993, 15.
43   For quartz and its spiritual associations in primitive cultures, see Eliade (1964), 47, 50–2, 125, 137–9, 339, 350, 599–600.
44   See G Cooney in *Archaeology Ireland*, 2/1989, 52–3.
45   See O'Kelly (1989), 124.
46   See Eogan (1986), 184–5.
47   Eogan (1986), 181–5.
48   M O'Sullivan in 'Brú na Bóinne' (supplement to *Archaeology Ireland* 3/1997), 21.
49   *ibid.* and in *UCD News* 12/1996, 9. See also M O'Sullivan in *JRSAI 123*, 17.
50   Maringer (1960), 181–6; Mohen (1990), 242–5; M O'Sullivan in 'Brú na Bóinne', 20–1.
51   See Bahn/Vertut (1988), 177; Kristensen (1960), 306–9; Eliade (1968), 158–63.
52   The leading academic adherent of this theory was Marija Gimbutas – see her entries on 'Megalithic Religion' and 'Prehistoric Religion' in Eliade (1987), 9, 336–44 and 11, 506–15. For a similar theory of A T Hatto, see Maringer (1956), 176–7; Bailey (1997), 26–8.
53   Eogan (1986), 179.
54   On such beliefs, see Frazer (1940), 294–5; E O James in Bleeker/Widengren (1969), 35–7.
55   M O'Sullivan in 'Brú na Bóinne', 20.
56   Eogan (1986), 146–72; Harbison (1988), 77–81; O'Sullivan (1993), 37–40. The combination of two circles, in such a way as gives the impression of an owl-face, is found in several megalithic carvings abroad, and also occurs on stones in Ireland – see Gelling/Davidson (1969), 106–11; Gimbutas in Eliade (1987), 9, 341–2. It has been suggested that this represents the female regenerative force in bird form, but all that can safely

be claimed is that it was another art motif which was disseminated broadly within the western European megalithic area.

57 Herity/Eogan (1977), 73–6.
58 Maringer (1956), 163–72; Piggott (1965), 48–50; Mohen (1990), 236–65.
59 For a discussion of this art and of its interpretations, see A Fleming in *World Archaeology 1*, 247–61; M O'Sullivan (1993) and in *JRSAI 116*, 68–83.
60 Maringer (1956), 108–14; Gimbutas (1982), 152–210; Bahn/Vertut (1988), 162–70.
61 O'Kelly (1982), 137, 139.
62 See Eliade (1958), 91–3, 124–53, 239–42.
63 See the interesting parallels adduced in Brennan (1980), 15–20.
64 *Ériu 11*, 188–92; *Ériu 12*, 142–7; *ZCP 19*, 53–8. The earliest written form of the name Aonghus was 'Óengus'.
65 Macalister (1941), 234. For other sun-symbolism of the Daghdha, see Chapter 2.
66 *Irische Texte 1*, 132.
67 Van Hamel (1933), 5.
68 See Bergh (1995), 124.
69 *Bibliotheca Historica* 2.47 – see Müllerus (1878), 116–17; Zwicker (1934), 4–5.
70 For Hecataeus and his works, see Pearson (1939), 25–108.
71 Some Classical writers treated of the Hyperboreans as lying far to the west – see Graves (1960), *1*, 80, 239, 281. The pseudo-Scymnus text, from about 100 BC, may also be based on Hecataeus, and here the Celts are in the role of the Hyperboreans – Zwicker (1934), 13.
72 Graves (1960), *1*, 76.
73 Homer, *Iliad* XX.219 – see Rieu (1950), 372.
74 There may have been some confusion in Diodorus' sources between the first element in *Hyperboreis* and *Ivernia*, later *Hibernia* or *Hiberia* (for Ireland). This would weigh against identification of the island with Britain, such as proposed by S Reinach in *Revue Celtique 12*, 163–7 and by Graves (1960), *1*, 80.
75 Herity/Eogan (1977), 27.
76 Mohen (1990), 259–63, 269 – where, however, the author confuses the solstices at Newgrange.
77 Eogan (1986), 43–3, 61, 176; O'Sullivan (1993), 20.
78 See Eogan (1986), 177–95.
79 For an anthropological discussion of these functions, see Firth (1975), 130–54.
80 Cooney/Grogan (1994), 67. For the function of human sacrifice generally, see Girard (1977), 1–38.
81 For an arrowhead in the hip-bone of a man at the portal tomb of Poulnabrone in Co. Clare, see Lynch (1981), 106.
82 See Eliade (1958), 111; H M Chadwick (1932) *1*, 601, 648, 656.
83 Estyn Evans (1942), 30.
84 Ó Súilleabháin (1967), 7–10.
85 This point emerges repeatedly from the over-all surveys, most specifically Cooney/Grogan (1994).

86 For a discussion of stone symbolism in primitive religion, see Eliade (1958), 216–38, 437–40; C-M Edsman in Eliade (1987), *14*, 49–53.

87 See G Cooney in *Archaeology Ireland* 2/1996, 29–30.

88 Wood-Martin (1902), 2, 206–61; Plummer (1910), *1*, cix; Ó Súilleabháin (1942), 21–2, 271–2, 394–5; Peete-Cross (1952), 32, 236, 299, 316, 432; Estyn Evans (1957), 298–302; Grinsell (1976), 54–61.

89 See Tylor (1930), 2, 98; Ó Súilleabháin (1942), 271–2; Ó hÓgáin (1995), 43.

90 References and discussion in Kristensen (1971), 62–77, 529. See also the entry on 'sun' by J R Bram in Eliade (1987), *14*, 132–43.

91 Ó Súilleabháin (1942), 251–2, 265; Ó hÓgáin (1995), 30–2, 88.

92 Maringer (1960), 108–14, 142–5, 155–7; Gimbutas (1974), 152–215.

93 *The World Atlas of Archaeology* (1985), 48–9; James (1962), 46–54; Maringer (1960), 198–200; Hutton (1991), 37–44, 101–3.

94 Raftery (1994), 24; Cooney/Grogan (1994), 155–6.

95 Von Sydow (1948), 192–3, 231–40.

96 See Aarne/Thompson (1961).

97 Thompson (1946), 272–8; Von Sydow (1948), 222–31.

98 Nilsson (1932), 40–3, 136–40, 146; Thompson (1946), 278–81.

99 For references, see Graves (1960), 2, 236–43.

100 Aarne/Thompson (1961), 104–6 (Type 313).

101 Aarne/Thompson (1961), 128–31 (Type 400).

102 Herity/Eogan (1977), 117–19; Harbison (1988), 100–2.

103 Herity/Eogan (1977), 114–23. For the 'beaker' culture in Britain, see Dyer (1990), 84–91.

104 A general discussion of Bronze Age burials in Cooney/Grogan (1994), 105–13, 144–8.

105 Herity/Eogan (1977), 123–32; O'Kelly (1989), 127–36.

106 Herity/Eogan (1977), 123–7; Cooney/Grogan (1994), 88–91.

107 Herity Eogan (1977), 125–6.

108 Chevalier/Gheerbrant (1996), 195–202. For instances of this in Irish literature and lore, see Peete Cross (1952), 179–80.

109 Ó Súilleabháin (1942), 240–2.

110 Herity/Eogan (1977), 117, 121.

111 O'Kelly (1989), 234–7; Hutton (1990), 117–18; S Ó Nualláin in Ryan (1991), 90–1; A Lynch in Ó Corráin (1994), 23–7.

112 Briard (1979), 56, 104; Brunaux (1988), 83.

113 Barrie Hartwell in *Archaeology Ireland* 4/1991, 12–15 and 4/1994, 10–13.

114 Harbison (1988), 93; E Grogan in 'Brú na Bóinne', 31.

115 G Eogan/H Roche in *Archaeology Ireland* 4/1993, 16–18.

116 Ó Ríordáin (1965), 75–80; A Sheridan, J Waddell in Ryan (1991), 50, 84–8; Harbison (1988), 85–6, 102–4.

117 E Grogan in Ryan (1991), 63; Grogan/Eogan (1987), 323–36. For the erection of tombs over earlier inhabited sites – apparently without ritual purpose – in the neolithic, see Cooney/Grogan (1994), 44, 64, 87.

118 For such deliberate antiquity, see Cooney/Grogan (1994), 79, 132.

119 G Cooney in *Archaeology Ireland*, 2/1996, 30.

120 Cooney/Grogan (1994), 67–8, 146–8, 155–6.

121 Maringer (1960), 20, 54, 130–2, 177–8, 190, 197; Brandon (1962), 10–14.
122 See Ó hÓgáin (1995), 12–19.
123 *ibid.*, 19–20
124 References cited in Cross (1952), 281–4 (motifs F541–F558).
125 For instances in shamanic cultures, see Lommel (1967), 39–71; Lowie (1970), 221–58; Eliade (1964), 3–32; Kiev (1964), 75–8, 473.
126 Waddell in Ryan (1991), 87; Cooney/Grogan (1994), 118, 135.
127 Herity/Eogan (1977), 81, 104, 135, 137; Harbison (1988), 103; John Waddell in Ryan (1991), 87. See also Dyer (1990), 85.
128 Maringer (1960), 14, 18, 50; Briard (1979), 14, 56; *World Atlas of Archaeology* (1985), 54.
129 See Smart (1971), 68–9.
130 See, for instance, the Old Testament *Book of Job* 1:21.
131 Herity/Eogan (1977), 149–53. For Bronze Age burial in Ireland generally, see O'Kelly (1989), 189–214; and for urns and their asociation with burial, see R M Kavanagh in *PRIA* 73C, 507–617 and 76C, 293–403.
132 See C Mount in *Archaeology Ireland*, 2/1991, 21–3 and in Waddell/Shee Twohig (1995), 97–112.
133 Cooney/Grogan (1994), 71, 108–10.
134 Van Gennep (1960); E O James in Bleeker/Widengren (1969), 23–4; Coon (1976), 341–76.
135 Examples from Irish folklore in Ó Súilleabháin (1967), 41–55.
136 James (1962), 54–68, 168–99; J R Porter in Davidson/Russell (1981), 215–38, 266–71.
137 For a general discussion of some of these issues, see Orme (1981), 218–54. For attitudes to the dead in other primitive cultures, see Frazer (1920), 238–9 and (1933–1934); M W Beckwith in Fiske (1923), 29–55; Hastings (1908–1926), 4, 411–511; Radin (1957), 219–53; Eliade (1987), 4, 251–9 and 5, 450–9.
138 Ó Súilleabháin (1942), 215–50, and (1967), 47–55.
139 Ó Súilleabháin (1967). For some primitive attitudes to the soul, see Radin (1957), 268–88.
140 This is in Irish tradition the November feast *Samhain*, Christianised as All Souls' Night – for a discussion of its importance in folklore, see Danaher (1972), 200–29.
141 Harbison (1988), 113–53.
142 M Cahill in Ryan (1985), 22–3.
143 *ibid.*, 80; Harbison (1988), 126–7; O'Kelly (1989), 178.
144 Herity/Eogan (1977), 111; G Eogan in Ó Corráin (1981), 147–62 and in Waddell/Shee Twohig (1995), 128–35; Hutton (1991). 103–7.
145 E A Anati in *JCHAS* 68, 1–15; R Bradley in Waddell/Shee Twohig (1995), 90–6.
146 Briard (1979), 26, 106–11, 128–9, 190.
147 For sun worship in the northern European Bronze Age, see Gelling/Davidson (1969), 9–26; Glob (1974), 99–125.
148 Cooney/Grogan (1994), 96–7, 137–42, 158–67, 247.
149 Herity/Eogan (1977), 178–9, 208–10; Eogan (1983); O'Kelly (1989), 184–6; Raftery (1994), 24–5. That there were discoveries of other

deposits, not appearing in the archaeological record, is quite likely. For a possible reflection of a notable mediaeval discovery, see Ronan O'Flaherty in *Archaeology Ireland*, 1/1996, 27–9.

150 Briard (1979), 196–202; Brunaux (1988), 91–5. For the deposition of hoards in general, see Bradley (1990).
151 Herity/Eogan (1977), 46.
152 R Meenan in 'Brú na Bóinne', 23.
153 E C R Armstrong in *JRSAI 47*, 21–36.
154 Eogan (1983), 117–42.
155 E E Evans in *UJA 10*, 59–62.
156 Ó Súilleabháin (1942), 32, 94.
157 See Piggott (1973), 322–3; Harding (1976); Dyer (1990), 116–32.
158 Harbison (1988), 152; Raftery (1994), 18–19, 32–4.
159 Herity/Eogan (1977), 222–3, 227–8; O'Kelly (1989), 309–25; Raftery (1994), 38–63.
160 See E Rynne in *Archaeology Ireland*, Spring 1991, 19–21.
161 O'Kelly (1989), 167–9; Raftery (1994), 26–32.
162 Harbison (1988), 155; Herity/Eogan (1977), 223, 234–8.
163 Raftery (1994), 59.

Chapter 2

1   Powell (1980), 21–2; see Tierney in *PRIA 60 C5*, 193.
2   See O'Rahilly (1946), 40–2, 385–7 and in *Ériu 14*, 7–28. See also J Pokorny in Ua Riain ed. (1940), 237–43. The term *Alba* since mediaeval times is taken to refer only to the northern part of Britain, Scotland.
3   See Rankin (1987), 2–8.
4   Tierney, *op. cit.*, 193.
5   In the poem *Ora Maritima*, written by Avienus in the 4th century AD – see the edition with introduction in Schulten (1922).
6   Powell (1980), 21–2.
7   *ibid.*, 22–4. For Pytheas, see Tierney, *op. cit.*, 195–6
8   In Irish the derivative is 'Cruithin', a term used for a section of the inhabitants of Britain and of Ireland (apparently the Picts) – see O'Rahilly (1946), 341–3, 444–52.
9   See K Jackson in Wainwright (1955), 158. Jackson also (*ibid.*) makes the interesting suggestion that 'Pritani' meant 'the people of the designs' and that the Celts of southern Britain may have borrowed the custom of painting or tattooing from an older indigenous population.
10 See Raftery (1994), 23, 141–6, 224–6
11 Herity/Eogan (1977), 224, 236–7; Raftery (1994), 225–8, 238.
12 For religion in general among the Celtic-speaking peoples, see P Mac Cana in Eliade (1987), 2, 148–66; A Ross, J Webster. M Green, and G A Wait in Green (1995), 423–511; M Green in Ahlqvist (1996), 21–37.
13 On this issue, see C Newman in *Archaeology Ireland*, 3/1993, 20–3.
14 For possible traces of pre-Celtic inhabitants in Ireland, see Mac Néill (1920), 61–82; Eoin Mac White in *ZCP 25*, 1–29.

15 See H Wagner in *ZCP* 42, 5–6.
16 See Childe (1940), 259–61; H Wagner in *ZCP* 42, 4–6; McCone (1996), 67–8 and in *Studia Celtica Japonica* 4, 37–50. For the alternative view, which would regard the Irish language as being derived from a much earlier proto-Celtic, see K H Schmidt in Ball/Fife (1993), 64–98.
17 Herity/Eogan (1977), 234–42; Raftery (1994), 147–77, 196–9.
18 Herity/Eogan (1977), 236–7.
19 Raftery (1984), 328–34.
20 See Brunaux (1988), 89–97.
21 Diodorus V, 27 – see Tierney, *op. cit.*, 249.
22 Strabo IV, 1, 13 – see Tierney, *op. cit.*, 262.
23 *ibid.*
24 Raftery (1994), 183; for Belenus see Green (1992), 30–1.
25 Filip (1977), 169; V Kruta in Moscati ed. (1991), 295.
26 Ross (1967), 87; Raftery (1994), 183.
27 Vouga (1925); Furger-Gunti (1984), 58–70.
28 Orosius V, 16 – see Davidson (1988), 62. For the Cimbri, see also Rankin (1987), 76–8, 125–8, 176–7.
29 Green (1986), 138–45; Dyer (1990), 158–9, Hutton (1991), 184–92, 230–2.
30 Fox (1946).
31 Hutton (1991), 187.
32 *ibid.*, 191–2.
33 Herity/Eogan (1977), 242.
34 Raftery (1994), 183 – see also O'Kelly (1989), 275–80.
35 R B Warner in Scott (1982).
36 Raftery (1994), 184.
37 E C R Armstrong *JRSAI* 53, 22–3.
38 See Mac Cana (1970), 100–1.
39 Diodorus V, 30 – see Tierney, *op. cit.*, 251.
40 See P Holmes in Ryan ed (1979), 165–88; O'Kelly (1989), 171–3; S Ó Duibhir in *Archaeology Ireland* 4/1988, 135–6.
41 See Joyce (1903), *1*, 147–8.
42 Stokes/Strachan (1901), 577.
43 Meid (1974), 9.
44 Raftery (1994), 184; Hutton (1991), 185–7; Powell (1980), 178–9, 182; Filip (1977), 169.
45 Herity/Eogan (1977), 204, 287; Piggott (1968), 67–70; O'Kelly (1989), 170–1.
46 Davidson (1988), 44–7; Green (1986), 141–7.
47 Mac Cana (1970), 10, 26–9, 38–9, 125.
48 See Powell (1980), 178–9.
49 See Raftery (1994), 183–5; Hutton (1991), 187
50 Herity/Eogan (1977), 242–4; O'Kelly (1989), 329–36; Raftery (1994), 189–99
51 Hutton (1991), 197–9, 238.
52 Raftery (1994), 80, 123, 199.
53 Raftery (1994), 195–7.
54 *ibid.*, 199.

55   MacCulloch (1911), 233–45; Davidson (1988), 45–68; Green (1986), 20–1 and (1992), 182–84.
56   Green (1986), 28–9; Dyer (1990), 150, 158; Hutton (1991), 192–6, 231–4, 393.
57   Raftery (1994), 199.
58   Ó Súilleabháin (1942), 483–4, 509–10. See Thompson (1955–1958), Motifs E291, F403.2.3.1.
59   Ó Súilleabháin (1942), 510. See Thompson (1955–1958), Motif E291.1.
60   Ó Súilleabháin (1942), 20.
61   S Ó Súilleabháin in *JRSAI 75*, 45–52.
62   Gwynn (1924), 18–21;
63   *ibid.*, 156–7 – see O'Curry (1873), *1*, dcxl–dcxli.
64   Servius on *Aeneid* III, 57 – see MacCulloch (1911), 234.
65   O'Grady (1892), *1*, 334.
66   Meyer (1912), 42 – see Stokes (1862), 17.
67   R I Best in *Ériu 3*, 149–73.
68   Van Hamel (1932), 52–61.
69   See Krappe (1927), 165–80.
70   Macalister (1940), 122–5.
71   *Y Cymmrodor 14*, 116–20; *Ériu 3*, 140–41. For a fascinating, if speculative, discussion of a preserved body, near Manchester, of a sacrificial victim from the Celtic era, who may have been a druid, see Ross/Robins (1989). For bog-bodies of sacrificial victims in Denmark from the same era, see Glob (1971).
72   Ó Súilleabháin (1942), 59–60, 336–7; Danaher (1972), 109–19, 190–9.
73   Bieler (1979), 132; Stokes (1887), 566–7; *Revue Celtique 13*, 52–3.
74   Stokes (1887), 74, 308, 566.
75   *Ériu 6*, 136–7. For the early origin of this tradition, which involves the king-figures Conaire and Lughaidh mac Con, see Chapter 6.
76   Mulchrone (1971), 33.
77   *Irische Texte 3*, 402–3, 424. See the discussion by G Toner in *Emania 8*, 60–2.
78   Greene (1955), 53.
79   *ibid.*, 54. For Maolodhrán in general, see Ó hÓgáin (1990), 292–3.
80   Cooney/Grogan (1994), 103–5, 131–2, 141.
81   Galfridus Monemutensis, *Historia Regum Britanniae VI*, 14 – see Thorpe (1966), 163.
82   Bromwich (1978), 88.
83   Magnusson/Pálsson (1969), 77–8, 255. See also Plummer (1910), *1*, cix–cx.
84   Williams (1930), 44–7; see Gantz (1976), 79–81.
85   Green (1986), 29–32, 216–20.
86   *ibid.*, 29; Hutton (1991), 194, 233–4.
87   Raftery (1994), 185; *Archaeology Ireland* 3/1993, 22.
88   Diodorus V, 29 – another synopsis of Posidonius' account is in Strabo IV, IV, 5. The custom is also referred to in Polybius III, 67; Livius X, 26 and XXIII, 24; and see Tierney, *op. cit.*, 250, 269; Jackson (1964), 35–7.
89   *de Bello Gallico*, V, 58.

90 For references to this, see Mac Piarais (1908), 5, 36; Jackson (1938), 73; Knott (1936), 45–6; Binchy (1970), 17.
91 *Revue Celtique 14*, 242–3; *Speculum 16*, 323–4.
92 Meyer (1910), 4–17.
93 Meyer (1912), 87–8; see also *Ériu 11*, 48–9, 58–61.
94 ZCP 1, 464–5. See also how the head of Sualdamh, father of the epical hero Cú Chulainn, spoke for a short while after he was decapitated – O'Rahilly (1976), 104.
95 C von Sydow in *Vetenskapssocietetens i Lund årsbok* (1920), 23–5.
96 *Ynglinga Saga* IV – see Davidson (1988), 77–8,
97 Ó Riain (1978), 25–30.
98 For other Irish heads chanting rhetorics, see Meyer (1910), 8; ZCP 20, 401.
99 Pettazzoni (1956), 196–219; Hutton (1991), 194–5 who, however, is doubtful concerning the significance of the heads.
100 Macalister (1956), 32, 112.
101 O'Rahilly (1946), 281–3, 514–15.
102 Williams (1930), 16.
103 *ibid.*, 99–101; P Sims-Williams in Matonis/Melia (1990), 62–3.
104 Ó hÓgáin (1982), 122–5, 168–202, 265–80.
105 See Pettazzoni (1956), 196–219.
106 Lucas (1973), 43–4; Raftery (1994), 185–6.
107 See O'Rahilly (1946), 481–4.
108 *de Bello Gallico* VI, 18 – see Tierney, *op. cit.*, 273. For a discussion of the division of the year among the Gauls, see Brunaux (1988), 45–6, 70.
109 Pettazzoni (1956), 213.
110 See the use of the word for 'night' (*oíche* in Irish, *nos* in Welsh) to indicate the eve of a festival.
111 Pettazzoni (1956), 471.
112 *Theogonia*, 508–20, 731–3, 741–50; see Evelyn-White (1959), 116–39.
113 *Odysseus, 4*, 564 – see Rieu (1946), p. 79.
114 See Rose (1974), 58–9.
115 Homer, *Odysseus, 1*, 52–4; Hyginus, *Fabula* 150 – see Graves (1960) *1*, 143–5.
116 Hesiod, *Theogonia*, 287–294, 981–3 – see Evelyn-White (1959), 100–1, 150–1; Pettazzoni (1956), 213; Graves (1960) 2, 132–3, 140, 392.
117 For discussion and references, see Graves (1960) 2, 132–5, 140–1.
118 *ibid.*, 135.
119 See Mohen (1990), 106, 126–7.
120 Scymnius, 188 – see Graves (1960) 2, 141.
121 Chadwick (1966), 32–42, 101–2.
122 *Moralia*, 419, 941 – see Brown (1943), 339–41.
123 In Hesiod's *Theogonia*, Cronus was the leader of the defeated Titans and with Briareus was confined to Tartarus, the underworld – see Grant (1962), 87–8, 99–106, 419; Graves (1960) 2, 387.
124 In his commentary on Hesiod – Brown, *ibid.* See also K Müller-Lisowski in *Béaloideas 18*, 149–50,
125 Walde/Pokorny (1930) *1*, 846–7.
126 K Müller-Lisowski in *Béaloideas 18*, 147–9.

127   Gwynn (1924), 310–1; Meyer (1919), 542.

128   Macalister (1956), 80–2, 106

129   Todd (1848), 248; Best/Bergin/O'Brien *et al* (1954–83), *3*, 520. The author of this poem was Máelmuru of Fahan in Co. Donegal (+887 AD).

130   Meyer (1895), *1*, 45–8.

131   Knott (1936), 9, 10, 22, 79.

132   O'Rahilly (1946), 127–9.

133   E Windisch in *Irische Texte 1*, 463; C-J Guyonvarc'h in *Ogam 11*, 284–5 and *12*, 49.

134   O'Brien (1962), 613–17; O'Rahilly (1946), 58–9, 467.

135   O'Rahilly (1946), 290–4; Green (1986), 172–3 and (1992), 30, 202.

136   Macalister (1941), 120–1. For Eochaidh meaning 'horseman', see RIA Dictionary s.v. 'echaid', 'oenechaid'.

137   O'Rahilly (1946), 292, 59.

138   *ibid.*, 320; Meyer (1912), 98; *Irische Texte 3*, 354–7.

139   Macalister (1941), 236.

140   For this postulated sky-god, see Walde/Pokorny (1930), *1*, 772–3; Buck (1949), 1464; Krappe (1978), 36–42; Eliade (1987), 7, 198–200; Mallory (1989), 128–9. Jupiter is from *Iu* (< Greek *Zev*, cognate with Umbrian *Iuve* i.e. Jove) + *Piter* (cognate with *Pater*); while Tyr (an alternative name for Odin) is from an earlier *Tiv-*.

141   See Chapter 1.

142   *Ériu 8*, 16.

143   *Irische Texte 3*, 354–6.

144   Gray (1982), 42–4.

145   *ibid.*, 28–30.

146   *ibid.*, 30, 70.

147   *ibid.*, 46, 54.

148   *ibid.*, 46–50.

149   ZCP *18*, 83–5.

150   Williams (1930), 44.

151   Watson (1941), 27–9.

152   O Bergin in *Mediaeval Studies for G S Loomis* (1927), 402–6.

153   Van Hamel (1933), 35–6; Gwynn (1924), 294, 454.

154   Stokes (1892), 8–9.

155   Gwynn (1924), 108.

156   O Bergin/R I Best in *Ériu 12*, 142–51.

157   de Vries (1961), 30–7; Mac Cana (1970), 29–32; Green (1992), 126–9.

158   de Vries (1961), 91–6; Thevenot (1968), 133–42; Mac Cana (1970), 44; Green (1989), 75–86 and (1992), 200.

159   Mac Cana (1970), 44, 49; Green (1992), 157–8.

160   For the motif of divine marriage in Celtic iconography, see Green (1989), 45–73. For possible Hindu parallels, see Dillon (1975), 138–42.

161   Gray (1982), 44.

162   Williams (1930), 35.

163   Gwynn (1906), 18. It is clear that the lady in question is the Mor-Ríoghain from the phrase in the poem referring to her, viz. *Dá Cích rígnai* ('the Two Paps of the queen', *rígnai* being a genitival form of *ríoghain*). The refer-

ence is to two smaller mounds to the west of the tumulus, which were associated with the Mor-Ríoghain – see note 177 below.

164 Green (1992), 178.
165 *ibid.*, 140, 146–7.
166 Mac Cana (1970), 83–5; Ross (1974), 270.
167 *Pace* Murphy (1953), 208–10, the alternative early form of the name 'Don' must be secondary to 'Dan-'; for which, see RIA Dictionary under 'Danann'.
168 Monier-Williams (1899), 468; Rees/Rees (1973), 365.
169 This parallel is discussed by O'Rahilly (1946), 308–17, who points out that the designation *trí dé Dána* is the older.
170 Walde/Pokorny (1930), *1*, 763; Pokorny (1959), *1*, 175.
171 Holder (1891), *1*, 1224–38; Jackson (1953), 379; Rees/Rees (1973), 52–3, 364–5.
172 Graves (1960), *1*, 200, 201–4. The name Danaoi was borne by a very early Greek tribe – see Nilsson (1927), 38. A derivation from the same root as the river Danube is cited in Frisk (1960), 347; and Snell (1991), 217.
173 See Ó hÓgáin (1990), 407–9.
174 Williams (1930), 67, 252–3. See also Gruffydd (1928); O'Rahilly (1946), 67, 308–17; Mac Cana (1970), 75–6; Rees/Rees (1973), 50–3.
175 *Irische Texte 3*, 288; Meyer (1912), 11.
176 RIA Dictionary, s. v. 'íath'.
177 Meyer (1912), 3.
178 RIA Dictionary, s.v. 'anae'.
179 Note the variations between the 'Anu' and 'Danu' forms listed in Gray (1982), 122. See also Macalister (1941), 182.
180 *ibid.*, 103, 130, 160, 188; Gray (1982), 122, 129. The earlier nominative form of the designation was written *Morrígu*. The standard form used here is that of the dative case (written in early Mss *Morrígain*).
181 Gwynn (1906), 18–19, 62–3.
182 See Ó hÓgáin (1990), 307–9.
183 Van Hamel (1933), 37
184 Williams (1930), 1–27.
185 See de Vries (1961), 123–7; Mac Cana (1970), 80–3.
186 Ó Ríordáin (1965), 43–5; Cooney/Grogan (1994), 102–3, 124, 132, 141.
187 RIA Contributions s.v. 'fulacht'.
188 See Ó hÓgáin (1990), 308–9.
189 See Graves (1960), *1*, 48–9, 203–4
190 Rees/Rees (1961), 52–3, 364–5.
191 The designation *fir trí ndéa*, used for the mythical followers of Danu – Gray (1982), 38 – meant either 'men of the three gods' or 'men of the three goddesses'. There are also frequent mentions of 'three gods of Danu' in the literature – this may be a later development, as argued by O'Rahilly (1946), 308–17, but it could also have been occasioned by a triplication of Danu.
192 de Vries (1961), 135–8.
193 Green (1992), 174.

194 Ross (1974), 265–71; Green (1986), 78–85 and (1992), 146–7, 155–6, 216.
195 Krappe (1978), 40–2, 50–2.
196 Faulkes (1987), 237 – s.v. 'Iord'.
197 Lemprière (1984), 663.
198 Graves (1960), *1*, 89–92.
199 Ions (1967), 15.

Chapter 3

1   Eliade (1964), 375–427.
2   *Vitae*, introduction, I – see Kendrick (1927), 75, 212.
3   Clement of Alexandria, *Stromata*, I, xv, 71 – see Kendrick (127), 106, 220; Chadwick (1966), 61–3. For 'shaman' see Eliade (1964), 495–6.
4   Piggott (1968), 56–7. For a fuller discussion of Celtic sanctuaries, see Brunaux (1988), 7–41, 116–19.
5   For the possibility that formal druidry originated at around this time, see Brunaux (1988), 114–15, 141–4.
6   See Walde/Pokorny (1927–30), *1*, 131–2 and 2, 330–2; C-J Guyonvarc'h in *Ogam 12*, 185–97.
7   Walde/Pokorny (1927), 2, 330–2.
8   RIA Dictionary s.v. 'neimed', 'fid-nemed'; O'Rahilly (1976), 113, 123; *Revue Celtique 20*, 178; Gwynn (1924), 166; Best/Bergin (1929), 130.
9   *Celtica 9*, 157–8; see Henry (1978), 144–5, 233–5.
10   *Archiv für celtische Lexikographie 1*, 272.
11   *De Bello Gallico*, VI, 13–21.
12   Walde/Pokorny (1930), *1*, 804–6; Le Roux/Guyonvarc'h (1986), 32.
13   J J Tierney in *PRIA 60 C5*.
14   *Geographica*, IV, 4 – see Kendrick (1927), 215; Tierney, *op. cit.*, 269.
15   Le Roux/Guyonvarc'h (1986), 425–43.
16   *ibid.*, 438–441; Henry (1978), 235.
17   *Germania*, VIII – see Mattingly/Handford (1970), 108. For a general discussion of the prophetess Veleda, see M J Enright in Ní Chatháin/Richter (1996), 219–27.
18   *Zeitschrift für vergleichende Sprachforschung 40*, 248; *Revue Celtique 17*, 276.
19   Walde/Pokorny (1930), *1*, 293–4.
20   See Ó hÓgáin (1982), 5–22, 335–415.
21   Tacitus, *Historiae*, IV, 54: Hippolytus, *Philosophumena*, I, xxv; see Kendrick (1927), 93, 105.
22   *Historiae*, V, 31, 2–5 – see Tierney, *op. cit.*, 251.
23   Ogilvie (1986), 87–8; Hutton (1990).
24   On this issue, see Rankin (1987), 286–9.
25   *De Situ Orbis*, III, 2 – see Kendrick (1927), 87.
26   *Geographica* IV, IV, 4 – see Tierney, *op. cit.*, 269.
27   *De Bello Gallico*, VI, 13 – see Tierney, *op. cit.*, 271.

28 For discussions and references, see Ó hÓgáin (1982), 15–22, 413–5, 419–20, 452–3; L Mac Mathúna in *Veröffentlichungen der Keltischen Kommission 2*, 225–38; Le Roux/Guyonvarc'h (1986), 88–97, 128–32, 199–205.

29 Macalister (1939), 42, 74.

30 O'Rahilly (1976), 20. Another prophecy by Cathbadh in Hull (1949), 44–5.

31 Ó Cathasaigh (1977), 122.

32 Dillon (1975), 123–4.

33 See Dillon (1953), 20; Ross (1967), 318–30; Ó Súilleabháin (1942), 292.

34 *Ériu 8*, 120–6.

35 Meyer (1912), 40.

36 *Ériu 8*, 120–3.

37 See Breatnach (1987), 28–60, 102–15

38 Macalister (1940), 8, 156 and (1941), 162–3 and (1956), 14–16; 36–8; O'Curry (1873), 2, 184–5; O'Rahilly (1946), 308–17. See also Le Roux/Guyonvarc'h (1986), 332–5. The Classical authors – in dividing the druids into three classes – may have been reflecting a similar triadic convention (see notes 14–15 above).

39 Mac Cana (1970), 48–9, 141; Dillon/Chadwick (1973), 28–30, 183.

40 Stokes (1905), 8.

41 For references see Le Roux/Guyonvarc'h (1986), 161–3; Ó hÓgáin (1982), 353–63, 449 and (1990), 22–3; 363–4; J F Nagy in Ahlqvist (1996), 129–48.

42 *Geographica*, IV, IV, 4 – see Tierney, *op. cit.*, 269; Kendrick (1927), 83, 215.

43 See Ó hÓgáin (1982), 352–3, 448.

44 Le Roux/Guyonbarc'h (1986), 77–87; O'Grady (1892), *1*, 341; Plummer (1910), *1*, clxi–clxiii; Watson (1941), 34; Caerwyn Williams/Ní Mhuiríosa (1979), 37–9; RIA Dictionary s.v. 'file'.

45 Kelly (1988), 54–5.

46 *ibid.*, 55.

47 Ó hÓgáin (1982), 326–31.

48 Dillon (1969), 6–8, 17–18.

49 e.g. O'Donovan (1865), *1*, 24. See also William/Ní Mhuiríosa (1979), 37–9.

50 O'Donovan (1865), *1*, 20; Watson (1941), 34.

51 Stokes (1905), 6.

52 *Irische Texte 3*, 51–2, 117–18; see also Williams/Ní Mhuiríosa (1979), 36–7.

53 Stokes/Strachan (1903), 2, 248–9. For Irish phrases in Anglo-Saxon charms, see Storms (1948), 303, 306.

54 Meyer (1912), 64 – see O'Donovan/Stokes (1868), 94–5.

55 *ibid.*

56 for references and discussion, see Ó hÓgáin (1982), 11–20, 418–20.

57 Meyer (1912), 40.

58 *ibid.*, 75–7.

59 *ibid.*, 28.

60 See O'Rahilly (1946), 336.

61   *ibid.*, 336–40.
62   See Chapter 4 re Fionn.
63   Atkinson (1901), 5, 56; *Anecdota from Irish Manuscripts 2*, 76; *Irische Texte 3*, 50; *Ériu 17*, 89; Meyer (1906), 16.
64   Ó hÓgáin (1982), 364–415.
65   *Orationes*, XLIX – see Kendrick (1927), 93.
66   *Historiae*, V, 31 – see Tierney, *op. cit.*, 251.
67   *ibid.*
68   Watson (1941), 11; O'Rahilly (1976), 104.
69   Henderson (1899), 20–2; Watson (1941), 6.
70   Hennessy/McCarthy (1887), 1, 56–7; O'Grady (1892), 1. 79.
71   Kelly (1988), 61.
72   Meyer (1912), 14–5.
73   *Revue Celtique 26*, 55; see *ZCP 21*, 324–5.
74   See Ó hÓgáin (1982), 281–306.
75   Stokes (1890), xxxix; *Archiv für celtische Lexikographie 1*, 272.
76   See D Ward in *The Journal of Indo-European Studies 1*, 127–44.
77   Several examples are cited in Ó hÓgáin (1982), 335–63.
78   *Revue Celtique 24*, 280.
79   Ó hÓgáin (1982), 321–34; Le Roux/Guyonvarc'h (1986), 205–12.
80   Meyer (1912), 58–60.
81   *Archiv für celtische Lexikographie 2*, 257, 269.
82   Gray (1982), 58.
83   O'Rahilly (1970), 13.
84   Knott (1936), 16.
85   See O'Curry (1873), 2, 184–90; O'Grady (1892), 1, 314; Le Roux/Guyonvarc'h (1986), 103–6.
86   *De Situ Orbis*, III, 2, 18–19; see Kendrick (1927), 87.
87   O'Donovan (1865), 1, 22.
88   Best/Bergin (1929), 294. There is a reference to a druid 'observing the stars' in an early Irish text, but this may be a Biblical borrowing – Ó hAodha (1978), 1.
89   For instances see Le Roux/Guyonvarc'h (1986), 103–15; Ó hÓgáin (1990), 105, 125, 159, 414.
90   Ó Cathasaigh (1977), 122.
91   Dillon (1969), 4–5 and (1975), 90–4; Le Roux/Guyonvarc'h (1986), 88–97.
92   Best/Bergin (1929), 302.
93   *Irische Texte 3*, 191.
94   XXIV, 103–4, XXIX, 52; see Kendrick (1927), 89–90.
95   See Ó Súilleabháin (1942), 396–9, 400–402, 406, 414, 422; Frazer (1920), 303, 354–5, 477, 518–19; T Davidson in *Gwerin 1*, 70. The mystical atmosphere of collecting herbs is well illustrated in a sampler from late Irish folklore in IFC 85:352–5.
96   Gray (1982), 50, 54. For other traditions of Dian Cécht, see Ó hÓgáin (1990), 156–7. For healing well, see also *Ériu 8*, 34.
97   O'Rahilly (1976), 97–9 and (1970), 101–4 and (1961), 113–16.
98   Meyer, *Death-Tales* (1906), 8; O'Rahilly (1961), 143.
99   Dillon (1953), 29.

100 *Irische Texte 3*, 366; O'Curry (1873), 2, 203–5.
101 *De Divinatione*, I, xli, 90 – see Kendrick (1927), 80.
102 *De Situ Orbis*, III, 2, 18–19 – see Kendrick (1927), 87.
103 O'Rahilly (1976), 19; Watson (1941), 16.
104 See Le Roux/Guyonvarc'h (1986), 55–9; Stokes (1905), 12; Dillon (1975), 96; Bieler (1979), 144.
105 *De Bello Gallico*, VI, 13–14; see Tierney, *op. cit.*, 271–2.
106 *Vitae*, introduction, 5 – see Kendrick (1927), 75.
107 See Meyer, *Triads* (1906); Bromwich (1961). For another triadic aspect of ideology among the Continental Celts, see Brunaux (1988), 128.
108 Meyer (1912), 64.
109 *Ériu 13*, 38.
110 Several examples cited in Ó hÓgáin (1982), 107–13.
111 Meyer (1912), 69–70; see Stokes/O'Donovan (1868), 102–3.
112 See note 22 above.
113 See C Watkins in Puhvel (1970), 1–17.
114 Calder (1917); Breatnach (1987); *Irische Texte 3*, 1–116. For the imagery of poetry as a learned trade in Irish tradition, see Ó hÓgáin (1982), 23–32.
115 McGrath (1979), 207–15.
116 *ibid.*, 13–63
117 O'Rahilly (1976), 19; *Revue Celtique 6*, 176–8; Hull (1949), 43–4.
118 *Revue Celtique 5*, 201. In the biographies of Irish saints, of course, this function of prophetic naming is taken over by especially wise clerics. An intermediary stage is reflected by the story of how a druid was told in a dream by three white-robed clerics what name to give to the baby St Brighid – Ó hAodha (1978), 1.
119 Le Roux/Guyonvarc'h (1986), 126–8.
120 See notes *supra* 29–31 and 145–149 *infra*.
121 Examples of these descriptions are cited in McManus (1991), 154–6.
122 *Pharsalia*, 1, 450–8; see Kendrick (1927), 88.
123 *Historia Naturalis*, XVI, 249 – see Kendrick (1927), 88–9.
124 Le Roux/Guyonvarc'h (1986), 32.
125 MacCulloch (1911), 199–200; Frazer (1940), 159–64; Friedrich (1970), 132–49.
126 Frazer (1940), 658–63.
127 See Ó hÓgáin (1995), 33–6.
128 See Le Roux/Guyonvarc'h (1986), 259–62.
129 Green (1992), 110. Mac Cana (1970), 124–5 is doubtful concerning the connection.
130 Ogilvie (1986), 95.
131 O'Rahilly (1949), 3, 516 – see also Chapter 4.
132 *ZCP 20*, 174; *ZCP 27*, 33–4; *Ériu 12*, 176; *Irische Texte 2*, 191, 247; Stokes (1877), 58; Meyer (1912), 48; Jackson (1938), 2, 86–7; Joynt (1941), 17; Meid (1967), 1, 7; O'Rahilly (1970), 54. See also *Ériu 11*, 194–6; Dillon (1953), 9; Cross (1952), 64.
133 See O Bergin in *Ériu 14*, 170; Thorburn (1989), 2, 50–4; Lucas (1989), 239–45.
134 *De Bello Gallico*, VI, 13 – see Tierney, *op. cit.*, 271.

135 *Historia Naturalis*, XXI, 13 – see Kendrick (1927), 90; Chadwick (1966), 15–16.
136 *Agricola*, XI, 4 – see Mattingly/Handford (1970), 62. For how easily it would have been for the Romans to subdue Ireland, *ibid.*, 74–5.
137 Meyer (1912), xiii–xvii.
138 Stokes (1905), 8.
139 O'Rahilly (1976), 2.
140 *Annali*, XIV, 30 – see Kendrick (1927), 92–3.
141 Gray (1982), 44.
142 *ibid.*
143 *Ériu 8*, 26.
144 Examples in Ó hÓgáin (1982), 105–6, 332–4.
145 O'Rahilly (1970), 5 and (1976), 2.
146 See Graves (1960), *1*, 48–9, 203–4.
147 Chadwick/Chadwick (1932–40) *1*, 448, 453 and *3*, 844; M J Enright in Ní Chatháin/Richter (1996), 225–6; H Wagner in *ZCP 31*, 50–1.
148 Chadwick (1966), 79–81.
149 Zwicker (1934), 97.
150 See Joyce (1903), *1*, 238; Plummer (1910), *1*, clix. The goddesses Bóinn and Brighid are referred to as druidesses in *ZCP 13*, 166 and *Revue Celtique 16*, 277. Other mentions of druidesses are in *Revue Celtique 5*, 198 and *26*, 156 and *29*, 112; *ZCP 8*, 104 and *12*, 252; Stokes (1900), 208.
151 O'Rahilly (1970), 57.
152 Ó hÓgáin (1982), 141–66.
153 See the discussion of Brighid in Chapter 4.
154 *Revue Celtique 40*, 416 and *43*, 298–300; *Ériu 8*, 26–8.
155 See O'Donovan (1865), *1*, 184, 190, 236–8.
156 RIA Dictionary, s.v. 'neimed'. See also C-J Guyonvarc'h in *Ogam 12*, 188–93; Ó hÓgáin (1990), 318.
157 Julius Caesar, *De Bello Gallico*, VI, 13.
158 O'Grady (1892) *1*, 73; Dinneen (1908–1914), *2*, 246–8.
159 Gwynn (1906), 44; *Revue Celtique 15*, 297.
160 *Ériu 4*, 152–4. The earlier form of the placename was *Uisniu*.
161 Van Hamel (1933), 43; a similar description in Meyer (1912), 12. Regarding a possible ancient fire-festival at Uisneach, see also D A Binchy in *Ériu 18*, 114–15, 129–30.

Chapter 4

1   See Ó hÓgáin (1990), 185–90, 237.
2   *Geographica* IV, IV, 4; see J J Tierney in *PRIA 60 C5*, 269.
3   *De Situ Orbis* III, 2, 18–19; see Kendrick (1927), 87–8.
4   *Factorum et dictorum libri*, II, 6, 10; see Kendrick (1927), 106.
5   M Bhreatnach in *Ériu 35*, 72–6
6   For this saint and his monastery, see Kenney (1929), 387–9.
7   Dillon (1953).

8   For Samhain as an otherworld-time in Irish folklore, see Danaher (1972), 200–29.

9   For a discussion of this aspect of human thought, see Eliade (1959), 68–113. For a constructive critique of Eliade's view, see Brandon (1965), 13–30.

10 Van Hamel (1941), 48–9.

11 *Ériu 11*, 188; Stokes (1900), 177, 189.

12 For these designations, see RIA Dictionary. The origin of the word *Eamhain* is discussed in Chapter 6.

13 e.g. *Irische Texte 3*, 193–8; *ZCP 17*, 193–205; see Dillon (1948), 101–31.

14 K Jackson in *Speculum 17*, 377–89.

15 See T Ó Cathasaigh in *Éigse 17*, 137–55; C-J Guyonvarc'h in *Ogam 14*, 329–40; Le Roux/Guyonvarc'h (1986), 280–1; P Sims-Williams in Matonis/Melia (1990), 57–81.

16 See Filip (1977), 28–50.

17 *ibid.*, 50–9.

18 Tertullian, *De Anima*, 57, 10; see P M Freeman in Mallory/Stockman (1994), 215.

19 See Carney (1955), 165–79.

20 Williams (1930), 9.

21 On this point, see MacCulloch (1911), 250; Chadwick (1932), 456, 473 and (1940), 845; Williams (1971), 36.

22 Best/Bergin (1929), 90–4, 129–32, 334–5; *Ériu 8*, 155–60. See also Williams/Ní Mhuiríosa (1979), 40–2; and for Scandinavian parallels Davidson (1943), 110–11 and (1988), 114–18, 149.

23 See Ó hÓgáin (1982), 168–78, 184–9.

24 E Ettlinger in *Études Celtique 6*, 30–61; Best/Bergin (1929), 128–9; *Revue Celtique 16*, 142 and *17*, 143 – see Plummer (1910), *1*, cix; Byrne (1973), 15–20; Powell (1980), 173.

25 These sites will be discussed in Chapter 6.

26 Meyer (1912), 98; *Irische Texte 3*, 356–7; see Ó hÓgáin (1990), 377.

27 *ZCP 3*, 245; Dinneen (1908), 326–32; Delargy (1969), 22 – see Olmsted (1992), 191–2. The Gaulish calendar found at Coligny gives *Giamon-* (with the same root as Irish *geimhreadh*, 'winter') and *Samon-* (corresponding to the Irish *Céad Shamhain*, 'first Samhain', an old designation for the May festival). This is discussed in detail by K R McCone in *Léachtaí Cholm Cille 11*, 139–41. For apparent divisions into 'bright' and 'dark' periods of months in the Coligny calendar, see Dillon (1975), 124.

28 *ZCP 19*, 55.

29 Macalister (1941), 120.

30 *ZCP 19*, 53–8. Other versions in Gwynn (1903–35), *2*, 18–21; *Ériu 11*, 188–92 and *12*, 142–7;

31 *Ériu 7*, 227. This is in a poem attributed to Cinaedh ua hArtacáin (+975 AD).

32 For a more inductive interpretation, see Sterckx (1986), where the Daghdha is taken to represent fecundity, Bóinn the world, and Aonghus life itself.

33 For examples, see J Waddell in Ó Corráin (1994).

34 *ZCP 19*, 55.

35 See Olmsted (1992), 89–90, table 57.
36 See Chapter 2, footnote 62.
37 See Holder (1896) *1*, 646–7; and O'Rahilly (1946), 2–3, who describes the name as a Co-ordinate compound. Dillon (1975), 122, interprets it as 'cow-finder' – for this other meaning of *vind*, see note 82 below.
38 The goddess was visualised in bovine form in several ancient cultures e.g. as Nut and Hathor in Egypt, Aditi in India, Audhumla in Scandinavia – see also James (1962), 82–5; Frankfort/Frankfort (1949), 17.
39 Gwynn (1913), 26–39, 286–8; *Revue Celtique 15*, 315–16, 456; *Irische Texte 3*, 195.
40 Knott (1936), 6; O'Donovan (1848), *1*, 90.
41 *Archiv für celtische Lexikographie 2*, 477; *Anecdota from Irish Manuscripts 5*, 25.
42 Stokes (1905), 28–9.
43 See Cross (1952), Motifs F394.1.1*, P427.3*, and *infra*.
44 See Gonda (1963), 76–93, 175, 189, 239–40; Dillon (1975), 121–3; RIA Dictionary s.v. 'Boänd'.
45 Griffith (1971), *2*, 108–357 passim.
46 Van Hamel (1932), 22.
47 *Anecdota from Irish Manuscripts 4*, 15.
48 *Ériu 13*, 38.
49 Binchy (1970), 12–4; Byrne (1973), 155.
50 Holder (1896), *1*, 533–43.
51 Ó hÓgáin (1990), 60–4. For a discussion of the origin of the cult of St Brighid, see Ó Catháin (1995).
52 Mac Cana (1970), 32; Thevenot (1968), 99–107; Green (1992), 47–8, 75–6.
53 Ó hÓgáin (1990), 231–2.
54 *ibid.*, 240–1. Goibhniu was an ancient Irish god of smithcraft – for him, see *ibid.*, 245–6.
55 ZCP 27, 28–37.
56 See Ó hÓgáin (1990), 67–9.
57 See Chapter 3, note 132.
58 *Bibliotheca*, V, 28 – see Tierney, *op. cit.*, 250.
59 Holder (1896), *1–3*; M. Lejeune in *Études Celtiques 22*, 92–177; Tovar (1961), 76–90; W Meid in *Current Trends in Linguistics 9*, 1190–1201; Olmsted (1992), 204–5.
60 Macalister (1945); McManus (1991); A Harvey in *Ériu 38*, 45–71.
61 *Celtica 12*, 9–10. References to the 'hidden' speech of the poets in RIA Dictionary s.v. 'fortchide'
62 O'Rahilly (1970), 13 and (1976), 9–10.
63 *Irische Texte 3*, 129. See also Meyer (1912), 49–50 where such inscriptions on timber are said to have accompanied burials. The literary allusions to *ogham* are listed in McManus (1991), 153–66.
64 Calder (1917), 187–8, 272–3.
65 Comyn (1902), 222; O'Rahilly (1970), 113.
66 *Heracles*, 1 – see Zwicker (1934), 78–80; for possible other traces of the cult of Ogmios, see Dillon/Chadwick (1973), 180–1; Ó hÓgáin (1982), 76–9; Rankin (1987), 283–5.

67 See C-J Guyonvarc'h in *Ogam 12*, 47–9. For such mercenaries in early Ireland, see K Meyer in *Ériu 4*, 208.

68 *Bibliotheca*, V, 28 – see Tierney, *op. cit.*, 250.

69 *De Bello Gallico*, VI, 14 – see Tierney, *op. cit.*, 272.

70 *Pharsalia*, I, 450–8; see Kendrick (1927), 88.

71 *Irische Texte 3*, 474–6; *ZCP 17*, 193–4; Vendryes (1953), 1–23, 27; Jackson (1938), 3–4.

72 For examples, see Henderson (1899), 44, 48;

73 For this in general see RIA Dictionary, s.v. 'féth'; Le Roux/Guyonvarc'h (1986), 183–5.

74 *Ériu 11*, 188; *Revue Celtique 5*, 202; Ó hÓgáin (1988), 199.

75 Stokes (1900), 143; Ó hÓgáin (1988), 265.

76 *ZCP 10*, 294.

77 Atkinson (1901), 90.

78 *ZCP 27*, 39–44.

79 *Irische Texte 3*, 356; Meyer (1912), 98; see O'Rahilly (1946), 318–20; Ó hÓgáin (1990), 377.

80 See Ó hÓgáin (1990), 40–1, 173–4, 286–8, 139–42.

81 Examples in Stokes (1887), 2, 325–6; Watson (1941), 25, 33; O'Rahilly (1961), 138, 141 and (1976), 113; Bieler (1979), 156. See also the white robe of the Continental druid described by Pliny in *Historia Naturalis* XVI, 249 – cited in Chapter 3.

82 Thurneysen (1946), 38; Jackson in Ó Cuív (1969), 5; P Mac Cana in Eliade (1987), 3, 164. The more usual Old Irish form of the verb is a deponent 'ro-finnadar', which seems to derive from the same stem by way of **vindnu-* (Thurneysen, *op. cit.*, 357).

83 Walde/Pokorny (1930), *1*, 236–9; Buck (1949), 1054; Mann (1987), 1534. H Wagner in *ZCP 31*, 23 makes the unusual suggestion that the adjective may have derived from the name. For the derivation of a character's name ('Vinda') from the same root in Sanskrit literature, see Monier-Williams (1899), 972.

84 See Vendryes (1974), R39; E P Hamp in *Bulletin of the Board of Celtic Studies 28*, 214; but cf. Walde/Pokorny (1930), *1*, 470.

85 *Irische Texte 1*, 68; *ZCP 12*, 365; Watson (1941), 33; *Ériu 13*, 51. Its cognate 'vindát-vat' had a similar function in Sanskrit literature – Monier-Williams (1899), 972.

86 Meyer (1912), 47; *Archiv für celtische Lexikographie 3*, 274; *ZCP 11*, 91; *Ériu 4*, 132. The semantic ranges covered by the word for truth (*fír*) and that for knowledge (*fiss*) in early Irish texts are very similar.

87 Holder (1896), 3, 341–4 etc; Whatmough (1970), 386, 693 etc; K H Schmidt in *ZCP 26*, 295–6.

88 Thevenot (1968), 110–12.

89 See Mac Cana (1970).

90 See Murphy (1953), lxxxii–lxxxiii. Cf. Holder (1896), 3, 344–5.

91 For these three characters, respectively, see Ó hÓgáin (1990), 210–11, 306–7, 224–5.

92 Ó hÓgáin (1988), 24–5, 52–60, 293.

93 O'Rahilly (1946), 337.

94 See Wallis Budge (1904), *1*, 466–99; Ions (1965), 71–4.

95 Nilsson (1927), 533–83.
96 See Jung/Kerenyi (1985), 25–69.
97 *ZCP 20*, 194–6.
98 *Irische Texte 3*, 188–90.
99 O'Brien (1962), 99.
100 *ZCP 19*, 48–51 and *20*, 196–7; O'Sullivan (1983), 1373 – see Ó hÓgáin (1988), 19–24 and (1990), 324.
101 Meyer (1895), *1*, 48.
102 See Ó hÓgáin (1988), 18–26.
103 *ibid.*, 27–51.
104 Gwynn (1906), 74. See also, in addition to the account of Morfhind (note 98 above) the importance attributed to a distance of nine waves at sea in the Irish mythological and hagiographical literature – Macalister (1956), 54; *Irische Texte 1*, 838; *Revue Celtique 2*, 201; Bernard/Atkinson (1898) *1, 25* = Stokes/Strachan (1903), 299.
105 *Revue Celtique 5*, 199–200.
106 Joynt (1936), 34–40; Ó Siochfhradha (1941), 74–80.
107 Ó hÓgáin (1988), 22, 99, 331.
108 Jung/Kerenyi (1985), 66–7.
109 Olrik (1919), 12–15, 437–45; Davidson (1964), 104–6.
110 H Wagner in *Ériu 23*, 136–7.
111 Hindu tradition has truth as a mighty blaze of light, found in a lake at the source of the river Ganges – Dillon (1975), 128, 132. For water as the universal mother, see Eliade (1958), 188–96.
112 For a discussion of this, see Patrick K Ford in Larson (1974), 67–74.
113 Bosley (1979), 191; Emin (1981), 109–10.
114 Vána (1983), 87.
115 Gwynn (1913), 26–9.
116 See note 26 above. Note the expression 'findgen grian' (literally 'the brightly-conceived sun') in *ZCP 11*, 109.
117 For a lady called Finda in an Irish heroic text, see O'Rahilly (1970), 105.
118 *Revue Celtique 17*, 175; see also O'Donovan (1842), 198.
119 O'Grady (1892), *1*, 332; see also Ó hÓgáin (1990), 283, 322–3.
120 See Ó hÓgáin (1990), 211–12.
121 See D J Ward in Puhvel (1970), 193–202; McCone (1990), 119.
122 See Ó hÓgáin (1982), 5–22, 80–93.
123 See O'Rahilly (1946), 278, 318–19; Williams (1930), 44; Bromwich (1961), 45, 406; Ó hÓgáin (1988), 16–17, 324. There are several echoes of the Irish Fionn, in association with the name Gwyn, in mediaeval Welsh literature. These can best be explained as survivals of borrowings from Leinster, perhaps prior to the 6th century AD when the Irish form of the name would still have been 'Vind-'. The transmutation of initial 'v' into 'gw' in Welsh began in the 6th century AD but was not completed until two hundred years later – cf. Jackson (1953), 385–94.
124 *Ériu 4*, 128–64; *Anecdota from Irish Manuscripts 1*, 24–39. Cf. Ó hÓgáin (1990), 224–5, 407.
125 Meyer (1895), 25–7.
126 Meyer (1910), 50.
127 Meyer (1912), 107.

128 Stokes (1905), 12.
129 *ibid.*, 12–15.
130 *ibid.*, 16–33.
131 *ibid.*, 52–8.
132 *Revue Celtique 14*, 245–6 and *25*, 344–6.
133 For the basic contrast between bright and dark in mystical thought, see Guénon (1962), 306–8.
134 Roider (1979) – see also Ó hÓgáin (1990), 167–8.
135 In the story of Culhwch and Olwen – Gantz (1976), 168.
136 Bromwich (1961), 403–4.
137 Williams (1930), 99–101; L Foster in Murphy (1953), 446.
138 Williams (1930), 2–6; see Gantz, 47–50. For these and other echoes of the myth in Irish and Welsh tradition, see Rees/Rees (1973), 283–6.
139 Ó hÓgáin (1988), 9–10, 52–5, 92–3.

Chapter 5

1   See Byrne (1973), 20.
2   Piggott (1968), 54–63.
3   There is an excellent résumé of the tradition of Tara in Bhreatnach (1995).
4   O'Kelly (1989), 109.
5   R M Kavanagh in *PRIA 76C*, 350–1, 388–9.
6   Herity/Eogan (1977), 67, 80, 144, 158, 166; O'Kelly (1989), 105–6, 204–5; Raftery (1994), 60–7.
7   Raftery (1994), 69–70.
8   S Caulfield in Ó Corráin (1981), 212.
9   Raftery (1994), 66–70.
10 Byrne (1973), 64.
11 Walde/Pokorny (1930), *1*, 219.
12 See C-J Guyonvarc'h in *Ogam 16*, 436–40.
13 Walde/Pokorny (1930), *1*, 298–304.
14 Macalister (1931), 134–6; Gray (1982), 24–5, 75.
15 See Gwynn (1924), 170–3; D A Binchy in *Ériu 18*, 136–8.
16 Binchy, *ibid.*
17 *Ériu 12*, 137–96. A later verse redaction in Gwynn (1906), 2–9.
18 See Ó Corráin/Maguire (1981), 90.
19 See Enright (1996), 260–82; see also note 70 *infra*.
20 de Vries (1961), 109–10.
21 *ibid.*, 49–50.
22 T F O'Rahilly in *Ériu 14*, 15–17; Henry (1978), 17.
23 *ZCP 17*, 143; Hogan (1910), 574.
24 O'Rahilly in *Ériu 14*, 14–21; Carney (1955), 334.
25 Zwicker (1934), 2–3, 95 – see McCone (1990), 109–10.
26 Dumézil (1973), 70–83.
27 *Ériu 2*, 176–85.
28 T S Ó Máille in *ZCP 17*, 136–9.
29 *ibid.*, 137–9; Dillon (1975), 106.

30 Hogan (1910), 488; Macalister (1956), 52.
31 *ibid.*, 82.
32 See references in O'Rahilly (1946), 74. One of these characters, Liath Luachra, is an elderly opponent of the young Fionn mac Cumhaill; while Fionn himself, in his older aspect, has symbolical grey hair – see Ó hÓgáin (1988), 16–24, 360 and (1990), 219–20. The Mór-Ríoghain is also grey-haired – see Dillon/Chadwick (1973), 183–4.
33 A full description of the roadway in Raftery (1996).
34 *Ériu 12*, 178.
35 For a fuller discussion of this roadway and the early literature, see D Ó hÓgáin in Raftery (1996), 359–66.
36 See Whitley Stokes in *Revue Celtique 16*, 308.
37 Aarne/Thompson (1961), 104–6 (Tale Type 313).
38 See von Sydow (1948), 210–12; discussed briefly in Chapter 1.
39 On this, see Seán de Búrca in *Studia Celtica 1*, 128–37.
40 Stokes (1905), 18.
41 Wheeler/Wheeler (1932), 100–4 and figures 113a-b.
42 For this and other interpretations, see J Carey in *ZCP 40*, 1–3.
43 Gray (1982), 24–5, 32–3, 130–1.
44 Bromwich (1961), 428.
45 See Chapter 4.
46 O'Brien (1962), 714–15.
47 See Ross (1974), 178, 232–3; Green (1992), 161–2.
48 O'Brien (1962), 117, 120.
49 O'Rahilly (1946), 516–17.
50 Webster (1986), 76–8; Green (1992), 140. Maponos appears as Mabon in mediaeval Welsh literature – see Bromwich (1961).
51 For a discussion of the name, see O'Rahilly (1946), 59–60.
52 *ibid.*, 59–60; Gruffydd (1928), 183–5.
53 Mac Néill (1908), 35, 135; Ó Cuív (1945), 6, 9 – see O'Rahilly (1946), 60; Ó hÓgáin (1990), 43–5. In some sources it is Balar's fellow Fomhoire leader Breas who is associated with Mizen Head – Macalister (1941), 228; Gray (1982), 134 – but these must reflect a later tradition.
54 Holder 2 (1896), 308–46; Thevenot (1968), 72–96.
55 See Mac Cana (1970), 27–9; H Wagner in *ZCP 31*, 22–5.
56 See MacCulloch (1911), 272–3; MacNeill (1962), 1, 390, 418.
57 Discussion and references in Ó hÓgáin (1990), 272–7.
58 For the plot in connection with characters such as Sargon, Cyros, Perseus, and Moses, see Rank (1914), 12–44; Krappe (1927), 1–43; Gruffydd (1928), 350–75; P Saintyves in P-L Couchoud (1928), 229–72.
59 Herodotus (1.107–130) in the 5th century BC tells it of Cyrus but not of Perseus, though he has several mentions of the latter. Perseus' slaying of the Medusa is referred to by Homer, Hesiod, and Pindar, as well as Herodotus, but the earliest known mention of the prophecy that he will kill his grandfather is by Apollodorus in the 2nd century BC. For references see Lemprière (1984), 212, 503–4.
60 The Cyclops was notorious in Greek literature since Homer's account of Polyphemus in the 8th century BC, but the actual image itself was of much

greater antiquity – see Krappe (1927), 19–26; Graves (1960), *1*, 32–3 and 2, 366–7; Bailey (1997), 147–8.

61   For figures in Greek mythology, such as Belus and Bellerophon, who may have suggested their own Bolerus to the Celts, see Rees/Rees (1961), 365–6.

62   Powell (1980), 148–9.

63   D Ó hÓgáin in *Léachtaí Cholm Cille* 25, 159–60.

64   Meyer (1912), 66–7; MacNeill (1962), 320–1.

65   Macalister (1941), 116–19, 128–9, 134–5.

66   See D A Binchy in *Ériu 18*, 123–4

67   R Thurneysen in *ZCP* 20, 369; see also Williams (1930), 148 who relates the Welsh word to commercial transactions.

68   D A Binchy in *Ériu 18*, 115–26.

69   The Welsh form of his name, Lleu Llawgyffes ('L. of the dexterous hand') would seem to be a slight departure from the original image – see Dillon (1975), 139–40.

70   *ZCP 20*, 213–27.

71   Gray (1982), 26–9.

72   For list of references, see Gray (1982), 122, 129.

73   Thurneysen (1946), 175, 303.

74   For these, see Ó hÓgáin (1990), 167–8, 224–5, 407.

75   Meyer (1895), 42–5.

76   Kurth (1893), 137, 150–6, 501 – see Ó hÓgáin (1990), 54.

77   Davidson (1988), 124–5.

78   Aarne/Thompson (1961), 292–3 – Type 873.

79   See Ó hÓgáin (1990), 374.

80   Gray (1982), 38.

81   *ibid.*, 66, 473.

82   *Pharsalia*.

83   Green (1992), 208–9.

84   O'Rahilly (1976), 23; Knott (1936), 21; Watson (1941), 45.

85   Best/Bergin/O'Brien (1954), *1*, 43

86   RIA Dictionary s.v. 'fomóir'; Gray (1982), 132.

87   *ibid.*, 34.

88   See O'Rahilly (1946), 483; Gray (1982), 134–5. Bres is described as scoring great victories over the Fomhoire in an early genealogical text – O'Brien (1962), 117.

89   O'Rahilly (1946), 313.

90   e.g. the contests between the Devas and Asuras in Sanskrit literature, between the Aesir and Vanir in Norse literature, and between the family of Zeus and the Titans in Greek literature.

91   Macalister (1939), 249 and (1940), 122–5, 128–31, 138–45; Van Hamel (1932), 21–2. Similar otherworld pillars are in Van Hamel (1941), 42; O'Meara (1981), 68–9.

92   On the sun-bower in Irish lore, see RIA Dictionary s.v. 'grianán'; and O'Rahilly (1946), 293.

93   Green (1986), 61–5 and (1992), 127–8.

94   Compare the 'house of Donn' discussed in Chapter 4.

95   Gray (1982).

96 G Murphy in *Éigse* 7, 191–8; Mac Cana (1980), 108–10.
97 A 7th-century Latin text has St Patrick overcoming a Cyclopic character – Bieler (1979), 102–7. This may be based on Lugh's defeat of Balar.
98 *Dian* meant 'swift'; and O'Rahilly (1946), 472–3 derives *cécht* from a Celtic **kenkt-* meaning 'step' or 'move on' as in Irish *céim*.
99 *Ériu 8*, 34–5, 44–5.
100 Meyer (1912), 36–7; *Irische Texte 3*, 358.
101 Stokes/Strachan (1903), 249.
102 Meyer (1912), 36; *Irische Texte 3*, 356.
103 Gray (1982), 50.
104 *Ériu 20*, 1–65. For other such references, see Gray (1982), 122–3.
105 Gray (1982), 42.
106 Stokes/Strachan (1903), 248. See also *Ériu 20*, 2.
107 He has a Welsh counterpart with a cognate name, Gofynion – see O'Rahilly (1946), 525–6.
108 Gray (1982), 50.
109 For the Gobán Saor, see Ó hÓgáin (1990), 241–3.
110 For evidence of such beliefs from remote antiquity, see Maringer (1960), 117–23, 189–97; Gimbutas (1982), 152–200; Briard (1979), 161–4, 190. For the goddess of the wilds among the Continental Celts, see Green (1992), 26, 33–4, 80. For the persistence of such ideas in some cultures, see A Chaudhri and C Blacker in Billington/Green (1996), 166–85.
111 See Ó Catháin (1995).
112 For her in the literature, see Murphy (1962), 74–83, 206–8; *Revue Celtique 49*, 440; Mac Cana (1980), 48, 58; Byrne (1973), 166–8, 211.
113 For her in folklore, see Ó hÓgáin (1990), 67–9; G Ó Crualaoich in *Béaloideas 56*, 153–78.
114 *Revue Celtique 25*, 344–9; *Ériu 11*, 152–3.
115 RIA Dictionary s.v. 'daighre'.
116 For Cernunnos, see Mac Cana (1970), 42–8; Green (1989), 86–102 and (1992), 59–61.
117 Bromwich (1961), 428, 441–3.
118 Kneen (1925), xxii.
119 See O'Rahilly (1946), 30; H Wagner in *ZCP 38*, 24.
120 See O'Rahilly (1946), 456–7. The Catuvellauni, who had established a very strong kingdom in the English midlands by the time of Julius Caesar, were Belgae in origin.
121 O'Rahilly (1946), 30–3.
122 See H Wagner in *ZCP 33*, 4–5 and *38*, 24. Another Celtic tribal name was Morini, meaning 'sea-people'.
123 J Pokorny in *ZCP 11*, 169–71; O'Rahilly (1946), 16, 31; A Mac an Bhaird in *Ainm 5*, 14.
124 For the characters Forgall Monach and Scenmenn Monach, see O'Rahilly (1946), 32–3.
125 'Manaw' must come from 'Manavia' or 'Manava' – Jackson (1953), 376. There is some difficulty in connecting the 'v' here with the 'p' of Monapia, which would normally have developed into a 'b' in early Welsh – *ibid.*, 394–6.

126 For such stories in Irish literature and folklore, see Ó hÓgáin (1990), 286–9.
127 RIA Dictionary s.v. 'emon' / 'emuin'.
128 Such otherworld islands could also be referred to in the plural (*emne*) – *ibid.*, s.v. 'Emain', 'Emne'.
129 Bieler (1979), 106 – the forms given are actually the accusative *Euniam* and the genitive *Huimnonn*.
130 This is obvious from the connections made in it between Manannán and a prince of that area, called Mongán mac Fiachnaí, who died in 624 AD. For Mongán, see Ó hÓgáin (1990), 301–4.
131 Mac Mathúna (1985), 33–4.
132 From this comes the term Avalon, meaning 'region of apples', in the later Arthurian literature.
133 Mac Mathúna (1985), 33–43; Meyer (1900), 79–80 and (1912), 78; *Irische Texte 3*, 193.

Chapter 6

1   Benveniste (1969), 2, 9–42
2   See Frazer (1940), 168–78, 264–93, 731.
3   *Ériu 9*, 52–4.
4   *ibid.*, 51.
5   *ZCP 11*, 82; see also Kelly (1976), 26.
6   Dillon (1975), 99; Brunaux (1988), 50–1. For an interesting reference by Livy to the good fortune associated with the reign of a Gaulish king, see McCone (1990), 108.
7   Binchy (1970), 15–16; Dillon (1975), 113. See also Chapter 3.
8   See Dillon (1975), 59–65, 96–7, 132–3.
9   *ibid.*, 104–5; Binchy (1970), 4–9.
10 *ibid.*, 25–7.
11 Kelly (1976), 6–11.
12 *ibid.*, 60 – see also Dillon (1975), 130–1.
13 In many cases, of course, the literature and the folklore used the concept of *geasa* merely as a means of developing a narrative plot. On the origins of this secondary function of *geasa*, see D Greene in Bekker-Nielsen (1979), 9–19.
14 O'Donovan (1847), 2–25; M Dillon in *PRIA 54 C1*, 1–25.
15 For discussion and references, see Reinhard (1933), 120–3; Ó hÓgáin (1990), 237. For the incidental nature of some *geasa*, see also A Maartje Draak in Bleeker/Widengren (1969), 641–2.
16 See M Carney in *Arv 13*, 173–9; Ó hÓgáin (1990), 254–5.
17 Dillon (1953), 9 – this must be derived from a common source with the description in Knott (1936), 4.
18 M Dillon in *PRIA 54 C1*, 27.
19 *Ériu 6*, 134.
20 See J Baudis in *Ériu 7*, 106.

21   For Cú Roí, the Daghdha, and Dáire respectively, see Ó hÓgáin (1990),
     139–42, 145–7, 147. For Dáire, see also Chapter 7.
22   *Ériu 2*, 1–14.
23   Henderson (1899), 102.
24   See Raftery (1994), 46–7.
25   O'Rahilly (1946), 117–29; see Knott (1936), xi. O'Rahilly, *ibid.*, 205, con-
     sidered the Érainn to be identical with a group of Belgae who had settled
     in Ireland in the centuries BC.
26   For references and discussion, see O'Rahilly in *Ériu 14*, 7–28 and (1946),
     53–7, 138–40.
27   For discussion and references, see Ó hÓgáin (1990), 277–9.
28   See Bieler (1979), 154–5; Meyer (1910), 28 and (1912), 75.
29   Knott (1936), 1–3. Eochaidh is here called Eochaidh Feidhleach – for the
     ultimate identity of him with Eochaidh Aireamh, see Chapter 5.
30   *Ériu 6*, 130–41.
31   Knott (1936).
32   *ibid.*, 8.
33   *Ériu 6*, 136.
34   O'Rahilly (1946), 119.
35   For the lore concerning Labhraidh, see Ó hÓgáin (1990), 267–9.
36   See O'Rahilly (1946), 103; H Wagner in *Ériu 26*, 25–6.
37   H Wagner in *Ériu 28*, 1–16.
38   ZCP 3, 1–14; *Revue Celtique 20*, 429–33; see Dillon (1946), 4–9; Ó
     hÓgáin (1990), 267–9.
39   See O'Rahilly (1946), 101–20; Byrne (1973), 130–6; Smyth (1982), 7–12.
40   Stokes (1900), 47–50.
41   See the discussion and note 120 below.
42   See Chapter 4.
43   Discussion and references in Ó hÓgáin (1990), 76–7.
44   For account of him and references, see Byrne (1973), 70–86 and Ó hÓgáin
     (1990), 322–4.
45   *Revue Celtique 24*, 190–207. Another version in *Ériu 4*, 91–111
46   See Thompson (1955–1958), motif D735; and the same motif in Cross
     (1952).
47   RIA Dictionary s.v. 'feis'; Carney (1955), 334; T F O'Rahilly in *Ériu 14*,
     15–17.
48   In a late mediaeval text, a similar story is told of one Lughaidh Laíghde
     gaining the kingship of Tara – *Irische Texte 3*, 318–21. This seems to refer
     to the tradition of Lughaidh mac Con as Tara king – see Ó hÓgáin (1990),
     278 and note 27 above.
49   O'Rahilly (1946), 282, 514–15.
50   Vendryes (1953). Also in Jackson (1938).
51   Pliny, *Historia Naturalis XVI*, 249 – quoted in Chapter 3.
52   For references, see Lincoln (1986), 41–5.
53   *ibid.*, 46–64.
54   O'Rahilly (1976), 124.
55   See Ó hÓgáin (1988), 98–100, 331, 342.
56   Meyer (1912), 11.
57   RIA Dictionary s.v. 'búan', 'Búanann'.

58 A T Lucas in *JCAHS 68*, 17–23. For a very early reference to the Bile Tartain, see *Revue Celtique 17*, 175.

59 Plummer (1910), *1*, civ; Byrne (1973), 27.

60 Gwynn (1913), 174–83.

61 Binchy (1970), 3–4; Dillon (1975), 100.

62 *ZCP 20*, 169–70.

63 For references, see Cross (1952), 306; Ó hÓgáin (1990), 177–8.

64 Gwynn (1913), 206–15; O'Grady (1892), 2, 483.

65 RIA Dictionary s.v. 'túaim'; Hogan (1910), 642.

66 Green (1992), 34–5, 148–9.

67 See S Ó Catháin in Josephson (1997), 253–4, 274–6. The name of the Welsh Arthur has a similar derivation.

68 Ó Cathasaigh (1977), 107–33. For the lore concerning Cormac in general, see Ó hÓgáin (1990), 119–27

69 *Ériu 16*, 84; *PMLA 60*, 341.

70 *Ériu 3*, 136; *ZCP 27*, 23.

71 *Ériu 16*, 38, 42.

72 Meyer (1912), 58–9. For blemishes of kings, see also Reinhard (1933), 118–19.

73 Frazer (1940), 265–74.

74 The Burgundians, whose culture was influenced by the Gauls, were reported to have had the custom of forcing a king to abdicate when he failed in battle – H Wagner in *ZCP 32*, 287–8.

75 O'Donovan (1865–1901), *4*, 52 – see also Binchy (1970), 21.

76 Best/Bergin (1929), 127.

77 Gwynn (1913), 20; *Irische Texte 1*, 81, 255; see D Binchy in *Ériu 18*, 126.

78 D D A Simpson in *Emania 6*, 31–3.

79 Herity/Eogan (1977), 46; O'Kelly (1989), 319; J P Mallory in Waddell/Shee Twohig (1995), 73–86.

80 Mallory (1985); O'Kelly (1989), 319–23; Raftery (1994), 74–9.

81 For correspondences between the Eamhain and Bronze Age henges in England, see Harbison (1988), 156–7.

82 For such concepts of sacred centre in cultures from different parts of the world, see Eliade (1959), 39–44.

83 RIA Dictionary s.v. 'Emain'.

84 O'Rahilly (1946), 12–13; J Pokorny in *ZCP 21*, 127 and *24*, 120.

85 See A Mac an Bhaird in *Ainm 5*, 11.

86 For *is*, meaning 'energetic' – which may have been a borrowing by the Continental Celts from the Illyrians – see Walde/Pokorny (1930), *1*, 4; Pokorny (1959), *1*, 299–301. For *omon*, meaning 'tree-bole' and later 'oak', see *ibid.*, *1*, 177 and RIA Dictionary ('omna').

87 Hennessy (1887), *1*, 66–7.

88 Gwynn (1913), 450–9 and (1924), 62–9. Other tellings listed in Ó hÓgáin (1990), 181. The horse is termed *ech mór* in Gwynn (1923), 64 and this is the identical designation given to the horse of the Gaulish sun-god (*epomarus*) – see Chapter 2.

89 For sepulchral tradition at Eamhain and a possible representation of the sun on a cairn there, see C J Lynn in *Emania 10*, 42, 47 and *Archaeology Ireland* 1/1993, 20–1.

90 Griffith (1971), *1*, 214–17; Dillon (1975), 107–8; Davidson (1988), 54–6. See also the lurid mediaeval description by Giraldus Cambrensis of a horse-sacrifice at the inauguration of an Ulster chief – Byrne (1973), 17–18; O'Meara (1982), 110.

91 The Greek earth-goddess Demeter and her consort Poseidon also appeared as a mare and stallion – Dillon (1975), 108.

92 Written usually as 'Emain Macha' in the old Mss.

93 Hence Ard Macha ('the high-point of the plain') i.e. Armagh in that same region.

94 Hogan (1892), 32; O'Rahilly (1976), 117–18.

95 RIA Dictionary – s.v. 'macha'.

96 Gray (1982), 128; Macalister (1941), 122.

97 Best/Bergin/O'Brien (1954), 79–85.

98 Stokes (1912), 41–2. The woman is here not given a name, but it is obvious that Macha is the one meant.

99 *ZCP 12*, 251–4; *Celtica 8*, 1–42; Best/O'Brien, *2* (1956), 467–8.

100 Green (1986), 91–4, 171–5 and (1992), 90–3.

101 Williams (1930), 9–12; see Gantz (1976), 52–4.

102 Thompson (1955–1958), motif F302; Hartland (1891), 240–327.

103 For this theory, see Ó hÓgáin (1990), 413–17.

104 Henderson (1899), 38–40; Best/O'Brien, *2* (156), 448–53; Van Hamel (1933), 73–117.

105 Macalister (1941), 188.

106 See the story of Atlante in Classical literature – Graves (1960), *1*, 266–7; and the 'Brünhilde'-type motifs in Aarne/Thompson (1961), 180–1, 187, (Types 513–14, 519).

107 See C J Lynn in *Emania 10*, 42. Many Celtic ritual sites abroad have entrances facing east – see J Webster in Green (1995), 459 – but this may also reflect solar orientation.

108 For sun-wise circumambulation by the Celts, see J J Tierney in *PRIA 60*, C5, 225, 247; Brunaux (1988), 27–8; J Webster in Green (1995), 459–60.

109 Gwynn (1924), 366.

110 J Puhvel in Puhvel (1970), 164–9.

111 Harbison (1988), 191–2; Raftery (1994), 70–1, 236; J Waddell in *Emania 5*, 5–18.

112 It reads VRAICCI MAQI MEDVVI – Macalister (1945), 16–17; see also G Olmsted in *Emania 10*, 11–16.

113 Perhaps it was a reader of this inscription in the late 7th century who invented the original oral story which lay behind *Táin Bó Fraích*, an epical tale in which Fraech is thought to be dead and is interred in the cave of Cruachu. Fraech, in archaic Irish, would have been Vraecah, from Celtic Vroecos.

114 *Ériu 5*, 232; see also Byrne (1973), 18–19, 83–4, 324.

115 *ZCP 18*, 168–70.

116 *ibid.*, 170–8.

117 O'Daly (1975), 48; Gwynn (1913), 382; Henderson (1899), 72. See also *Revue Celtique 10*, 212–28;

118 Herity/Eogan (1977), 46, 84; Harbison (1988), 157.

119 For the archaeology of Aillinn, see B Wailes in Harding ed. (1976), 319–38 and in *Emania* 7, 10–21.
120 O'Brien (1962), 22–3.
121 Meyer (1913–1914), 2, 6–7; Byrne (1973), 134.
122 O'Kelly (1989), 316–19; Raftery (1994), 71–4.
123 See Byrne (1973), 176–82, 327–8.
124 For him, see Ó hÓgáin (1990), 182–3.
125 *Irische Texte* 3, 302–4. A later and somewhat altered version in Jackson (1938), 1–2.
126 Jackson (1938), 5–39.
127 O'Daly (1975), 82. For Lughaidh mac Con in general, see Ó hÓgáin (1990), 277–9.
128 *Irische Texte* 2, 208; ZCP 4, 39; Meyer (1910), 72; *Revue Celtique* 3, 346. See RIA Dictionary: 'enech'.
129 O'Daly (1975), 60–1, 82–5.
130 Stokes/Strachan (1903), 335; ZCP 8, 299.
131 O'Rahilly (1946), 300.
132 O'Daly (1975), 48.
133 Stokes (1900), 47–50.
134 For the practice among the Celts of applying divine names to kings, see O'Rahilly in *Irish Historical Studies* 1, 308.
135 H Wagner in ZCP 38, 21.
136 J Pokorny in *Celtica* 3, 307–8; H Wagner in *Ériu* 28, 10–11.
137 O'Daly (1975), 64, 120.
138 See O'Rahilly (1946), 288, 290.
139 *ibid.*, 288; Byrne (1973), 177; O'Daly (1975), 153.
140 O'Rahilly (1946), 286–9.
141 *ibid.*, 289–90.
142 For Danu/Anu see Chapter 2.
143 O'Daly (1975), 38–9. This contradicts the literary idea that an Irish king should be without blemish, a factor which suggests that – as we have said – the nickname predates the application of this story to Ailill.
144 See the discussion and source-list in Ó hÓgáin (1990), 20–2.
145 Grogan/Eogan (1987).

Chapter 7

1 Chadwick (1961), 16–19; de Paor (1993), 19–21, 227.
2 Stilicho, later Emperor of Rome, repulsed one such massive raid by the Irish on the coast of Britain in the year AD 399 – see Byrne (1973), 76.
3 *ibid.*, 35.
4 See O'Rahilly (1946), 216–17.
5 For accounts of Niall's birth and career, see *Otia Merseiana* 2, 75–6; *Revue Celtique* 24, 190–207; O'Grady (1892) 1, 326–36; *Ériu* 4, 91–111.
6 For Niall's death, see *Otia Merseiana* 2, 84–92; *Revue Celtique* 15, 295–7; Gwynn (1906), 36–41; O'Brien (1962), 122.

7 This Latin text is edited in Conneely (1993), 25–50, with translation on pp 63–76.
8 Conneely (1993), 34–5.
9 Stokes (1905), 16–17. For other examples of such references, see D A Binchy in *Ériu* 16, 38, 42; Ó hÓgáin (1982), 210–11.
10 See Carney (1973), 7–13, 116–19.
11 Conneely (1993), 47, 74.
12 *ibid.*, 32, 65.
13 *ibid.*, 41, 70.
14 *ibid.*, 40, 70.
15 *Book of Job* 1:21. For other echoes of Job in the *Confessio*, see Conneely (1993), 46, 52.
16 The phrase occurs in the form *gratias agamus Domino Deo nostro* ('let us render thanks to the Lord our God') in the Preface of the Roman Mass and would therefore have been known to Patrick – see Addis/Arnold, Scannell (1928), 527.
17 Bieler (1979), 110–11.
18 *ibid.*, 1–2.
19 *ibid.*, 112–13.
20 O'Brien (1962), 580–1.
21 O'Rahilly (1946), 7.
22 Walde/Pokorny (1930), *1*, 861; Mann (1984–7), 183, 192; RIA Dictionary, s.v. 'dáir', 'Dáire'.
23 see Chapter 2.
24 For the cauldron of the Daghdha, see Gray (1982), 24–5; ZCP *18*, 83.
25 Gray (1982), 44.
26 This is discussed by me in more detail in Mac Conmara (1997), 174–84.
27 Colgrave (1968), 126–8. See also Carney (1973), 142–52.
28 Bieler (1979), 108–11.
29 *ibid.*, 154–5.
30 For references, see Ó hÓgáin (1985), 241–3, 248–50, 340–1 and (1990), 114, 127, 139, 352.
31 Bieler (1979), 102–7.
32 For them, see R Sharpe in *Ériu 30*, 75–92.
33 See M E Byrne in *Ériu 11*, 97–102.
34 Knott (1936), 44.
35 Chapter 2 – see also O'Rahilly (1946), 58–9.
36 Walde/Pokorny (1927), 2, 446–7. The ordinary Irish word for the sun (*grian*) is derived from a root meaning 'heat'.
37 Conneely (1993), 49, 76.
38 Perowne (1975), 94.
39 R Browning in Heer (1973), 13–19.
40 Meyer (1912), 63.
41 *Revue Celtique 20*, 418–19. See also the reference – some centuries later – to an apostate Irish priest who 'made an altar of crystal, and made on it the carving of sun and moon' – *Revue Celtique 20*, 428.
42 Bieler (1979), 84–7. This is Muirchú's account; that by Tíreachán – *ibid.*, 130–1 – is much shorter.
43 RIA Dictionary, s.v. 'áed'; O'Rahilly (1946), 58–61, 66, 319–20, 547.

44 Bieler (1979), 130–1.

45 *ibid.*, 84–97.

46 *ibid.*, 84.

47 In the passage quoted above, Muirchú states that Benineus 'experienced what has been said of the three young men'. This phrase (excluded here) refers to the youths who emerged unscathed from the furnace in Babylon (*Daniel* 3).

48 Luke 23.31.

49 Bieler (1979), 62, 124, 138. See also *ibid.*, 17, 39–42.

50 Stokes (1905), 100, 186–8, 198–202.

51 Mochta is reported to have died in 535 AD. There are accounts of him in Bury (1905), 309–10; Kenney (1929), 350–1; Heist (1965), 394–400.

52 Carney (1973), 115–17.

53 This festival, and its tradition, is discussed in detail by MacNeill (1962).

54 RIA Dictionary s.v. 'creth', 'cruth'. It derives from an Indo-European root **quer-*, meaning 'to 'make' – see Walde/Pokorny (1930), *1*, 517–18; H Wagner in *Celtica* 6, 214–15; D Ward in *The Journal of Indo-European Studies 1*, 140.

55 Bieler (1979), 130–3.

56 *ibid.*, 88–91. For a translation of the passage in the *Acts of Peter*, see James (1924), 331–2.

57 Bieler (1979), 74–7.

58 See *ibid.*, 200; and Carney (1967), 2–3, 97–8. That this Irish text is the original is indicated by its alliteration and punning, neither of which qualities are obvious from Muirchú's Latin version.

59 The Irish text is in Mulchrone (1939), 22, but the fifth line is missing. For this line, Carney (1967), 2 proposes *Canfaid míchrábud*, but this lacks the alliteration and ambiguity inherent in the proposed *Canfaid cáidi*, which is an equally accurate translation of Muirchú's *incantabit nefas*. In the third line the Irish manuscript reads 'a bratt tollcend', but 'tí' has been suggested by Carney in place of 'bratt' because it suits the alliteration better and has the exact same meaning. A further six lines are cited in the Irish text, but these are probably later additions.

60 In line with this interpretation, Muirchú quotes the answer in his Latin text, not as '*amen, amen*' but as '*fiat, fiat*' – on this, see Carney (1967), 97–8.

61 The tendency towards rhyme in the metre would also indicate a 6th-century Christian origin – for rhyme in early Irish poetry, see Henry (1978), 142–59.

62 Henry (1940), 109–10; Murphy (1953), lxi–lxiii.

63 Stokes (1900), 148. See also a similar prophecy attributed to Fionn at a different location – *ibid.*, 52.

64 Conneely (1993), 41–4, 70–2.

65 *ibid.*, 46–7, 74.

66 *ibid.*, 47, 74.

67 *ibid.*, 43, 72.

68 See Byrne (1973), 78–82.

69 Bieler (1979), 132–3.

70 *ibid.*, 138–45.

71 *ibid.*, 96–9.
72 *ibid.*, 132–3.
73 *ibid.*, 132–3.
74 *ibid.*, 130–1.
75 *ibid.*, 84–91.
76 de Paor (1993), 135–6.
77 *ibid.*, 92–3, 176–7.
78 O'Donovan (1865–1901), *3*, 7–8
79 Meyer (1912), 64.
80 O'Brien (1962), 80–1; Ó hAodha (1978), 42.
81 Bollandus/Henschenius (1863), February 1, 135–41. Translation in de Paor (1993), 207–24 and by Seán Connolly in *JSRAI 117*, 5–27. For Cogitosus and his name, see Felim Ó Briain in *ZCP 36*, 112–37.
82 For St Brigid's Feastday in folklore, see Danaher (1972), 13–37.
83 Bollandus/Henschenius (1863), 118–20; Ó hAodha (1978), 1.
84 Bollandus/Henschenius (1863), 156; Ó hAodha (1978), x, 36.
85 Stokes (1905), 28. See also Ó hÓgáin (1982), 259, 277–9; and Chapter 4 above.
86 Danaher (1972), 31–3, 108–9.
87 Anderson/Anderson (1961).
88 *ibid.*, 502.
89 Bernard/Atkinson (1898), *1*, 62–89. Reference to the dragon is on p. 69.
90 Anderson/Anderson (1961), 386–9.
91 For a discussion of this and other legends of saints and water-monsters in Gaelic tradition, see D Ó hÓgáin in *Béaloideas 51*, 87–125.
92 Anderson/Anderson (1961), 278–83.
93 *ibid.*, 75.
94 See Aarne/Thompson (1961), Type 934A – p 329; Kenneth Jackson in Ua Riain (1940), 535–50.
95 *ibid.*, 6–7, 94–5.
96 These accounts of Diarmaid are in O'Grady (1892), *1*, 66–84; *ZCP 7*, 305–7. For further sources, see Ó hÓgáin (1990), 158–61.
97 For further accounts of this celebrated king, see Macalister (1956), 384–7; Best/Lawlor (1931), 102–7; P Walsh in *Irisleabhar Muighe Nuadhat* (1926), 3–11; Ó Cadhlaigh (1950); Byrne (1973), 87–105.
98 Binchy (1970), 11.
99 The occasion for the development of this legend of Ruadhán and Diarmaid may have been a curse put on the king of Tara, Aedh Oirdnidhe, by Columban monks in the year 816 – Hennessy (1887–1901), *1*, 308.
100 O'Grady (1892), 1, 66–71; Plummer (1910), 2, 245–9 and (1922), 1, 88, 321–5, 363; Heist (1965), 163–5.
101 Binchy (1970), 17; Dillon (19), 118–20.
102 Other references to such fasting by saints and others in Plummer (1910), 1, cxx–cxxi.
103 Van Hamel (1933), 15.
104 Todd (1867), 100 – see V Hull in ZCP 29, 190–1;
105 Book of Jonah 3.6–8.
106 For Beag and traditions of him, see Ó hÓgáin (1990), 47–8.

107 The poem is edited and translated by W Stokes in *Revue Celtique 20–21*. For a recent dicussion, see Henry (1978), 191–212. For Dallán Forgaill, see Ó hÓgáin (1990), 148–50.

108 Stokes (1905), 9.

109 Hogan (1910), 589.

110 O'Brien (1962) 279–80.

111 Meyer (1912), 49.

112 O'Brien (1962), 279–80; O'Rahilly (1946), 521; Gwynn 4 (1924), 188.

113 *ZCP 14*, 157. Note also the name *Roth mac Rí-ghoill* ('Roth son of the one-eyed King') given to his fosterfather in O'Brien (1962), 279–80.

114 *Revue Celtique 43*, 62.

115 *Irische Texte 3*, 408; *ZCP 14*, 163. Both of these texts, though belonging to the mediaeval period, seem to be based on earlier tradition.

116 *Ériu 4*, 173–81; *ZCP 14*, 145–63. Discussions in Kenney (1929), 749–53; MacNamara (1975), 64–7.

117 O'Brien (1962), 279–80, 285–6, 385.

118 *ibid.*, 205.

119 For the miracles and wondrous deeds attributed to Irish saints, see Plummer (1910), *1*, cxxix–clxxxviii. For other references, see Ó hÓgáin (1990), 379–83.

120 Plummer (1896), *1*, 266.

121 Plummer (1910), *1*, cxxxv, clxxiii–iv.

122 For examples and full discussion of this, see Ó hÓgáin (1982), 281–414.

123 For a full discussion of the magical powers of poets in folklore, see Ó hÓgáin (1982).

124 Plummer (1912), *1*, 253 and *2*, 234; *Revue Celtique 13*, 84.

125 Plummer (1910), *2*, 146, 149; and (1922), *1*, 185, 215; Heist (1965), 238. A similar miracle by St Ailbhe – de Paor (1993), 230.

126 For the concept of sacred space, see Eliade (1959), 20–65.

127 For the marking of boundaries in Irish religious and secular lore, see Ó hÓgáin (1985), 41–6, 326 and in *Béaloideas 60–61*, 65–6.

128 See J Loth in *Revue Celtque 33*, 254–8; Wood-Martin (1902), *2*, 51–7.

129 Many examples of these meanings are cited in RIA Dictionary s.v. *dess, desse, dessel, túaisceartach, túaisre, túaisrendae, túaithbel, túath*. See here also another word for 'left', *clé*.

130 Examples in O'Rahilly (1976), *1*, 25, 42; Best/O'Brien (1956), *2*, 443–4.

131 Meyer (1912), 94.

132 Stokes (1900), 122, 221.

133 RIA Dictionary s.v. *túaithe, túaithech, túathaid*.

134 e.g. *Revue Celtique 3*, 176; *Irische Texte 3*, 415; Best/Bergin (1929), 239; Van Hamel (1933), 72.

135 Mark 16:19.

136 Matthew 25:33.

137 Stokes/Strachan (1901–3), *2*, 254.

138 Plummer (1922), *1*, 236.

139 Stokes (1890), 93.

140 O'Kelleher/Schoepperle (1918), 182–4. The Cathach and its case survive, and are respectively in the Royal Irish Academy and the National Museum in Dublin.

141 Wood-Martin (1902), 2, 58–67; Plummer (1922), 248; Meyer (1911), 58.
142 1. Kings 18.32; 2. Kings 1.10.
143 *ACL 1*, 268.
144 *ACL 2*, 482
145 Watson (1941), 1; *Ériu 11*, 188.
146 Dillon (1953), 29 – see also Ó Raithbheartaigh (1932), 197–201.
147 Macalister (1941), 106–8; see also Van Hamel (1933), 72–3.
148 Best/Bergin (1929), 80; Ó Súilleabháin (1942), 518 – see also Macalister (1941), 240–1.
149 Jackson (1990), 4.
150 See Wood-Martin (1902), 2, 51–7; Ó Súilleabháin (1942), 229–31, 278.
151 For these holy wells in general, see Wood-Martin (1902), 2, 46–115.
152 Bieler (1979), 152–5.
153 Gwynn (1913), 252–3 and (1924), 300–1.
154 *ibid.*, 228–31, 518.
155 For him, and his alter-egos, see O'Daly (1975), 74–7, 153; Ó hÓgáin (1990), 277–9.
156 O'Hanlon (1875), 8, 69–70.
157 Kenney (1929), 398–9; Heist (1965), 131, 382; Ó hÓgáin (1990), 300–1.
158 See the illuminating dicussion of this background by P Ó Riain in *ZCP 36*, 138–55.
159 Many miraculous accounts of saints' deeds at fountains are cited in Plummer (1910), 1, cxlix–clii.
160 See Wood-Martin (1902), 2, 108–13; Ó Súilleabháin (1942), 279.
161 See Chapter 5.
162 See Wood-Martin (1902), 2, 81–90; Ó Súilleabháin (1942), 279–80.
163 See Chapters 3 and 6.
164 Heist (1965), 163; Plummer (1922), 1, 320–1.
165 For earlier sources on the four major festivals, see Le Roux/Guyonvarc'h (1986), 231–59. For these and other Irish traditional festivals in folk tradition, see Danaher (1972). Full studies of two of the primary festivals have been published – for St Brigid's festival see Ó Catháin (1995), and for Lughnasa see MacNeill (1962).

Bibliography

Periodicals

Ainm: Bulletin of the Ulster Place-Name Society (Belfast, 1986–)
Anecdota from Irish Manuscripts 1–5 (Halle, 1907–1913)
Archaeology Ireland (Dublin, 1987–)
ACL = Archiv für Celtische Lexikographie 1–3 (Halle, 1898–1907)
Arv (Stockholm, 1945–)
Béaloideas: Journal of the Folklore of Ireland Society (Dublin, 1927)
Bulletin of the Board of Celtic Studies (Cardiff, 1921–)
Celtica (Dublin, 1946–)
Current Trends in Linguistics (The Hague, 1966–)
Éigse (Dublin, 1939–)
Emania (Belfast, 1987–)
Ériu (Dublin, 1904–)
Études Celtiques (Paris, 1936–)
Irish Historical Studies (Dublin, 1938–)
Irische Texte 1–4 (Leipzig, 1880–1909)
Irisleabhar Muighe Nuadhat (Maynooth, 1907–)
JCHAS = Journal of the Cork Historical and Archaeological Society (Cork, 1892–)
Journal of Indo-European Studies (Hattiesburg, 1973–)
JRSAI = Journal of the Royal Society of Antiquaries of Ireland (Dublin, 1890–)
Léachtaí Cholm Cille (Maynooth, 1970–)
Ogam (Rennes, 1948–)
Otia Merseiana 1–4 (Liverpool, 1899–1904)
PMLA = Publications of the Modern Language Association of America (Wisconsin, 1884–)
PRIA = Proceedings of the Royal Irish Academy (Dublin, 1836–)
Revue Celtique 1–55 (Paris, 1870–1934)
Speculum (Cambridge, Massachussetts, 1926–)
Studia Celtica (Cardiff, 1966–)
Studia Celtica Japonica (Toyohashi, 1988–)
UCD News (Dublin, 1976–)
UJA = Ulster Journal of Archaeology, 3rd Series (Belfast, 1938–)
Veröffentlichungen der keltischen Kommission (Vienna, 1981–)
World Archaeology (Oxford, 1969–)
Y Cymmrodor 1–50 (London, 1877–1951)
ZCP = Zeitschrift für celtische Philologie (Halle, 1896–)
Zeitschrift für vergleichende Sprachforschung (Berlin, 1852–)

Books

Aarne, Antti / Thompson, Stith, *The Types of the Folktale* (Helsinki, 1961)
Addis, W E / Arnold, Thomas / Scannell, T B, *A Catholic Dictionary* (London, 1928)

Ahlqvist, Anders, *et al*, eds., *Celtica Helsingiensia* (Helsinki, 1996)

Anderson Alan O / Anderson, Marjorie O, *Adomnan's Life of Columba* (Edinburgh, 1961)

Atkinson, Robert, *The Ancient Laws of Ireland, 5* (Dublin, 1901)

Bahn, Paul G / Vertut, Jean, *Images of the Ice Age* (Leicester, 1988)

Bailey, Adrian, *The Caves of the Sun* (London, 1997)

Ball, Martin J / Fife, James, eds., *The Celtic Languages* (London, 1993)

Bekker-Nielsen, H, *et al*, eds., *Medieval Narrative: a Symposium* (Odense, 1979)

Benveniste, Émile, *Le Vocabulaire des Institutions Indo-Européannes 1–2* (Paris, 1969)

Bergh, Stefan, *Landscape of the Monuments* (Stockholm, 1995)

Bernard, J H / Atkinson, Robert, *The Irish Liber Hymnorum 1–2* (London, 1898)

Best, R I / Bergin, Osborn, *Lebor na hUidre* (Dublin, 1929)

Best, Richard / Bergin, Osborn / O'Brien, M A / O'Sullivan, Anne, *The Book of Leinster, 1–6* (Dublin, 1954–1983)

Best, Richard / Lawlor, H J, *The Martyrology of Tallaght* (London, 1931)

Bhreathnach, Edel, *Tara: A Select Bibliography* (Dublin, 1995)

Bieler, Ludwig, *The Patrician Texts in the Book of Armagh* (Dublin, 1979)

Billington, Sandra / Green, Miranda, eds., *The Concept of the Goddess* (London, 1996)

Binchy, Daniel A, *Celtic and Anglo-Saxon Kingship* (Oxford, 1970)

Bleeker, C Jouco / Widengren, Geo, eds., *Historia Religionum, 1* (Leiden, 1969)

Bollandus, Johannes / Henschenius, Godefridus, *Acta Sanctorum* [Feb 1] (Paris, 1863)

Bosley, Keith, *The Elek Book of Oriental Verse* (London, 1979)

Bradley, Richard, *The Passage of Arms* (Cambridge, 1990)

Brandon, S G F, *Man and his Destiny in the Great Religions* (Manchester, 1962)

——*History, Time and Deity* (Manchester, 1965)

Breatnach, Liam, *Uraicecht na Ríar* (Dublin, 1987)

Brennan, Martin, *The Boyne Valley Vision* (Portlaoise, 1980)

Briard, Jacques, *The Bronze Age in Barbarian Europe* (London, 1979)

Bromley, Yu V, *Theoretical Ethnography* (Moscow, 1984)

Bromwich, Rachel, *Trioedd Ynys Prydain* (Cardiff, 1961)

Brown, Arthur C L, *The Origin of the Grail Legend* (Cambridge, 1943)

Brunaux, Jean Louis, *The Celtic Gauls: Gods, Rites and Sanctuaries* (London, 1988)

Buck, Carl Darling, *Dictionary of Selected Synonyms in the Principal Indo-European Languages* (Chicago, 1949)

Bury, J B, *The Life of St Patrick* (London, 1905)

Byrne, Francis J, *Irish Kings and High-Kings* (London, 1973)

Caerwyn Williams, J E / Ní Mhuiríosa, Máirín, *Traidisiún Liteartha na nGael* (Dublin, 1979)

Calder, George, *Auraicept na n-Éces* (Edinburgh, 1917)

Campbell, Joseph, *The Way of the Animal Powers* (London, 1983)

Carney, James, *Studies in Irish Literature and History* (Dublin, 1955)

——*Medieval Irish Lyrics* (Dublin, 1967)

——*The Problem of St Patrick* (Dublin, 1973)

Chadwick, H M / Chadwick, N K, *The Growth of Literature 1–3* (Cambridge, 1932–1940)
Chadwick, N K, *The Age of the Saints* (London, 1961)
——*The Druids* (Cardiff, 1966)
——*The Celts* (Middlesex, 1970)
Chevalier, Jean / Gheerbrant, Alain, *A Dictionary of Symbols* (London, 1996)
Childe, V Gordon, *Prehistoric Communities of the British Isles* (London, 1940)
——*The Prehistory of European Society* (Middlesex, 1958)
Colgrave, Bertram, *The Earliest Life of Gregory the Great* (Lawrence, 1968)
Collins, John J, *Primitive Religion* (New Jersey, 1978)
Comyn, David, *Foras Feasa ar Éirinn, 1* (London, 1902)
Conneely, Daniel, *The Letters of Saint Patrick* (Maynooth, 1993)
Coon, Carleton S, *The Hunting Peoples* (Middlesex, 1976)
Cooney, Gabriel / Grogan, Eoin, *Irish Prehistory, a Social Perspective* (Dublin, 1994)
Couchoud, P-L, *Congrés d'histoire du Christianisme* (Paris, 1928)
Cross, Tom Peete, *Motif-Index of Early Irish Literature* (Bloomington, 1952)
Danaher, Kevin, *The Year in Ireland* (Dublin, 1972)
Davidson, H R Ellis, *The Road to Hel* (Cambridge, 1943)
——*Gods and Myths of Northern Europe* (Middlesex, 1964)
——*Saxo Grammaticus, 1* (Cambridge, 1979)
——*Myths and Symbols in Pagan Europe* (Manchester, 1988)
de Paor, Liam, *Saint Patrick's World* (Dublin, 1993)
de Vries, Jan, *Keltische Religion* (Stuttgart, 1961)
Delargy, J H, *The Gaelic Story-teller* (Chicago, 1969)
Dillon, Myles, *The Cycles of the Kings* (London, 1946)
——*Early Irish Literature* (Chicago, 1948)
——*Serglige Con Culainn* (Dublin, 1953)
——*The Archaism of Irish Tradition* (Chicago, 1969)
——*Celts and Aryans* (Simla, 1975)
Dillon, Myles / Chadwick, Nora, *The Celtic Realms* (London, 1973)
Dinneen, Patrick S, *Foras Feasa ar Éirinn 2–4* (London, 1908–1914)
Dumézil, Georges, *The Destiny of a King* (Chicago, 1973)
Dyer, James, *Ancient Britain* (London, 1990)
Eliade, Mircea, *Patterns in Comparative Religion* (London, 1958)
——*The Sacred and the Profane* (London, 1959)
——*Shamanism* (Princeton, 1964)
——ed., *The Encyclopaedia of Religion 1–16* (New York, 1987)
Eluère, Christiane, *The Celts: First Masters of Europe* (London, 1992)
Emin, Gevorg, *Seven Songs about Armenia* (Moscow, 1981)
Enright, Michael J, *Lady with a Mead Cup* (Dublin, 1996)
Eogan, George, *Hoards of the Irish Later Bronze Age* (Dublin, 1983)
——*Knowth and the Passage-Tombs of Ireland* (London, 1986)
Estyn Evans, E, *Irish Heritage* (Dundalk, 1932)
——*Irish Folk Ways* (London, 1957)
Evans-Pritchard, E E, *Theories of Primitive Religion* (Oxford, 1965)
——*A History of Anthropological Thought* (London, 1981)
Evelyn-White, Hugh G, *Hesiod, the Homeric Hymns, and Homerica* (London, 1959)

Faulkes, Anthony, *Snorri Snurluson: Edda* (London, 1987)
Ferguson, John, *Greek and Roman Religion: A Source Book* (New Jersey, 1980)
Filip, Jan, *Celtic Civilisation and Its Heritage* (Prague, 1977)
Firth, Raymond, *Symbols, Public and Private* (New York, 1973)
——*Human Types* (London, 1975)
Fiske, Christabel Forsyth, ed., *Vassar Mediaeval Studies* (London, 1923)
Fox, C, *A Find of the Early Iron Age from Llyn Cerrig Bach* (Cardiff, 1946)
Frankfort, Henri / Frankfort, H A, *Before Philosophy* (Middlesex, 1949)
Frazer, James G, *The Golden Bough, 12* [index] (London, 1920)
——*The Fear of the Dead in Primitive Religion 1–2* (London, 1933–4)
——*The Golden Bough* [abridged] (New York, 1940)
Friedrich, Paul, *Proto-Indo-European Trees* (Chicago, 1970)
Frisk, Hjalmar, *Griechisches Etymologisches Wörterbuch, 1* (Heidelberg, 1960)
Gantz, Jeffrey, *The Mabinogion* (Middlesex, 1976)
Gelling, Peter / Ellis Davidson, H R, *The Chariot of the Sun* (London, 1969)
Gimbutas, Marija, *The Goddesses and Gods of Old Europe* (London, 1982)
Girard, Réne, *Violence and the Sacred* (Baltimore, 1977)
Glob, P V, *The Bog People* (London, 1971)
——*The Mound People* (London, 1974)
Gonda, Jan, *The Vision of the Vedic Poets* (The Hague, 1963)
Gougaud, Louis, *Christianity in Celtic Lands* (London, 1932)
Michael Grant, *Myths of the Greeks and Romans* (New York, 1962)
Graves, Robert, *The Greek Myths 1–2* (Middlesex, 1960)
Gray, Elizabeth A, *Cath Muige Tuired* (Dublin, 1982)
Green, Miranda, *The Gods of the Celts* (Gloucester, 1986)
——*Symbol and Image in Celtic Religious Art* (London, 1989)
——*Dictionary of Celtic Myth and Legend* (London, 1992)
——ed., *The Celtic World* (London, 1995)
Greene, David, *Fingal Rónáin and Other Stories* (Dublin, 1955)
Griffith, Ralph T H, *The Hymns of the Rgveda* (Varanasi, 1971)
Grinsell, Leslie V, *Folklore of Prehistoric Sites in Britain* (London, 1976)
Gruffydd, W J, *Math Vab Mathonwy* (Cardiff, 1928)
Guénon, René, *Symboles Fondamentaux de la Science Sacrée* (Paris, 1079)
Gwynn, Edward J, *The Metrical Dindshenchas 1–4* (Dublin, 1903, 1906, 1913, 1924)
Harbison, Peter, *The Archaeology of Ireland* (London, 1976)
——*Pre-Christian Ireland* (London, 1988)
Harding, D W, ed., *Hillforts: Later Prehistoric Earthworks in Britain and Ireland* (London, 1976)
Hastings, James, ed., *Encyclopaedia of Religion and Ethics 1–13* (Edinburgh, 1908–1926)
Heer, Friedrich, *The Fires of Faith* (New York, 1973)
Heist, W W, *Vitae Sanctorum Hiberniae* (Brussels, 1965)
Henderson, George, *Fled Bricrend* (London, 1899)
Hennessy, William M / McCarthy, Bartholomew, *Annals of Ulster 1–4* (London, 1887–1901)
Henry, P L, *Saoithiúlacht na Sean-Ghaeilge* (Dublin, 1978)
Herity, Michael, *Irish Passage Graves* (Dublin, 1974)

Herity, Michael / Eogan, George, *Ireland in Prehistory* (London, 1977)
Hogan, Edmund, *Onomasticon Goedelicum* (Dublin, 1910)
Holder, Alfred, *Alt-Celtischer Sprachschatz 1–3* (Leipzig, 1896)
Hutton, Ronald, *The Pagan Religions of the Ancient British Isles* (Oxford, 1991)
Ions, Veronica, *Egyptian Mythology* (London, 1965)
——*Indian Mythology* (London, 1967)
Jackson, Kenneth, *Cath Maighe Léna* (Dublin, 1938)
——*Language and History in Early Britain* (Edinburgh, 1953)
——*The Oldest Irish Tradition* (Cambridge, 1964)
——*Aislinge Meic Con Glinne* (Dublin, 1990)
James, E O, *The Ancient Gods* (London, 1962)
——*The Tree of Life: an Archaeological Study* (Leiden, 1966)
James, M R, *The Apocryphal New Testament* (Oxford, 1924)
Josephson, Folke, ed., *Celts and Vikings* (Göteborg, 1997)
Joyce, Patrick W, *A Social History of Ancient Ireland 1–2* (London, 1903)
Joynt, Maud, *Feis Tighe Chonáin* (Dublin, 1936)
Jung C G / Kerenyi, C, *Science of Mythology* (London, 1985)
Kiev, Ari, ed. *Magic, Faith, and Healing* (New York, 1964)
Kelly, Fergus, *Audacht Morainn* (Dublin, 1976)
——*A Guide to Early Irish Law* (Dublin, 1988)
Kendrick, T D, *The Druids* (London, 1927)
Kenney, James F, *The Sources for the Early History of Ireland: Ecclesiastical* (New York, 1929)
Kneen, J J, *The Place-Names of the Isle of Man* (Douglas, 1925)
Knott, Eleanor, *Togail Bruidne Da Dearga* (Dublin, 1936)
Krappe, Alexander H, *Balor with the Evil Eye* (Columbia, 1927)
——*Mythologie Universelle* (New York, 1978)
Kristensen, W Brede, *The Meaning of Religion* (The Hague, 1960)
Kurth, Godefroid, *Histoire Poétique des Mérovingiens* (Paris, 1893)
Laing, Lloyd, *Celtic Britain* (London, 1979).
Larson, Gerald, ed. *Myth in Indo-European Antiquity* (Berkeley, 1974)
Le Roux, Francoise, *La Souveraineté Guerrière de l'Irlande* (Rennes, 1983)
Le Roux, Francoise / Guyonvarc'h, Christian-J, *Les Druides* (Ouest-France, 1986)
Lemprière, J, *Classical Dictionary* (London, 1984)
Lincoln, Bruce, *Myth, Cosmos, and Society* (Cambridge, Mass., 1986)
Lommel, Andreas, *The World of the Early Hunters* (London, 1967)
Loomis, C S, *Medieval Studies in Memory of Gertrude Schoepperle Loomis* (Paris, 1927)
Lowie, Robert H, *Primitive Religion* (New York, 1970)
Lucas, A T, *Treasures of Ireland* (Dublin, 1973)
——*Cattle in Ancient Ireland* (Kilkenny, 1989)
Lynch, Ann, *Man and Environment in South-West Ireland* (Oxford, 1981)
McMann, Jean, *Loughcrew: The Cairns* (Oldcastle, 1993)
Mac Cana, Proinsias, *Celtic Mythology* (London, 1970)
——*The Learned Tales of Medieval Ireland* (Dublin, 1980)
Mac Conmara, Máirtín / Ní Thiarnaigh, Éilís, eds., *Cothú an Dúchais* (Dublin, 1997)

Mac Mathúna, Séamas, *Immram Brain* (Tübingen, 1985)
Mac Néill, Eoin, *Duanaire Finn, 1* (Dublin, 1908)
——*Phases of Irish History* (Dublin, 1920)
Mac Piarais, Pádraig, *Bruidhean Chaorthainn* (Dublin, 1908)
Macalister, R A Stewart, *Lebor Gabála Érenn 1–5* (London, 1938, 1939, 1940, 1941, 1956)
——*Corpus Inscriptionum Insularum Celticarum 1–2* (Dublin, 1945–1949)
MacCulloch, J A, *The Religion of the Ancient Celts* (Edinburgh, 1911)
MacNamara, Martin, *The Apocrypha in the Irish Church* (Dublin, 1975)
MacNeill, Máire, *The Festival of Lughnasa* (Oxford, 1962)
Magnusson, Magnus / Pálsson, Hermann, *Laxdaela Saga* (Middlesex, 1969)
Malinowski, Bronislaw, *Magic, Science and Religion* (London, 1974)
Mallory, J P, *Navan Fort: the Ancient Capital of Ulster* (Belfast, 1985)
——*In Search of the Indo-Europeans* (London, 1989)
Mallory, J P / Stockman, G, eds., *Ulidia* (Belfast, 1994)
Mann, Stuart E, *An Indo-European Comparative Dictionary* (Hamburg, 1987)
Maringer, Johannes, *The Gods of Prehistoric Man* (London, 1960)
Matonis, A T E / Melia, Daniel F, eds., *A Festschrift for Eric P Hamp* (Van Nuys, 1990)
Mattingly, H / Handford S A, *Tacitus: the Agricola and the Germania* (Middlesex, 1970)
McCone, Kim, *Pagan Past and Christian Present in Early Irish Literature* (Maynooth, 1990)
——*Towards a Relative Chronology of Ancient and Medieval Celtic Sound Change* (Maynooth, 1996)
McGrath, Fergal, *Education in Ancient and Medieval Ireland* (Dublin, 1979)
MacManus, Damien, *A Guide to Ogam* (Maynooth, 1991)
Meid, Wolfgang, *Táin Bó Fraích* (Dublin, 1967)
Meyer, Kuno, *Hibernica Minora* (Oxford, 1894)
——*The Voyage of Bran, 1* (London, 1895).
——*The Death-Tales of the Ulster Heroes* (Dublin, 1906)
——*The Triads of Ireland* (Dublin, 1906)
——*Fianaigecht* (Dublin, 1910)
——*Betha Colmáin maic Lúacháin* (Dublin, 1911)
——*Sanas Cormaic* (Halle, 1912 = Anecdota 4)
——*Über die älteste Irische Dichtung 1–2* (Berlin, 1913–1914)
Mohen, Jean-Pierre, *The World of Megaliths* (New York, 1990)
Monier-Williams, Monier, *A Sanskrit-English Dictionary* (Oxford, 1899)
Moscati, Sabatino, *et al*, eds., *The Celts* (Venice, 1991)
Mulchrone, Kathleen, *Caithréim Cellaig* (Dublin, 1971)
Müllerus, Carolus, *Diodori Siculi, 1* (Paris, 1878)
Murphy, Gerard, *Duanaire Finn 3* (London, 1953)
——*Early Irish Lyrics* (Oxford, 1962)
Ní Chatháin, Próinséas / Richter, Michael, eds., *Ireland and Europe in the early Middle Ages* (Stuttgart, 1996)
Nilsson, Martin P, *The Minoan-Mycenaean Religion* (Lund, 1927)
——*The Mycenaean Origin of Greek Mythology* (Cambridge, 1932)
Ó Cadhlaigh, Cormac, *Diarmaid mac Chearbhaill* (Dublin, 1950)
Ó Catháin, Séamas, *The Festival of Brigit* (Dublin, 1995)

Ó Corráin, Donnchadh, ed., *Irish Antiquity* (Dublin, 1994)
Ó Corráin, Donnchadh / Maguire, Fidelma, *Gaelic Personal Names* (Dublin, 1981)
Ó Cuív, Brian, *Cath Muighe Tuireadh* (Dublin, 1945)
——ed., *A View of the Irish Language* (Dublin, 1969)
Ó hAodha, Donncha, *Bethu Brigte* (Dublin, 1978)
Ó hÓgáin, Dáithí, *An File* (Dublin, 1982)
——*The Hero in Irish Folk History* (Dublin, 1985)
——*Fionn mac Cumhaill* (Dublin, 1988)
——*Myth, Legend and Romance* (London, 1990)
——*Irish Superstitions* (Dublin, 1995)
Ó Raithbheartaigh, Toirdhealbhach, *Genealogical Tracts* (Dublin, 1932)
Ó Riain, Pádraig, *Cath Almaine* (Dublin, 1978)
Ó Ríordáin, Seán P, *Antiquities of the Irish Countryside* (London, 1965)
Ó Ríordáin, Seán P / Daniel, Glyn, *New Grange* (London, 1964)
Ó Siochfhradha, *Laoithe na Féinne* (Dublin, 1941)
Ó Súilleabháin, Seán, *A Handbook of Irish Folklore* (Dublin, 1942)
——*Irish Wake Amusements* (Cork, 1967)
——*Irish Folk Custom and Belief* (Dublin, 1967)
O'Brien, Michael A, *Corpus Genealogiarum Hiberniae* (Dublin, 1962)
O'Curry, Eugene, *Manners and Customs of the Ancient Irish 1–3* (Dublin, 1873)
O'Daly, Máirín, *Cath Maige Mucrama* (Dublin, 1975 = Irish Texts Society 50)
O'Donovan, John, *The Battle of Magh Rath* (Dublin, 1842)
——*Leabhar na gCeart, or the Book of Rights* (Dublin, 1847)
——*Annála Ríoghachta Éireann 1–7* (Dublin, 1848–1851)
——*The Ancient Laws of Ireland, 1–4* (Dublin, 1865–1891)
O'Grady, Standish Hayes, *Silva Gadelica 1–2* (London, 1892)
O'Hanlon, John, *Lives of the Irish Saints* (Dublin, 1875)
O'Kelly, Claire, *Illustrated Guide to Newgrange* (Wexford, 1971)
O'Kelly, Michael J, *Newgrange* (London, 1982)
——*Early Ireland* (Cambridge, 1989)
O'Meara, John J, *The Voyage of Saint Brendan* (Dublin, 1981)
——*The History and Topography of Ireland: Gerald of Wales* (Middlesex, 1982)
O'Rahilly, Cecile, *The Stowe Version of Táin Bó Cuailnge* (Dublin, 1961)
——*Táin Bó Cuailgne from the Book of Leinster* (Dublin, 1970)
——*Táin Bó Cuailnge: Recension 1* (Dublin, 1976)
O'Rahilly, Thomas F, *Early Irish History and Mythology* (Dublin, 1946)
O'Sullivan, Muiris, *Megalithic Art in Ireland* (Dublin, 1993)
Ogilvie, R M, *The Romans and their Gods* (London, 1969)
Olmsted, Garrett, *The Gaulish Calendar* (Bonn, 1992)
Olrik, Axel, *The Heroic Legends of Denmark* (New York, 1919)
Opie, Iona / Tatem, Moira, *A Dictionary of Superstitions* (Oxford, 1992)
Orme, Byrony, *Anthropology for Archaeologists* (London, 1981)
Oskamp, H P A, *The Voyage of Máel Dúin* (Groningen, 1970)
Pearson, Lionel, *Early Ionian Historians* (Oxford, 1939)
Perowne, Stewart, *Roman Mythology* (London, 1969)
Pettazzoni, Raffaele, *The All-Knowing God* (London, 1956)

Pfeiffer, John E, *The Creative Explosion* (New York, 1982)
Piggott, Stuart, *Ancient Europe* (Edinburgh, 1965)
——*The Druids* (London, 1968)
Plummer, Carolus, *Venerabilis Baedae 1–2* (Oxford, 1896)
——*Vitae Sanctorum Hiberniae 1–2* (Oxford, 1910)
——*Bethada Náem nÉrenn 1–2* (Oxford, 1922)
Pokorny, Julius, *Indogermanisches Etymologisches Wörterbuch 1–2* (Bern, 1959)
Powell, T G E, *The Celts* (London, 1980)
Puhvel, Jaan, ed., *Myth and Law Among the Indo-Europeans* (Berkeley, 1970)
Radin, Paul, *The World of Primitive Man* (London, 1953)
——*Primitive Man as Philosopher* (New York, 1957)
Raftery, Barry, *La Tène in Ireland* (Marburg, 1984)
——*Pagan Celtic Ireland* (London, 1994)
——*Trackway Excavations in the Mountdillon Bogs* (Dublin, 1996)
Rank, Otto, *The Myth of the Birth of the Hero* (New York, 1914)
Rankin, H D, *Celts and the Classical World* (London, 1987)
Rees, Alwyn / Rees, Brinley, *Celtic Heritage* (Carmarthenshire, 1973)
Reinhard, John Revell, *The Survival of Geis in Mediaeval Romance* (Halle, 1933)
Renfrew, Colin, *Archaeology and Language* (London, 1987)
RIA Dictionary i.e. Royal Irish Academy, *Contributions to a Dictionary of the Irish Language* (Dublin, 1913–1975)
Rieu, E V, *Homer: The Odyssey* (Middlesex, 1946)
——*Homer: The Iliad* (Middlesex, 1950)
Roider, Ulrike, *De Chophur in Da Muccida* (Innsbruck, 1979)
Rose, H J, *Gods and Heroes of the Greeks* (London, 1974)
Ross, Anne, *Pagan Celtic Britain* (London, 1967)
——*Everyday Life of the Pagan Celts* (London, 1970)
Ross, Anne / Robins, Don, *The Life and Death of a Druid Prince* (London, 1989)
Ryan, Michael, ed., *The Origins of Metallurgy in Atlantic Europe* (Dublin, 1979)
——ed., *Seoda na hÉireann* (Dublin, 1985).
——ed., *The Illustrated Archaeology of Ireland* (Dublin, 1991)
Schulten, Adolf, *Avieni Ora Maritima* (Berlin, 1922)
Scott, B G, ed., *Studies in Early Ireland* (Belfast, 1982)
Smart, Ninian, *The Religious Experience of Mankind* (Glasgow, 1971)
Smyth, Alfred P, *Celtic Leinster* (Dublin, 1982)
Snell, Bruno, *Lexikon des Frühgriechischen Epos* (Göttingen, 1991)
Sterckz, Claude, *Elements de Cosmogonie Celtique* (Brussels, 1986)
Stokes, Whitley, *Three Irish Glossaries* (London, 1862)
——*The Tripartite Life of Patrick 1–2* (London, 1887)
——*Lives of the Saints from the Book of Lismore* (Oxford, 1890)
——*The Bodleian Dinnshenchas* (London, 1892)
——*Acallamh na Senórach* (Leipzig, 1900 = *Irische Texte 4*) *The Colloquy of the Two Sages* (Paris, 1905)
Stokes, Whitley / O'Donovan, John, *Cormac's Glossary* (Calcutta, 1868)

Stokes, Whitley / Strachan, John, *Thesaurus Palaeohibernicus 1–2* (Cambridge, 1901–1903)

Sydow, C W von, *Selected Papers on Folklore* (Copenhagen, 1948)

Thevenot, Émile, *Divinités et sanctuaires de la Gaule* (Paris, 1968)

Thorburn, Archibald, *Thorburn's Mammals* (New York, 1989)

Thorpe, Lewis, *Geoffrey of Monmouth: The History of the Kings of Britain* (Middlesex, 1966)

Thurneysen, Rudolf, *A Grammar of Old Irish* (Dublin, 1946)

Todd, James H, *The War of the Gaedhil with the Gaill* (Dublin, 1867)

Tovar, A, *The Ancient Languages of Spain and Portugal* (New York, 1961)

Turville-Petre, E O G, *Myth and Religion of the North* (London, 1964)

Tylor, Edward B, *Anthropology 1–2* (London, 1930)

Ua Riain, Eoin, *Féil-sgríbhinn Eoin Mhic Néill* (Dublin, 1940)

Van Gennep, Arnold, *The Rites of Passage* (London, 1960)

Van Hamel, A G, *Compert Con Culainn* (Dublin, 1933)

——*Lebor Bretnach* (Dublin, 1932)

——*Immrama* (Dublin, 1941)

Vána, Zdenek, *The World of the Ancient Slavs* (London, 1983)

Vendryes, Joseph, *Airne Fíngein* (Dublin, 1953)

——*Lexique Étymologique de l'Irlandais Ancien* (Paris, 1959–)

Vouga, Paul, *La Tène* (Leipzig, 1925)

Waddell, John / Shee Twohig, Elizabeth, *Ireland in the Bronze Age* (Dublin, 1995)

Wainwright, F T, *The Problem of the Picts* (Edinburgh, 1955)

Walde, Alois / Pokorny, Julius, *Vergleichendes Wörterbuch der Indogermanischen Sprachen 1–2* (Berlin, 1930)

Wallis-Budge, E A, *The Gods of the Egyptians, 1* (London, 1904)

Watson, J Carmichael, *Mesca Uladh* (Dublin, 1941)

Webster, Graham, *The British Celts and their Gods under Rome* (London, 1986)

Whatmough, Joshua, *The Dialects of Ancient Gaul* (Harvard, 1970)

Wheeler, R E M / Wheeler T V, *Excavations of the Prehistoric, Roman, and Post-Roman Site at Lydney Park* (Oxford, 1932)

Williams, Ifor, *Pedeir Keinc y Mabinogi* (Cardiff, 1930)

Wood-Martin, W G, *Traces of the Elder Faiths of Ireland 1–2* (London, 1902)

——*The World Atlas of Archaeology* – pub. Mitchell Beazley (London, 1985)

Zwicker, Ioannes, *Fontes Historiae Religionis Celticae 1–2* (Berlin, Bonn, 1934–1935)

Printed and bound by CPI Group (UK) Ltd, Croydon, CR0 4YY

25/03/2025

14647332-0004